D1443579

# ICE TIME

## A Portrait of Figure Skating

# ICE TIME

## A Portrait of Figure Skating

### DEBBI WILKES
#### and
#### Greg Cable

Prentice Hall Canada Inc.
Scarborough, Ontario

**Canadian Cataloguing in Publication Data**

Wilkes, Debbi
    Ice time: a portrait of figure skating

ISBN: 0-13-185117-9

1. Skating - Canada. I. Cable, Greg.T
II. Title.

GV850.4.W55 1994 796.91′2′0971 C94-932518-X

Prentice-Hall, Inc., Englewood Cliffs, New Jersey
Prentice-Hall International (UK) Limited, London
Prentice-Hall of Australia, Pty. Limited, Sydney
Prentice-Hall Hispanoamericana, S.A., Mexico City
Prentice-Hall of India Private Limited, New Delhi
Prentice-Hall of Japan, Inc., Tokyo
Simon & Schuster Asia Private Limited, Singapore
Editora Prentice-Hall do Brasil, Ltda., Rio de Janeiro

ISBN 0-13-185117-9


Copy Editor: Karen Rolfe
Production Coordinator: Anita Boyle
Cover Design: Carole Giguère
Interior Design: Julie Fletcher
Cover Image: Duomo Photography/The Image Bank
Page Layout: Hermia Chung


1 2 3 4 5 BG 98 97 96 95 94

Printed and bound in Canada.

Every reasonable effort has been made to obtain permissions for all
articles and data used in this edition. If errors or omissions have
occurred, they will be corrected in future editions provided written
notification has been received by the publisher.

To Bruce and Ruth Wilkes for their faith and for
teaching me to always be the best I can be

To Sue and Rob for their support

To John, Chris and Jilly for their love

and

To Guy Revell for
wonderful moments of
ice time

–DW

To Judy, Linda and Nairn

–GC

# Acknowledgements

We wish to thank the many people from the skating world who so generously shared their time, talents, opinions and memories. Without them, this book would never have come to life: Barbara Ann Scott, Frannie Dafoe, Toller Cranston, Brian Orser, Josée Chouinard and Elvis Stojko; Marg and Bruce Hyland, Sheldon Galbraith, Ozzie Colson, Louis Stong and Kerry Leitch; Sandra Bezic; David Dore; Johnny Esaw and Doug Beeforth; Kevin Albrecht; Mel Matthews; Sue Wilkes; Dorothy Hallis; Eric Anweiler; and Irene Stojko.

We thank Dr. Howard Winston; Chris Kapalowski for her help with research; and Simon Cable, Tobin Cable, Melissa Cable and Linn Aosjia for handling a massive transcribing job quickly and well.

We thank Herb Hilderley and Ken Proctor of Prentice Hall for their strong belief in the idea; David Jolliffe for his profound patience and his expertise in seeing the book through to production; and the sales, marketing and production staff for their outstanding efforts in bringing the book to the public.

And we thank John Darroch for his timely intervention which got this thing going in the first place

Debbi Wilkes and Greg Cable
Toronto
November 1994

The ice was thick in the parking lot of the Northlands Coliseum in Edmonton. In the record-cold North American winter of 1994, January was particulary miserable. The CTV television crew covering the Canadian Figure Skating Championships was not allowed to park close to the stage door of the Coliseum, so along with Rod Black, Brian Orser and Lynn Nightingale, I had a fair hike from the car. For some reason, I hadn't worn my snow boots, so I slipped and slid the distance in black pumps totally unsuited to the frigid conditions.

As a crew, we had already spent a week in Edmonton covering the practices, the personalities and the politics that are involved in any championship event. We were a good and experienced group. Between Brian, Lynn and I, we counted 14 Canadian championships, seven World medals and three Olympic medals. While Brian was new to the broadcast team as the on-air analyst, the rest of us had covered endless competitions over the years, nationally and internationally.

This Canadians was different, however. An Olympic year always means that the competition has an extra edge; this Olympic year especially, coming just two years after the Albertville Games. The turnover of skaters at the end of an Olympiad is an enduring cycle, but many who otherwise would have retired in 1992 decided to stick around. Adding to the excitement, Olympic gold medalists and legends of the sport—Gordeeva and Grinkov, Brian Boitano, Viktor Petrenko, Katarina Witt and Torvill and Dean—would be returning to the Games after years of skating professionally. The prospect of being part of what looked to be the greatest competition in figure skating history was a terrific motivator for the top competitors at the national championships.

We had already seen Shae-Lynn Bourne and Victor Kraatz start to defend their ice dance title, the first fruits to bloom from the garden planted during the brilliant career of Tracy Wilson and Rob McCall.

We had seen Isabelle Brasseur and Lloyd Eisler win their fifth pairs championship. They had begun as a "rag-doll pair" and retained some of that style, but recognized that the best pairs skaters need more nowadays. They understood what needed to be done and struggled to take on new dimensions with what, for Lloyd at least, was foreign to him. He stretched himself to take on a softer side. Isabelle has grown up in their years together. They began in 1987, staying together eight years, longer than many marriages. She began as just a little puppet he could manipulate without a say because he was the one with the national and international experience. He had already won a bronze medal at the Worlds with Kathy Matousek. But Izzie grew from being a partner with no say to being someone who directed the pair in a positive way, bringing a femininity and chemistry that brought out his masculinity. The stories they put down on the ice started to make sense. They became world champions because of it.

In 1992, in Albertville, they reclaimed a place on the pairs Olympic podium that had almost seemed Canada's by right in the years after the Second World War. Canadian pairs had won medals in four of the first five post-war Olympiads—1948, 1956, 1960 and 1964. But at the 1964 Games in Innsbruck, Soviet pairs skaters claimed the gold medal spot—a place they and their Russian successors have yet to relinquish—and changed pairs skating forever.

Still to come over the weekend was the women's competition. With the Queen of Canadian skaters, Barbara Ann Scott, among the sold-out crowd in the Coliseum, Josée Chouinard and Karen Preston would skate against a field of twelve up-and-comers, battling for the two spots on the Olympic team. Karen had been Canadian champion in 1989 and 1992, Josée had won in 1991, they had both lost to Lisa Sergeant in 1990 and Josée had regained the title in 1993, rushing off the ice into her mother's arms saying, "Enfin. Enfin. Enfin."

Josée had made a rather ballsy move at the beginning of the skating season. In July, she left the coach she had worked with since she was nine and moved to Toronto to train with Louis Stong, the coach of, among others, Karen Preston. In early season competitions, she had already shown that during her time with Louis she had become a skater.

People had been trying for years to tell Karen Preston that she had to do more than jump, spin and look pretty, but she gave no sign that she had reached the stage where she was willing to take the final Salchow over the boards into who she is and let herself come out on the ice. The human Karen Preston appeared every once in a while, but there were only glimpses and fleeting ones at that.

But on this night, the men were to skate their short programs. There were three places available on the Olympic team. Kurt Browning and Elvis Stojko were shoo-ins, of course, but who would emerge as the men's champion was the talk of the event. Elvis had been an also-ran for years, skating in Kurt's shadow. Kurt had always been allowed to beat him, even when he didn't deserve to, which probably had less to do with Elvis than with a system where there isn't room for two world champions from the same country. What do you do with them? The star system barely exists in Canada anyway, so when we have the best and second best in the world, who gets first dibs?

Opposites in personalities both on and off the ice, Kurt and Elvis were always very aware of each other and aware of the talents each had and the other needed. Kurt was never inhibited. He could do anything, tried anything and loved it. The bigger the challenge, the better. Elvis became a more studied individual. Athletically, he'd try anything, but personally, in the spotlight at centre ice, he seemed for a very long time to be uncomfortable. Kurt had a long history of success and was so gregarious and outgoing that most people couldn't help but love him right away. Elvis remained much quieter, more conservative and introspective. When he was very young, an interview with him was a dreaded assignment. He was so shy he couldn't say anything. Every question was answered with a simple yes or no.

At the Canadian championships in Sudbury in 1990, Elvis was a jumping machine and Kurt couldn't stand up. Yet at that moment the judges felt—based on the detail and choreography of the program, the musical selections, the mood changes and artistic flair—that even Kurt's bad skating was better than Elvis' best. Elvis was still skate, skate, jump, skate, skate, jump, with a bit of footwork thrown in here and there. Jumps and spins are important, but they are not the only thing. Coming out of those championships, he was determined to change his reputation and he did, although it took him years to be accepted. But he won the bronze to Kurt's silver in the 1992 Worlds and the silver to Kurt's gold in 1993.

In those years, Elvis was taking control and starting to change. He knew what had to be done. It was just a question of being comfortable while he was doing it. Competing against someone like Kurt, who could do absolutely everything, and believing as Elvis did that he could only do one thing, he often relied on what had always worked before. If you have beaten everybody with jumps and spins, why expose yourself to being creative? How do you make that artistic leap when you believe that you are only an athlete?

During the early nineties, he timidly took artistic steps but in a direction that was a little too safe. To take such steps is a decision that can only be made by the individual. No one can show a skater how to do it. Skaters can talk and share the ideas that have helped other artists, but the step itself can't be forced.

Now it came down to this night of the short program, with the long program still to come. Many suspected that Kurt, four-time world champion and Canada's great hope for a first Olympic men's gold, had stayed in amateur competition two years too long, his natural exit from the field being after the Albertville Games.

I don't usually go to practices on broadcast days. I've already seen everyone's program and 9:00 am to midnight days are not my cup of tea. But Rod Black phoned early in the morning and suggested we take in the men practicing their short program at the Northern Alberta Institute of Technology. We made our way to the arena, expecting to sit up in the stands to get a good view as we would usually do. To our amazement, the place was packed, without a seat to be had anywhere. We stood by the boards, close to Elvis' coach, Doug Leigh. A little further down was Uschi Keszler, a talented choreographer—although she prefers the term "stylist"— who had been trying to do with Elvis what she had done with Brian Orser: make him a world champion.

An unflagging lobbyist for her skaters, particularly with media people, Uschi had been telling me for years that Elvis was evolving rapidly, but had not yet truly been "born." She believed that when his moment arrived, he would change men's figure skating forever, as Don Jackson had done, as Toller Cranston, Brian Orser and Kurt Browning had done. I had my doubts.

As various competitors went through their routines, Elvis came over to speak to Doug Leigh. He said, "I don't feel like doing the short program. Why don't we do the long?"

Doug said, "Sure, if you like. You're the boss."

The music from the soundtrack of *Dragon: The Bruce Lee Story* began. Elvis went into character and into his routine. He nailed every jump, performed every spin, his footwork was dazzling and as the music reached its end he stood alone at centre ice, his face looking skyward, his hand palm-up in a classic martial arts pose that he slowly withdrew, staying in character all the while.

The audience went nuts and I found myself standing at the side of the boards with tears streaming down my face. I went over to Uschi and said, "You know I never really believed you until now."

That night we made our way across the frozen lot to the Coliseum. As we went in, Elvis and his girlfriend were dropped at the door, Elvis in a non-descript track suit and carrying a huge skating bag. He followed us in, kissed his girlfriend good-by, then headed to the dressing rooms along a corridor packed with fans, officials, reporters and a CTV camera.

He walked on calmly and, as he did, time seemed to stand still. The sound in the corridor fell into a hush. As one, all heads and the camera turned to focus on this lone and somewhat serene figure. Louis Stong, Kurt Browning's coach, looked over to me and just raised his eyebrows. Everyone knew that something was going to happen here tonight.

Figure skaters always look a little precious. Gliding on ice on a couple of thin, sharp blades imposes a posture of control. Carving intricate patterns and figures on ice demands a delicacy and precision that adds to the effect. Competitive skaters show an unnatural early maturity, an over-eagerness to please and a preference for the perfect little costume that all accentuate the preciousness. But the image masks the fact that figure skating is one of the most brutal sports around. If other athletes took the pounding figure skaters do they'd be on the disabled list for months. Skaters go fast, jump high, fall hard without pads, but they always get up and keep going.

The season begins in July for competitive skaters and serious skaters who may not be at the national or international level. Summer school programs are often designed so a skater can choose four or eight weeks of training. For family or financial reasons, some might only skate for one month, generally August, but serious skaters skate all summer.

After having time off, or at least slowing down significantly in June, the first couple of weeks back on the ice are spent getting your legs back. When you have skated five or six days a week, every week, then have taken time off, you feel as if you are skating on someone else's legs. Your feet don't work, your skates don't feel right, your body is not in shape or in tune. It doesn't take long to lose the edge. The first week in a summer school is spent finding yourself again.

During the time off, the skaters, coach, or both, have searched for new material, new music, new ideas about how the skaters will present themselves in the upcoming season. The aim is to show progress by trying new elements or putting a new face on the artistic side of a performance. Good coaches always have their ears open and usually have an incredible library of musical material.

The consultation process begins, trying to put pieces together so that they make sense musically and can also fulfill the requirements of a good program—musical variety and changes of pace, mood, tempo and rhythm. One spot will say "footwork," another will say, "I need a jump." With so many considerations involved, it may take the better part of a month to lay the music down. Changes may still be made as work on the program begins. Choreographically, certain things emerge.

For a short program, a skater has up to two minutes and 40 seconds to do the eight required elements. To some, that seems like a long time, but those elements of set jumps and spins have to be connected by steps that cover all parts of the ice. To do that well, a skater needs every second of the time. A skater can't just go out and skate around in a circle, do a double Axel, skate in another circle, then do a triple whatever. A program is a jigsaw puzzle that sometimes comes together very easily and at other times is a nightmare of chopping, changing and rearranging. To get a good program done is a long and tiresome process.

It's a wonder that so many people put up with the hard work and pain of training. But skating's unique combination of delicacy and brutality, of artistry and athletics, is enticing. Many are drawn to it by the fact that alone among sports—other than mixed doubles in tennis—skating does not just involve men against men and women against women, but a man and a woman against other couples. There are many aspects of the skating world that attract people to the doing or viewing of it. Thousands want to get on the roller coaster ride of elite competition and live the skater's life.

Skating is a sport Canadians have always done well in. The creator of modern figure skating, Jackson Haines, was Canadian born and a star pupil of his in Vienna was Louis Rubenstein from Montreal. Rubenstein is considered to be the first world champion, although the competition he won in St. Petersburg, Russia, took place in 1892, two years before the International Skating Union, the sport's governing body, was established, with Canada the only non-European founding member. In the first half of this century, Canadian skaters like Montgomery Wilson, Melville Rogers and two sisters from Toronto, Maude and Cecil Smith, had a big following in Europe.

Cecil Smith and Melville Rogers skated as a pair in the first Winter Olympic Games in Chamonix in 1924 and were thought by the audience and press to be medal material. The judges placed them seventh. But skating in Canada, as in the United States and much of Europe, was still considered a leisure activity of the well-off.

Then came Sonja Henie. She skated at Chamonix too. She was eleven years old at the time and already the Norwegian champion. She didn't place, but a great French skater, Pierre Brunet, looked at her and said, "This is the future." She was. Starting in 1927, she won ten consecutive world championships and three Olympic gold medals. She had some stiff competition several times, especially in the first Worlds held in North America, the 1930 championships in Madison Square Garden in New York. Cecil Smith did well in figures and caused a stir in the free skate by wearing white boots, a brash innovation that Sonja adopted a few months later. Sonja kept the title, with Cecil Smith coming second and long-time American champion, Maribel Vinson, coming third. Cecil's silver was the first medal Canada had ever won in world competition.

After the 1936 Olympics, Sonja turned professional and revolutionized skating. She practically invented the modern ice show, touring nine American cities to sell-out crowds in her first year. Then she set out to be a movie star. No other sport has had its growth in popularity so closely tied to the mass media. Her string of eleven movies changed how people looked at figure skating. The movies also helped shape the perception in a large part of the North American population that skating, which began as essentially a man's sport, was a woman's sport and a woman's activity. She was the first Ice Queen, a fixture of American culture ever since.

The movies were forgettable but great box office successes. Some of the most handsome leading men of the day stumbled across the ice after her, trying to look graceful. She was loved by millions. Skaters thought she was a first-class bitch. The Canadian men's figure skating champion of 1936 and 1937—a cousin of Cecil Smith's—saw her in action in the 1940s. Osborne Colson had gone off to the States after he won his championships, spending eight years as a pro, skating singles and pairs in the ice shows of the day. He also had the pleasure of pushing Joan Crawford across the ice into the arms of another skater in the Hollywood feature *Ice Follies* with Jimmy Stewart. One night he watched Sonja sweetly collecting bouquets of roses from the adoring crowd, flashing the smile that had made her famous on screens around the world. When she got behind the curtain, she flung the roses to the floor, slashing and chopping them madly with her blades before stomping off saying, "Orchids. Orchids. Only orchids for Sonja."

She also had a talent for going through skating partners at a great rate, the men always dressed in black sequins so they would fade into the background as she worked her magic on the ice. She skated—and had a grand affair—with Stewart Reburn, a Canadian pairs champion with Louise Bertram. They didn't really have the lifts for pairs, but they were the forerunners of free dance and took New York by storm in the thirties. Reburn was featured in the movie *Second Fiddle* and in Sonja's live show, but he came back to Canada to join the RCAF in 1939. More than a few male skaters refused to have anything to do with her. Eventually, her eye landed on Murray Galbraith. He and his brother, Sheldon, the sons of a Winnipeg businessman and hockey player, had grown up in California. They had both won Pacific coast skating titles, but they could never get past Bobby Speck in the national championships, so they went into showbusiness, becoming stars skating a "shadow pair" in Ice Follies. With Sheldon in the navy, Murray Galbraith was available but would only work with her on two conditions: equal billing and five per cent of the show. She didn't like it, but she agreed.

Whatever her personality quirks, she was an inspiration. Hundreds of rinks were built because of her. Thousands of young girls took to the ice because of her.

One of the inspired was an Ottawa girl, Barbara Ann Scott. She says, "I was always fascinated with skating and, of course, I saw every one of Sonja's movies 49 times. I just loved to skate and I liked to compete, always." As a little girl she would write Santa Claus every year. "I always asked for one-runner skates and a horse. When I was six, I received the skates. I was so disappointed the boots were black and not white like Sonja's."

She started lessons that year at Ottawa's Minto Club with a famed European coach, Gus Lussi. Within a few years, another legendary coach, Otto Gold, was teaching her figures. Barbara Ann had a gift for them. Many skaters spend years trying to get their gold test in figures. Barbara Ann had hers at age ten. By 1945, she was Canadian champion and North American champion, beating American skater Gretchen Merrill. That summer, Otto Gold was running the first summer skating school in Canada at the Granite Club in Kitchener. Barbara Ann and her mother were surprised to find Gretchen Merrill training there too. Otto Gold gave Merrill extra attention and never made her do her program although the other skaters had to. Mrs. Scott had it out with him. He forthwith refused to teach Barbara Ann.

For over a year, she had no teacher. But the European and world championships were starting up again in Europe after being cancelled during the war and the Canadian Figure Skating Association wanted her to compete. They just had to find her a coach, which is how Sheldon Galbraith showed up in a frosted quonset hut in Ottawa dressed in California clothes just weeks before Barbara Ann was to go to Europe. With his brother Murray skating with Sonja Henie, Sheldon thought he'd try teaching. His first pupil was the best skater in the world.

In 1947 and 1948, she was Canadian champion, North American champion, European champion, world champion and Olympic champion, a feat never duplicated before and impossible to repeat now. The North American championships are no more and, after her and Dick Button's triumphs in 1948, North Americans were never again allowed to compete for the European title.

Canadians loved her and she returned the emotion when she turned professional. "It was right after the war and people were looking for something to be happy about," she says. "I guess they adopted me as their little girl or something. Their pleasure came through what I did. I wanted to tour my own country and in those days, instead of putting up bronze war memorials, most of the small communities put up memorial arenas, so we put a tour together. Ozzie Colson was the choreographer and director, which was quite an experience. We played almost all the little towns and cities across Canada." She took over from Sonja Henie as the star of the Hollywood Ice Revue and went on the road for seven years. She never made movies, but she was a star, the first bona fide woman star in Canadian sport.

She was an inspiration to generations of skaters. I was only a few months old when she won her first world championship, but she became an inspiration to me, drawing me from the cozy confines of small town Ontario into the bizarre life of world competition. Unionville is now a yuppyish enclave in the expanse of suburbia spreading north from Toronto, but in the early 1950s, when I was a wee little bambina, the sign on Highway 7 announced the town's population as 603. It stayed 603 for as long as I can remember. We lived in a farmhouse on a five-acre piece of land on the highway, land that was sort of farmed, though not in the traditional sense.

My dad was a salesman who considered himself something of a gentleman farmer.

Everything about Unionville was small town. My school was a big old place with strange combinations of grades in each of its four rooms. There were few organized activities for children to participate in, mainly because there weren't enough kids to fill organized teams. When my one girlfriend from the farm moved away, my mother started worrying about my becoming a tomboy and thought I should do something "feminine." She decided I would join the skating club at the Unionville arena, a ramshackle old barn used mainly for hockey. Hockey players got all the prime ice time, but figure skating classes could be worked in at odd hours of the day.

It was traumatic when she first took me to the rink at the ripe age of five. She pushed me onto the ice with double runners laced to my galoshes. I stood there and bawled until she took me off, crying out, "These skates won't skate."

She changed her plan and had my sister, Susan, take me out on a pond at the back of the property with real figure skates. I couldn't stand up at first and was terrified of the toe picks, but Sue taught me to push a chair along. She was a pretty good skater, skating on hockey skates, and I toddled along after her while she teased me mercilessly. I started thinking that skating might not be too bad.

The next year, my mum took me back to the arena for group lessons. Partway through the year, the club teacher, Christine Kennedy, told my parents I should have private lessons. She started me off by having me crawl around the ice, lie on it, touch it, hug it, even lick it so I would realize what it was. It had a tinny taste from absorbing the reek of ammonia that always filled the building. In all the years after, the ice never frightened me. I didn't like to fall, and almost never did fall, not because I was afraid of hurting myself but because a fall might send something askew. After all, the hair had to be perfect and falling was so ungraceful.

The club put on an ice show carnival every year to raise money for the upcoming season. The show at the end of my first season was built around the story of Peter Pan. Incredibly to me, I was asked to skate a solo as Tinkerbell. I had a ballet tutu with lots of netting. My sister sat up night after night pasting over a thousand silver sequins onto the tutu so I would sparkle. I had a silver crown my mother had made and that my dad had wired with batteries connected to a little light in the crown. There came a moment in the show when Tinkerbell had to lead all the children to Neverneverland.

All the lights in the rink went out. I reached under my tutu and flipped a switch. The light in my crown blinked in the darkness and off we went to the enchanted land. It was magic.

That was the first of some great roles—Gretel, Captain Hook, a Red Lobster, the Cowardly Lion from Oz—and it wasn't long before I would race around the large living room in the farmhouse, jumping from couches to chairs, spinning around in the centre, thinking all the while that this was going to be my Olympic program. The same music—*The Teddy Bear's Picnic*—always played on the hi-fi while I bounced and danced away. My mother would stick her head out of the kitchen once in a while, sometimes getting pretty upset at my using the furniture like a trampoline, but usually just watching in silence. One day, I said, "Mummy, come and watch me skate. I'm going to be a champion."

That was a turning point for me and for my parents. They suddenly started to make fairly serious commitments with their time and their money. I became wild to get to any show with skating in the title. I went to every Hollywood Ice Revue with Barbara Ann Scott and Ice Capades that I could. For hours I'd go through stacks of Ice Capades programs my mother collected. The skating was beautiful, but it was the showbiz that attracted me, the lights and colours and sequins and staging. The theatrics appealed to my imagination.

After two years, I tried my preliminary figure test and failed. My teacher said I was too light so no one could see my tracings. I tried it with drapery weights attached to my costume. Failed again. But one night around this time, my mother awakened my father from his after-dinner nap and told him he had to go to the annual meeting of the Unionville Skating Club. He wasn't much of joiner and certainly wasn't interested in getting involved in "that women's thing," but he went. He came out of the meeting as president. He took to the new position with his usual style. When he had first come from Britain in the twenties, he ran out of money working his way across Canada and made a few bucks boxing. In the middle of a bout in Fort William, he saw my mother in the audience. He said, "I'm going to marry you." Then he knocked his opponent out of the ring and left him sprawling at her feet. He decided I really didn't need to pass the preliminary test. I was much too good for that.

He and my mother decided I would move on to post-season training, which meant a trek to the Metropolitan Figure Skating School at Weston arena on the shores of the Humber River. In the days before Highway 401, it was a long drive three times a week, all to try to pass this test, which I never did. After so many failures, my dad decided I was too good for the beginner test anyway, so I would go on to the next level, which wouldn't be allowed today. We made the change from community level teaching to a more experienced group of coaches, led by Marg Roberts and Bruce Hyland. They were former waltz champions of Canada and silver medalists in pairs who had performed in all the shows with Barbara Ann.

I skated around the Weston rink having a wonderful time. The other kids skated rings around me. There were some really good skaters at the school, including Guy Revell from Newmarket who was already on his sixth test. Marg noticed my dad always encouraging me from the boards. One day, she went over to talk to him, then skated over to Bruce with an incredulous look on her face. She said, "That gentleman over there wants that little blonde girl over there to skate with Guy!"

Bruce said, "Well, maybe someday."

Bruce was never one to close the door on potential or opportunity. In 1951, teaching in Oakville, he and Marg had been called to the home of Henry Jelinek to talk about his children. He asked Marg and Bruce if they could make his children world champions. Otto and Maria Jelinek were about ten. Bruce said, "It depends how much they want it." Mr. Jelinek asked how long it would take. Bruce says, "I didn't even have pairs skaters other than a couple of little kids. I said ten years, but I really had no idea what I was saying."

My dad always told me that there was no one easier to sell than another salesman. He convinced Bruce to come and teach in Unionville. Marg took a little longer to convince, but they both came to this club in the middle of nowhere. They brought some of their best skaters with them, like Louis Stong, Marijane Lennie and the rebel of the group, Mel Matthews. Their "western contingent" of Otto and Maria would often come up from Oakville to skate with us too. Marg and Bruce's arrival marked the beginning of a productive period and an internationally well-respected reputation for the Unionville Skating Club.

Bruce remembers my dad as a democratic dictator. "When he ran the club, it was really not a presidency with a group of directors. He chose every member of the club directors that did something. One person was good on money, another person was good on building props, another was good on music. That's how he built this skating club that was so successful in this little rink that was so bad, with snow flying through the walls and snow drifts right on the seats."

It really was a dreadful arena. When the club put on shows, the musical director would wear gloves to play a piano brought in on the back of a truck. As we rehearsed in the 20-below weather inside the building, he'd get up every once in a while and cry out, "Why am I here?" The carnivals Marg and Bruce put on every year eventually were right up there with Ice Capades in my mind. They were asked to take the shows on tour sometimes. Other clubs wanted us to come and perform in their buildings. Logistically and economically the idea was ridiculous, but the club developed a reputation for putting on the best shows around. Unionville became a model for small community clubs that thought they could never compete against the Granite or other fancy clubs that seemed to carry so much clout.

Dad decided that Unionville would offer to host the Central Ontario sectional championships in 1958. The first sectionals had been held just the year before, hosted by the much older and high-profile Toronto Skating Club. Remarkably, he got the go-ahead. The competitors and their families were billeted in local homes, the ladies of the village made endless sandwiches, the skaters all changed in one big room and the parents huddled around the arena's sole pot-bellied stove in a vain attempt to keep warm, often singeing their clothes in the process. It was a good competition, with four future champions—Petra Burka, Paul Huehnergard, Ken Ormsby and Guy Revell—in the novice division alone.

I had been doing some pairs skating with a boy named Brian Bailie for carnival purposes and to see if I had any pairs potential. Marg and Bruce said, "You're the president's daughter, why don't you compete?" I had just turned eleven and wasn't sure I wanted to do it, but Marg knew I was highly competitive and always knew the right words to say. "Look, it's a lot easier than doing tests. You don't have to reach any standards. You just have to be better than the next guy." An ambiguous standard meant nothing to me. Beating the next guy I could understand.

We entered the junior pairs event, equivalent to novice level today, and won. There was only one senior pair, equivalent to junior level Canadians, who were going to perform in the finals on the last night of competition. Marg and Bruce thought we should give this other couple some competition before they moved on to the national championships in Ottawa. The only problem was that we had to be on the ice for half a minute longer and we had no music and no program. Dad got out his records—old '78s—and made a new master disc that extended the slow part of our junior program with the strains of *As Time Goes By*. We re-worked the choreography in our driveway.

The word had spread through the village after our win on the Saturday and the arena was full for the Sunday night finals. Having never skated our program, we went out in the senior competition and won that too. The other pair was rather miffed. Our win meant they couldn't go to the nationals. We didn't feel we could participate either, after winning more by fluke than anything else, but Marg and Bruce thought we should go to Ottawa, sit in the stands and at least watch what went on. We did and my eyes were opened. This was the big time.

With the success of the sectionals, my dad got the bug. He was bitten. Things went crazy. I was suddenly skating ten months of the year, full time.

I was a pairs skater because I couldn't jump. I was very petite when I started to skate, and did not have the musculature or body proportion of the typical athlete. Physical limitations would never have allowed me to be a good jumper—too much leg and too wild. But in those days, an inability to jump wasn't limiting. You just moved into pairs where a single Axel or double Salchow was a big deal. I was good in other ways. I did have a musicality that was more appropriate for pairs than singles skating. Pairs skating since Dafoe and Bowden and Wagner and Paul had became a lyrical love story and I could tell stories. I loved to act. Any one of the traditional feminine roles was well within my reach.

Guy was a guest skater at our carnival in April that year. He was an outstanding free skater who could do double Axels, but found dealing with his nerves very tough. I couldn't skate that well, but I was tough as nails. We decided to try it together. Marg and Bruce started working with us in the fall of 1958. Six months later, we were on our way to the Canadian championships in Rouyn-Noranda, Quebec. That was a thrill. We had had very little experience and the other couples were a lot older, but we won the junior Canadian title and were asked by the Canadian Figure Skating Association to represent Canada in the North American championships in Toronto. That was a big step. We placed fifth out of six, but it was a wonderful experience and unusual in that for most skaters it's a long, slogging process to get to an international competition. I would like to think our rapid rise was because we had such enormous talent, but it was really because the competition was so poor.

Our performances are embarrassing to watch now, the skating is so old fashioned, but we had great lifts and skated very fast for those times. Other than the lifts, our strongest point was that Bruce had a very innovative way of hearing music. His competitors always skated to the most beautiful melodies and had a way of reaching deep inside themselves and feeling what the music meant. I had trouble understanding that—it's hard to convince an eleven-year-old to be passionate about music—but Guy, being six years older, had an intense understanding of what Bruce meant. He was a wonderful foil. He would treat me like a little Dresden doll, playing the very manly role to the skinny beanpole with the princessy look. It played well, until I grew. When we started, I could fit under his arm. When we ended, he could almost fit under mine.

Guy was responsible for our success. He had the vision and the desire. I did too, but I was a kid. He was a slave driver, the one who wanted it so badly and could see what had to be done to get there. He taught me more about skating than any coach ever did. He was so patient. The man in a pair always gets badly battered when learning new lifts and twists. We were learning a double twist lift, no big deal now but hot stuff in those days. Guy had the vision that it could be done and that we were going to be the first ones to do it. What it required was a back entrance by both of us. Then I picked and he lifted and twisted me so that I floated free. I had to twist two rotations in the air, then he would catch me and set me down. Naturally, I couldn't find the end of the rotation for quite some time and kept coming down on the top of his head with the point of my elbow. His head was so swollen and bruised he couldn't comb his hair for weeks, yet no pain was too great and no move too hard that he wouldn't try it again and again. He drove me crazy.

"I'm done, I don't want to do it any more."

"No, one more, try it again, get your leg this way. It's the only way we're going to win."

He was driven. He would never stop during a performance no matter what disaster might have befallen us, and there were a few. Once, his costume flew apart during a skate. Once, mine opened up down the back from neck to derriere. He wouldn't stop. In St. Andrews-by-the-Sea, we were the closing number in the opening show of the Lord Beaverbrook Arena. A minute into the number, the flat pad under the ball of his foot came loose. The only thing holding his blade to his boot were a couple of screws on the heel. Even today I hate to imagine the force put on those screws. He felt it was important for me to know we were in a crisis situation, so he said, "My blade's off."

He was my link from the top of the lift to the ice. If his blade was off, how could he keep me steady? "Let's stop."

"No, we're not stopping." He would not alter the program one bit. We finished the program without a moment's twinge or hesitation. He was determined. His nerves sometimes got the better of him and he'd forget the program. I'd mumble in his ear, "Down the other way, we're going to do the outside spiral, this is where the spins go." We rotated in opposite directions, so I would nod to let him know I had landed the double Salchow. Sometimes I lied. But he was wonderful to skate with and was also a great friend. We would travel all over Ontario to competitions, exhibitions and carnivals. We'd finish a performance in Sarnia or somewhere, hop in the car and he'd drive home with me asleep on my little pillow in the back seat so I could get to school fresh the next morning.

After winning the junior title and finishing up our first year together, we had to get serious about finding a place to train. Since Unionville had such a dumpy little arena used almost entirely for hockey, it was not a viable solution. Bruce also coached at the Toronto Cricket Club and felt we should become members to take advantage of the great ice time it offered. Few rinks around the world, let alone in Canada, had an ice surface designated solely for figure skating and the Toronto Cricket was one of them. No hockey allowed. We wouldn't have to buy ice by the hour, which became very expensive. We would have some continuity, with a schedule that was much the same every day so Bruce could see us regularly.

We were asked to represent the Cricket Club, but there was no way my parents would allow that. They were true to their roots and to the loyalty and support we had had from Unionville and the township of Markham. My dad said, "Absolutely not" and I was very glad he did. Representing Unionville meant a lot to me, a feeling that went beyond being a big fish in a little puddle. I felt like a fish out of water at the Cricket Club. It was scary to walk into a place like that with all its linen tablecloths, fur coats and rich skating history, formerly as the Toronto Skating Club. I felt unsophisticated, a total hick, as if I didn't wear the right clothes, speak properly or look right. Everyone seemed to be smarter, blonder, taller, better looking. This was a different world. My parents put in an application, the lobbying procedure began and eventually we were allowed to train there.

At the 1960 Canadians in Regina, we came third to Wagner and Paul and Otto and Maria. There were only spots for two Canadian pairs at the Squaw Valley Olympics—Wagner and Paul easily beat the European champions, Marika Kilius and Hans-Jürgen Bäumler, for the gold and Otto and Maria came fourth—but we got to join them at the Worlds in Vancouver in March.

These first Worlds for me marked the beginning of an incredible year in so many ways. I had just turned thirteen. People were starting to notice us and I was starting to notice a few things about how the skating world and the real world operated. We almost didn't make the competition. During a practice three days before heading west, Bruce yelled at me for not putting enough effort into a scissor lift, so on the next try I kicked my leg up with a little extra energy. Guy lost his balance and I took off. Guy crumpled to the ice on the net side of the blue line, I soared and landed flat on my back on the far side of the red line. I cracked my tailbone and every muscle I had seemed to seize up. My dad called in a physiotherapist, an unusual move then, and worked like a demon himself to get me skating again. We made it to Vancouver.

The championships were the culmination of my dad's dreams for me and, for one of the few competitions of my career, both my parents came, my mum to look after me and my dad to do some public relations for us and help keep Guy's nerves under control.

I had a great time. I tried to make friends with a Soviet pairs skater, Liudmila Belousova, who was skating with Oleg Protopopov. They had just come from being the first Soviet pair to skate in an Olympics, placing ninth. I thought Liudmila was my age and that we'd have great fun together. She turned out to be twenty-five. I also got word from the CFSA through my mother that I should watch out who my friends were. Guy and I placed eleventh out of the twelve pairs competing. Wagner and Paul kept the world title they'd had since 1957. The big surprise was the Jelineks' second-place finish, ahead of Kilius and Bäumler. I was very happy about that, not only because of Otto and Maria, but because Marika Kilius, the German ice princess, was the most hateful person I had ever met. Years afterward, when Marg thought my competitive instinct needed a boost, she just whispered in my ear, "Marika Kilius."

My father died that July. A few weeks later, my mother sat in the dining room with some friends who were trying to help organize what had to be done if I was going to keep skating. She put her head in her hands and said, "I don't know how I can continue this. I can't afford to go on."

I remember feeling a great sense of relief. I was starting to feel the enormous pressure of where I was headed and thought, "I have an out. I don't have to do this anymore." I said, "It's okay, mummy. I don't need to skate. I can give it up."

She said, "Oh, you have to. You have to do it for your father."

He wasn't physically there cracking the whip anymore, but he was still there symbolically and it was a burden. I never told my mother, but I thought in a sense I was lucky he had died. He had been pushing with such strength and fervor, I probably would have rebelled eventually and told him, "I'm not doing this. These are your goals, not mine." It wasn't that I didn't want to skate and achieve. I loved everything about it. It was strictly a reaction to pressure and a reluctance to do such very hard work. My mother felt a responsibility to him that we try to finish what he had started and she was a much better politician, a better manipulator in a sense, than he was.

I continued to skate. I don't know how she managed to pay for everything, but she did. People in the community, through the Unionville club, moved mountains with fund raisers and other kinds of help. Whether some of it was under the table, I never knew.

Fresh from my fourteenth birthday, we went to Lachine for the Canadians, expecting to stay one lock step behind the Jelineks as they moved up the ranks to become champions. But a pair from the Toronto Cricket Club, Gertie Desjardins and Maurice Lafrance, beat us to come in second. This was a little shock to the system. We suspected that some muscle-flexing by the Cricket Club was involved, seeing as how we were sure our performance was better, but we were soon off to the North American championships and we didn't think the reach of the Cricket Club could extend to Philadelphia.

Our team looked good going into the event. We all expected Don Jackson and the Jelineks to win, although it wasn't likely that our women's champion, Wendy Griner, would get past Laurence Owen, one of the daughters of American champions Maribel Vinson and Guy Owen. Laurence was wonderful. She had a fresh, wholesome look, but didn't fit into any mold. She was carefree and joyous on the ice. She had wonderful rosy cheeks, beautiful big eyes and a short shag haircut that feathered over her face and fluttered when she skated. I was totally enchanted by her.

Her sister, Maribel Owen, was a different story. She and her partner, Dudley Richards—Dudley Dahrling, as we all called him—were the pairs champions. They were very lovey-dovey both on and off the ice and had all the lah-dee-da affectations I equated with the Boston Beacon Hill crowd. They bugged me. Of course, they were the competition, which may have coloured my attitude, but they seemed to me to be more like dancers than pair skaters. They couldn't do lifts very well, while lifts were our big thing. Because I was tiny at this point, Guy could pitch me into the air with great abandon. Maribel and Dudley couldn't come close. I thought they were just showboats and was quite disgusted with them. We also felt that Otto and Maria would easily win the title and that even though we were better than the Americans, we would never be allowed to be second.

The few days of competition were eventful. Bruce got a call from Marg in Toronto that he was a father for a second time. Then Otto and Maria fell during practice. Otto's head slammed into the ice, knocking him unconscious for almost an hour, and, as he went down, Maria dropped from six feet up onto his prone body. As she came down, his skate blade slashed her thigh. There was blood all over the ice as the medical team scrambled to get them to hospital fast.

Not surprisingly, the rumour started flying around that they might not be able to compete. Guy had me out on the ice almost immediately. We truly did want Otto and Maria to skate, but if they couldn't we might just win this thing. We worked our tails off.

In what was one of the gutsiest performances in skating history, Otto and Maria did skate, stitches and all, and did win the title. They were dazzling. But our intensified training paid off. We skated one of our best skates ever. Some observers thought that if there was ever a night for us to move ahead in the protocol, this was it. We were great. Then we waited. Our abysmal marks were posted. In the stands, my sister saw a man standing, waving his arms. It was long-time coach and former French pairs champion Pierre Brunet leading the crowd in a long, sustained "boooo."

I went upstairs to the dressing room where my mother was waiting. It was the only time I ever cried over such searing disappointment, the only time I ever threw anything in frustration at the unfairness of it all. I knew how Maribel and Dudley had skated. I knew we were better. Mum yanked me aside fairly quickly, saying, "We will not have any of that nonsense of throwing things and crying because of how you were placed. The only job you can do is go out and skate. If you skate well, good for you. But where you place is up to the judges and you will accept it gracefully and with good sportsmanship."

It was a lot to handle, especially since I also had to deal with our almost immediate departure for the world championships in Prague. Not only was this my first trip to Europe, but we were going behind the Iron Curtain, a scary proposition during the darkest days of the Cold War. What made it even more frightening was that this would be the first time Otto and Maria had returned to Czechoslovakia since their childhood escape after the Communist takeover. Maria would be living with my mother and me while we were there. The Canadian government and the Internationl Skating Union had intervened and demanded guarantees that the Jelineks would be safe in Czechoslovakia and would not be detained. The ISU even threatened to move the championships if assurances weren't given. But despite the Czech promises, we didn't know whether we should let them out of our sight. My mother knew a Czechoslovakian woman in Toronto who had returned to her homeland and had never been allowed out again.

Another concern was that my mother's visa hadn't arrived in Canada before we left and I wasn't going anywhere without her. It still hadn't arrived when the Canadian and American teams flew together to New York to catch our flights to Europe. We were going through Amsterdam and the Americans through Brussels. They would leave after us but would get to Prague first and would wait for us so the whole North American contingent could go as a group into the city.

At the New York airport, we heard that the visa had been tracked down and was on its way, but as the time of our flight got closer, there was still no sign of it. My mother said "Now look, if the visa doesn't get here, I'll just go with the Americans. But I'll be there in Prague. Don't worry." I did. The visa arrived just as we were boarding the plane.

When we got to Prague, nothing much was happening at the airport. There was no sign of the American team anywhere, so I went up to an official-looking woman to find out what was going on. To a fourteen-year-old's eye in 1961, she was exactly what a communist would look like. She wore a grey hat over greyish hair, a long grey sacky coat and heels that looked more like old ladies' sensible shoes. She peered at me rather coldly through glasses with thick Coke-bottle lenses. I said, "We can't find our friends. Where are the Americans?"

She said, "I'm sorry, the Americans have all been killed." Then she turned and walked away.

The word spread quickly through the airport, but we couldn't get any information. No one would tell us anything. In my imagination, I thought they had all been lined up against a wall and shot. Eventually we learned that the plane had gone down on its approach to the Brussels airport. The entire team—along with friends, parents, some of the finest coaches in the United States and young alternates who had decided to go just to observe—were among the 73 people who died.

We were all in shock. My mind started thinking about how close my mother had been to being on that plane. With dad having died just months before, I felt for a moment what it might be like to be an orphan. We were shepherded onto a bus for a long journey into downtown Prague. The trip was long not because of traffic—there were hardly any cars at all, nobody could afford them—but because a million people had taken to the streets to protest the death of an African leader, Patrice Lamumba. They carried huge black and white signs splattered with blood-red paint and obvious anti-American slogans. They rocked the bus back and forth as it inched its way along the main streets. I couldn't figure out what this was about at all.

We stayed in Prague for a few days, continuing to skate and not knowing what was happening with the championships. After practices, I would go back to my room at the Jalta Hotel to find my mother and her Toronto friend writing notes to each other, then burning them in the ashtray. It was like a spy movie. We stayed about a week, gradually realizing that the other teams were not arriving. Eventually, we learned that the competition, despite American requests to carry on, had been cancelled and that we were allowed to leave. We went to Switzerland to skate for a while, came home, then soon left for Boston for a memorial fund-raiser for the American skating team.

At the 1962 Canadians in Toronto, Gertie Desjardins and Maurice Lafrance beat us again to come in second to Otto and Maria. Then we were off to Prague again to skate in a new rink that was the most beautiful building I ever performed in. It had a huge capacity under a ceiling painted blue with white doves surrounding a slogan that apparently said something like "sport for peace."

The Czechoslovakian people were very kind and showed great respect and admiration for all the athletes. They seemed to take a special liking to Guy and me. They would come to practices with little gifts, mainly crystal glass. They gave me a nickname that meant "little water spider" because I was so skinny with such long legs. I took great offence to it, but everyone else seemed to think it was nice. We would sign hundreds of autographs every day and were swarmed as we left the building.

It was the best Worlds ever for Canada. Don Jackson landed his triple Lutz and became champion of the world. Wendy Griner won the silver. And in a wonderfully emotional moment for the Prague fans, Otto and Maria became world champions too. Guy and I placed fourth, much higher than Gertie and Moe.

Soon after, Otto and Maria retired from competition and joined the Ice Capades, so the race was on to become the new Canadian champions. Rather than looking at our skating and what we needed to do to be first, we chose to push responsibility for losing onto unfair judges. We felt that the way the skating industry was, if you had the support of the Toronto Cricket Club machine behind you, you were probably going to place higher than if you were from dumpy little Unionville. I used to feel that the judges were all Toronto Cricket and as long as we were competing against a Toronto Cricket team, we would never win. I didn't think our Canadian championship performances were that bad. I felt, rightly or wrongly, that we were camping in the wrong tent. It seemed to me a better indication of our talent and skill when we were more highly placed at the Worlds than we were in our own country.

It was also unnerving that we always seemed to draw first place to skate. We felt that almost no one could win skating first out of the warmup because the judges were saving their higher marks for later in the roster. In those days, pairs only skated one program—there was no short program until 1964—and if you skated first, it was doomsday. It would send Guy for a loop. The script he made for himself was "if we skate first out of warmup, we can't win."

The 1963 Canadian championships were at the Royal Glenora Club in Edmonton. All kinds of people were being fed information about how Gertie and Moe were the likely winners. That ticked me off. I thought, "What do we have to do? We beat them at the Worlds." Even back in those days when the sport wasn't that big, the local newspapers would cover national skating events. Figure skating being such a beautifully photogenic sport, skaters in action always made for a great front page. When we arrived in Edmonton, there was a picture of Gertie and Moe in the paper under the caption: "The Favourites." Everybody walked around on eggshells, not wanting to show us the paper in case it tipped us in a bad direction. My mother showed it to me. She knew if anything was going to jump-start my motor, it would be that.

Again we drew first place to skate. We felt the draw was fixed. Guy was freaking out. Everything was against us. The big Cricket machine was going to run right over us. We didn't skate very well. It wasn't disastrous, but we weren't top notch. Fortunately, Gertie and Moe didn't skate very well either. It was a squeaker, but we beat them four judges to three. Once we had the title, we started to relax and improve. The experience also fixed our idea about skating first out of the warmup. Important, yes, recipe for doom, maybe not.

Two weeks later, we were in Vancouver for the North Americans. At the end of a practice in the Vancouver Coliseum, I was standing by the boards when I saw the imposing figure of Gertie and Moe's coach, Sheldon Galbraith, approaching. He had always terrified me, so my knees were trembling and my heart was pounding. He said in a deep, menacing voice, "You know, you may have won the Canadians. But we've been working very hard and we're going to beat you this time."

I was frozen to the spot. I thought that was a terrible thing for an adult to say to a sixteen-year-old, but it was warfare as far as he was concerned. I shot back, "Well that's fine, Mr. Galbraith, I hope you have because we've been working just as hard to stay ahead." Then I ran off to my mother almost in tears. The encounter was frightening, but the message was just the sort of negative motivation I needed to really put the boots to Gertie and Moe. I became so confident that the day of the competition, walking along the street in Vancouver and seeing the trophy in the window of the local Birks store, I said to my mother, "That's going to be ours tonight." My mother thought my bubble would burst right there on the spot. We won on every judge.

As Canadian and North American champions, Guy and I got quite a build-up in Europe for the Worlds in Cortina d'Ampezzo in 1963. We appeared on the cover of *Bundt*—the equivalent of Life magazine—and were talked about as the inheritors of the Dafoe and Bowden and Wagner and Paul tradition. The ISU was apparently behind the hype, part of the early marketing efforts for the European Tour of Champions to come. On photo day at an outdoor rink near our Cortina hotel, we went into one of our patented lifts for the benefit of the world press. Guy raised me up parallel to the ice. I continued right on over, going pile driver-style head first onto the ice. My memory is still shaky about what happened next, but I am told the ISU representatives insisted that we compete despite the injury. Paralysis in half my face put an end to that idea. Then they insisted we at least skate in the tour. The Canadian government intervened and quickly got me on connecting flights back to a hospital in Toronto. Doctors there decided there was no concussion because I wasn't getting dizzy. It took them a few days to realize that skaters don't get dizzy. The constant rotation and spinning develops a finely tuned inner balance.

I recovered soon enough for us to make some guest appearances at springtime carnivals. The fractured skull wasn't the only problem I had with my head. It was swelling for other reasons. We performed in Northern Ontario and, because we thought the place was a two-horse town that wasn't very important, we didn't skate in a very important way. We flopped around the ice and made a joke out of it. When we came off the ice, my mother was waiting. She went up one side of us and down the other about how inconsiderate, thoughtless and unprofessional we were, how we didn't deserve the word "champion" behind our name so disgustingly selfish and arrogant had we been. She made us realize that every audience is important. That helped us to add a little gloss to our performances for the next year when we were headed for the Olympic Games in Austria.

Our skate at the 1964 Canadians in North Bay was our best ever. We easily kept the title and even got a few sixes. It was also the high point for the Unionville Club. The correspondent for the local paper raved about the championships and wrote, "And so Unionville's coach, Bruce Hyland, who had three entries, had two firsts, Senior Pairs and Junior Pairs, and one second, Senior Dance." She also noted, "A young lad from Lachine easily took the Junior Men's Singles; remember his name, Toller Cranston, for future reference."

At Innsbruk, Guy and I had to be considered for one of the top three spots, but no one had seen us at Cortina and people forget fast. No one knew what we could do so Bruce threw himself into the all-important "off-ice political work." He says, "It was just little groups talking. 'Hey, have you seen Debbi and Guy? She had an injury but now she's doing great.' We had to get the news out."

Every day he would come back to the village and say, "Okay, we're up another placing."

He was adamant about the structure and procedure during practice. He would never let us do anything that wasn't working and we had to do our best trick right away so the judges on the sidelines could see it. It would always be the twist.

It was a real battle for medals and the battle for the top places on the podium was fierce. There was an intense focus on the pairs competition. The Austrian and German federations were all-powerful in those days and the German federation had the reigning world champions in Kilius and Bäumler. But Liudmila and Oleg Protopopov were threatening the German lead, the first time a Soviet pair had ever done so. Cold War politics made the rivalry a matter of east-west honour. The local Austrian crowd was rabidly pro-German. At the Games' opening ceremonies, people were selling postcards of Kilius and Bäumler proclaiming them Olympic champions.

Pairs still skated only one Olympic program. It was all or nothing. We skated ninth. The Protopopovs were just before us, but there was a warmup between their skate and ours. We were skating first out of the warmup again. We stood at the side of the boards staring out at this great white sheet of ice waiting for our names to be called. Usually we were very silent. Guy was always supportive and always gave my hand a little squeeze. But the Olympics is a different beast. I have never since felt anything as scary or thrilling. The Olympics can tease out the very worst in people. Guy looked over with a stark look in his eyes and said, "Now don't you blow this."

I picked my jaw up off the floor long enough to say something equally horrible. "You just stand up and do your job and I'll do mine." And with that, we skated out before the Olympic judges.

We apologized to each other afterward. It wasn't such a bad skate, although not our absolute best. Our slow part, which was very Protopopov-like, went over wonderfully well. Guy, who almost never fell, fell on a double loop jump, but I don't think it had much effect on the standings. No one was going to beat the Protopopovs that night, although it was very close.

It was the end of an era on the podium. For one thing, along with Petra Burka who won bronze a few nights later, we became the last Olympian skaters from Canada to stand on the podium in front of a Union Jack. For another, the pendulum of skating dominance swung the last few degrees away from North America and into Europe. The Protopopovs' gold medal was the first-ever skating medal for the Soviet Union. Their place atop the pairs podium has been handed down like a Soviet-Russian heirloom ever since.

One factor that made them champions was that the Canadian judge gave us second place and Kilius and Bäumler third. Suzy Morrow, the pairs silver medalist in the 1948 Games, was a very experienced judge and wasn't the only one who placed us second, but the fury of the crowd focused on her. She wore a red wool coat when she judged. The headlines in the paper the next day called her the 'Red Devil'. The reaction in Innsbruk was bad enough, but it got worse when we went on to the Worlds in Dortmund, Germany. An angry crowd was waiting for our team bus when we arrived. They were ready to tear Suzy apart. She switched outfits with Marg Hyland and quickly walked out with the kids with Marg's hat pulled down over her face. Marg sauntered out in the red coat and said, "Hi, everybody."

Everyone stared at her. "Who are you?"

She said, "I'm just one of the mothers."

The German fans were soothed when Kilius and Bäumler defeated the Protopopovs to remain world champions. Guy and I won the bronze again, skating in gold beaded outfits that were the talk of the competition.

Two years later, the German Olympic Committee declared that Kilius and Bäumler were professionals before the Games and retroactively disqualified them from competition. Guy and I returned our bronze medals, which were passed on to the fourth-place American team, Vivian and Ronald Joseph, while we were sent the silver. I have official documents stating that we won bronze and silver medals in the same event and no Canadian or International Olympic organization has been in touch to clarify the standings. The ISU never stripped Kilius and Bäumler of their world title and the word is that they have been rehabilitated and are back in the record books as having won Olympic silver. But I still have the medal.

While we were in Dortmund, my mother and I told Marg that Guy was negotiating with Ice Capades. I was faced with the prospect of retiring. I was just 17 and couldn't imagine living on the road. I needed to get more education and do something productive. But Guy was 23 and joining the show was a wonderful move for him. He had a long career with Capades, skating with Gertie Desjardins. They made a great pair.

My mother was approached, unofficially, but with the encouragement of the Canadian Figure Skating Association, and told that there was someone who would sponsor my skating. Everything would be paid for if I would continue, which meant finding a new partner and going through all the building stages again. Apparently, the sponsorship hinged on my skating with Maurice Lafrance and being coached by Sheldon Galbraith. I said, "No, it's Bruce or nobody." But really, that was never a factor. I just didn't want to do it anymore. My mother left the decision to me and I considered it for a long time, maybe ten seconds. We were third in the world, which wasn't too shabby. I could never see beating the Protopopovs, who were in a class by themselves. I couldn't imagine staying for another four years. It didn't make sense to linger in this strange, make-believe world of elite competition where the only thing to talk about was skating. It was a very short career—six years—for a high level athlete. I'd do it all again, every second of it. It was fabulous. But I felt it was time to move on and get a life.

As it turned out, the life still played out in the skating world. Skating has that effect on people. The love affair with the sport never ends. The competitive part was thrilling, but it was just a moment in time. The circle hasn't closed yet on the glorious adventure that offered so much more than medals.

W hat skaters need most is ice time. The rink is the skater's world. It is where small children and mature competitors spend hour after hour, day after day, all year long to learn new skills, to practice, practice and practice again and to perfect their skating technique. Canada is blessed with some of the best winter facilities anywhere, with even the smallest town having an arena that is often the focus of community life. That gives Canadian skaters a critical edge in world competition.

Ice time is expensive and sometimes hard to come by simply because there is one other great popular ice sport that Canadians are rather good at. For arena managers, more than ice is involved with hockey. There is extra revenue from the snack bar and pro shop when teams and fans pile in, so naturally hockey gets more prime ice time, often leaving figure skaters the choice of working in the wee hours of the morning, the late hours at night or other times the hockey players don't want. The rink is their world too, although beyond the basic essential elements of ice, boots and blades it is a very different world indeed.

Even in those basics, there are differences that have to be catered to. Hockey players like their ice much colder and harder than figure skaters do, with a temperature anywhere between 15 to 19 degrees Fahrenheit. Ice that cold turns grey and the tracings of figures are hard to see. Ice that cold has no give and is terrifying to fall on without all the pads that hockey players wear. Figure skaters like the ice to be a little spongier, to have a bounce, with a temperature of around 25 degrees Fahrenheit, soft but not so soft that puddles form on the surface. Figure skaters like the ice fairly thin too because thick ice becomes too white. Thin ice is darker and tracings show up much more easily.

The figure skating blade is wider, longer and less round than a hockey skate blade and the hollow ground between the inside and outside edge is much greater. Figure skaters need more connection to the ice. Blades are much more than a means of transportation. They are anchors that allow skaters to make tight turns with their bodies leaning toward the ice at very sharp angles.

Beginning skaters often think they should shave their toe picks off, but the picks are there for a reason. A large toe pick is essential in free skating because the picks are used in the same way that toes are used for walking, namely for balance. For higher level figures, the toe picks may be shaved off, because there is a certain look to the tracing and the turns that is easier to achieve without them. A skater can get a better-looking edge and a better appearance of the print on the ice.

There are always modifications to accommodate personal style. Through trial and error, a skater begins to find out what blade works well. Tradition is also involved. Because there have been so few changes in blade design, what worked for Barbara Ann Scott will probably work for Elvis Stojko, even though the requirements are considerably different. With figure blades, coaches have a history of using a favourite throughout their skating careers and are likely to recommend the same blade to their students. Custom is passed on from coach to skater and when the skater becomes a coach, the tradition continues.

The construction and design of the boot has not changed much either. There has been very little research on how the boot can better absorb the shock of big jumps. The thought has been that the boots have to be like concrete for skaters to land the jumps safely, but something's got to give on re-entry to the ice and if it isn't the boot, it's the body. The pounding and banging that comes from the torqueing of the body as it tries to get out of multiple rotations produces ligament damage, tendon tears, shin splints and other long-term injuries.

There are not that many high-quality boots in the world, so there is not a lot of choice. Most skaters go with custom-made boots. Skaters' feet do not look pretty. Deformities are not uncommon after being stuffed into hard leather for so many years. Lumps, bumps, calluses and "skater's heels"—huge bumps on the back of the heel that can be terribly painful—have to be accommodated in the boot design. The boot becomes critical not just for its strength, but its comfort.

Skaters shop around for the kind of combination that works well for them. My boots were custom-made by John Knebli, still one of the best bootmakers in the world, who would make very careful allowances for a thin heel and a wider area on the ball of the foot, taking many special measurements. Putting my foot in the boot was like putting it in cement. My foot couldn't bend, move, twist or turn. Blisters developed and started to bleed. There would be localized, specific areas of pain, but also general aching just from putting the boot on. The boot would be so stiff at the top of the laces that I couldn't bear to have anyone even look at my shin, it would be so bruised.

It can take a week of "hamburger feet" before skates start to feel comfortable. Sometimes boots break down before the season is over, the strength of the leather deteriorating to the point where creases appear on the sides. Instead of holding the foot up, the leather flops, which means you'll kill yourself.

Skaters might have to go through that twice a year, so they always try to break in boots when there isn't a critical event coming up.

Landing a jump takes skill. You're falling from two to three feet up in the air onto a tiny fraction of an inch of a steel blade and moving across the ice, skating always on a curve. If the jump is done well, the body stays right over the skate so that when you land you're well-balanced. But that's not always what happens. The boot becomes even more important landing a bad jump. Just as you anticipate where a corner will be when you're riding a bicycle but can always make minor adjustments doing the turn, you need to be able to make instant adjustments to the landing so that you can hold it without putting the other foot down, without having to step forward prematurely and without crumbling in a heap on the ice. A boot that is doing its job holds the skater like a root holds a tree.

Pairs skaters have the most dangerous and difficult elements to do in terms of a boot withstanding force. Throws—where the man assists the woman off the ice, then hurls her through the air where she has to do triples or doubles by herself and then land—happen at a much greater speed, over a much greater distance and at a much greater height than any single skater ever has to deal with. The chance of a bad injury may be no greater for pairs skaters, but the constant pounding takes a toll. The skaters doing triples in a throw are not the Brownings and Stojkos who are accustomed to doing triples. They are women who are not as physically prepared and would never do them on their own as singles skaters.

Throws are frightening. I don't know that I would have ever done them had they been part of a skater's artillery in my day. It's one thing to be lifted and carried six feet off the ice, which takes a certain kind of mentality—the worst falls happen in those moves—but it is quite another to be pitched twenty feet across the rink.

Skating on both edges at the same time is called a flat and it is not something skaters want to do. The idea is to be skating on one edge or the other at all times. Certain moves could be done on a flat or in a straight line for artistic effect, but they are few and far between. The rule is one foot, one edge, always skating curves.

The blade's rocker is rounded from toe to heel and blades have different radiuses. The deeper the rocker, the better the blade for jumping. A coach will often force a timid skater into a blade with a deeper rocker because once you roll onto the front of the blade, you're committed. You are going into the air whether you want to or not, which has an effect on the timing, rhythm and psychology of the jump.

Sharpening is very much by choice. Normally a skater doing figures will want a duller edge than someone who is free skating. When you are doing figures, you are generally going very slowly and want to maintain a constant speed around the figure. Too much sharpening on the edge tends to slow you down. Too little sharpening also slows you down. Some people skate figures on very dull skates. A dull sharpening especially for figures—a satin finish— makes the edge extremely smooth so there is no impediment, no friction from the blade itself, no nicks picking up extra bits of ice. A satin finish doesn't have the same depth a free skate sharpening would have, but is not really dull either. Many young skaters trying a figure sharpening for the first time cannot hold an edge at all. They skid around the circle, feeling as if they have no connection with the ice.

Free skating puts much more stress on the sharpening. When you're going at incredibly fast speeds on incredibly deep edges, you need a very sharp blade to hang on. There is nothing worse than pushing and feeling as if there is nothing to push with and that you are slipping off the edge.

Amateurs need perfect sharpening, proper ice quality, the building temperature just right, positive vibes coming from the audience. Older skaters with experience can skate no matter where they are, what the conditions or how dull their blades. I've seen coaches I admire skating beautifully around the rink and not only do they not have any edges, their boots are held on with string. Real skating is when you can do it no matter what. You worry less about the frills and more about the basics.

My figure coach invented little games a child could understand. She would say, "Now don't skate on top of the ice. You look like you're skating on eggshells." She would talk about cotton balls being on top of the ice and that I seemed to be skating as if I were afraid I would disturb them. "Get down under those cotton balls. Skate three inches under the ice."

Once I passed my gold figure test, Marg said, "Now you'll learn how to skate."

I was very miffed. "What do you mean? I won an Olympic medal. I've got my gold test and you're telling me I'm just going to learn how to skate?"

She was right. Get into the ice, feel like you're skating three inches under. When I was skating, my tracing was so light it was a struggle to see it. Now I step down on a figure and it looks likes someone has taken a white pen and carved out a print in the ice. I'm not different, I've just learned a lot more about what is important. Get into the ice. Use your knees and press into it.

I used to think that by lifting up, I would put less pressure on the ice, have less friction and go faster. But it doesn't work that way. The more a skater is into the ice, the greater the speed. Some people have now made plain, straight skating—stroking—an art form all its own. When skaters talk about other skaters, they don't want to see jumps and tricks and spins. They want to see stroking that is loose, easy, powerful, in control, with no body language reflecting effort above the waist.

As a coach, I say to my younger students, "Sit with me behind the boards and we'll watch other skaters skate around the rink. But we're going to watch from where we can only see from the waist up. Then we'll talk about whether they're good skaters." Looking at the best skaters from that vantage point, you are not aware that they are pushing. They stay on one level just moving through space as if there were no friction at all. Poor skaters bob up and down, their bodies bending forward, their shoulders heaving. The power comes from the hips and upper legs, with a little help from the lower back. The artistic moves come from the waist up.

Kurt Browning has outstanding "run to the blade,"meaning on one push with the same amount of power, he can cover twice the distance anyone else can. His blade has a magical property. While other skaters have to push hard, he can skate around the rink with almost no effort. His secret is a great body, great contact with the ice and a "good foot." He feels the ice, kissing it as he goes along with a very gentle touch, but he skates three inches under. His foot skates, not his body, with little intellectual direction. His brain doesn't have to tell him, "Okay, now be here, lean there, balance now." He moves so naturally. It's called talent.

A good foot also shows itself in figures. Skaters may trace a perfect circle which, if you break it down small enough, is a series of straight lines. But one skater's series will be very round, continuous, with a smoothness to it like railway tracks going around a curve. Another skater's circle may also seem perfectly round, but the edge will appear to lurch through the circle in short movements. With a very smooth skater, the texture and colour of the tracing is uniform all the way around. The lurching foot leaves a tracing that is light-dark-light-dark-light-dark. The difference is subtle to the untrained eye. To the trained eye, it's glaring.

When figures were important, there were very unlikely champions, the most famous being Trixie Shuba of Austria. The best free skate move she could do was a basic double flip or double Lutz, yet she won the Olympic gold and two world championships. In 1972, she placed ninth in the free skate portion of the program, but kept the title because figures were worth 60 per cent. She went on the world tour of champions, doing what she did best. When she came out for her exhibition number at Maple Leaf Gardens, she skated figures and was booed out of the building. She made the rules change almost single-handedly.

Marg Hyland sat in on the meeting in Ljubliana, Yugoslavia in 1970 when Sonia Bianchetti from Italy first suggested dropping figures at the Worlds and Olympics. Jacques Favart, the ISU president said "No way. That's ridiculous, that's where figure skating is based and that's the way it's going to be." Marg says, "Sonia thought they should be eliminated because it took too much time and the North Americans had more ice time and more practice and they always did well in figures. That was the whole thing. It was ice time."

But with derision greeting the world champion, the ISU realized something had to be done. The value of figures in the overall mark was gradually decreased until 1990, when they were eliminated all together for senior events, opening the door for a crop of magnificent free skaters to burst forth.

It's a shame that figures have been eliminated. At low levels, skaters are still tested on them, but the incentive to do figures is just not there anymore now that they do not have to be done in competition. The good thing about their loss is that it has reduced ice time for just about everyone. Skaters no longer need to train six, seven or eight hours a day, with three or four of them spent on figures, followed by three hours of free skating. The reduction in ice time has allowed skaters to have more of a life apart from skating. Because of the enormous expense of the sport, many skaters, even with financial contributions from sponsors, the CFSA or the government, still have to work to support themselves. Now kids work half-days, train half a day, then have a bit of a life at night.

Skating figures is a lovely, lovely feeling, very quiet, almost dreamy. Free skating is energy-plus. The two worked well back-to-back, rather like learning scales on piano and then cutting loose by playing pieces. Figures taught muscle control and developed quality edges. Carving eights, threes and other figures requires intense concentration. The best "figure" skaters are either blessed with that gift or soon have to develop it. One of the most blessed of all time was Barbara Ann Scott. When she was tracing in practice or competition, a bomb could go off beside her and neither the noise nor the shock wave of the blast would have put her off stride.

The skill developed partly from the cold, precise, relentless coaching of Otto Gold. "He had eyes that would bore right through you," she says. "He was a taskmaster. He did not like any frills in free skating. If you moved your arms as a ballet dancer, he'd take off his gloves and throw them at you. He wanted it strictly business-like. He trained both Mary Rose Thacker and me and he had us both skate to the same music, the polka from *The Bartered Bride*. We called it 'The Battered Wives' and we both skated to it for two years in a row. We never had choreography. Mary Rose just did an Axel. I did all the double jumps. No one ever believes that, but in 1942 in Winnipeg I opened my program with a double Lutz. I was the first one ever to do that."

Under Sheldon Galbraith's direction, her abilities and presentation grew, but skating figures was what were valued then and they were the basis of her success. Sheldon says, "She would have beat every boy in the world. There wasn't one who could hold her. Dick Button could never have held her. That doesn't mean he couldn't have beat her in free skating, but he wouldn't have been near after the figures. She was doing 12 figures, two days, six tracings. The second day, she crucified her competitors."

Tracing figures is not valued highly in skating anymore, but Barbara Ann kicked off almost half a century of contributions to the sport by Canadians, contributions that are way out of proportion to the size of our population. Canadian women have played a part, although as a sport women's skating has been in the doldrums for years, despite the attention it gets from the media. Petra Burka was the first to do a triple Salchow in competition, helping her become the country's second woman world champion. Karen Magnussen was more well rounded. She was smart, a gifted communicator, good at everything and had determination and a tremendous work ethic. If figures had not been part of the mix, Lynn Nightingale would have been world champion. As a free skater, she performed exquisite programs where time just seemed to stand still. Liz Manley is probably the most talented women's skater Canada has ever produced, even though with her good-sized self-destruct button she was always unpredictable. Her silver-medal performance at the Calgary Olympics under enormous pressure was a triumph, although she really should have won the gold. She was that good that night. Josée Chouinard, but for her nerves, could have made an impact. At her best, she skates with great poise and grace, and is vivacious, very musical and lady-like.

With a few exceptions, men's skating before Don Jackson won the world championship in 1962 was a snore and a bore, a lackluster, unartistic series of jumps and spins put together with as little imagination as possible. Donnie skated to a fantasy of *Carmen* and married athletic elements and artistry. Now men's skating has become the benchmark of excellence and the beacon showing skating where it will go.

Canadians have always been the first to do things in competition. Donnie Jackson, the first triple Lutz. Vern Taylor, the first triple Axel. Brian Orser, the first triple combination. Kurt Browning the first quad. Elvis Stojko the first quad combination. Others, of course, have had tremendous influence. Britain's John Curry took it in the direction of classical ballet. Robin Cousins has added more to skating since he retired than he did as an amateur, not to underestimate his impact then. He was beautiful, lyrical, long, flowing, quite tall for a skater. He had a bit of the Curry in him, but in a more athletic way and with a more manly look.

Toller Cranston had a touch of the same style, but with no real ballet training to back it up. He was just so different from everyone else. That was apparent from the moment he packed up his skates and paints in Montreal and at 16 took a train to Toronto, arriving fat, out of condition and with no conception of the need for training. "I had no idea," he says. "I thought you just hoped for a good day on the night of the competition. I didn't know about going through your program."

He skated at the Toronto Cricket Club, coached by Ellen Burka, for several weeks before telling her, "I am not like the other people. I am an artist. I am going back to Montreal because I cannot be inspired here." Fortunately, Ellen prevailed upon him to stay. In 1974, he won a bronze medal at the Worlds. That year and the next, he took the gold as free skating champion of the world. Twenty years later, he is still one of the greatest names in skating, as sought after today as he was then. He talks quite openly about not being a very good skater. He says he's just a show hag who will continue as long as he can throw his body around in the air. He figures no one really cares now whether he goes off a poor edge, has a bad take-off or loses his balance at some point. Just fight back and land the jump.

He found his own vocabulary very early on. He says, "I sacrificed refinement for aesthetics, for passion. Even if it came out in a regular or ugly or unaesthetic way, I tried to be passionate about what I did. And in my defense, I actually believed it."

All his positions are a little out of the ordinary. In skating, it is called "Tollering around." There are a great many typical Toller moves that are slightly balletic, very stretched. Extravagant hand and arm movements are keys to his artistry. The arms explode, the hands speak a language of their own. Sometimes his hands are the only thing I watch. In stroking, his shoulders wave, then he goes into distorted positions that somehow work, performed with a sense of show. Very grand flamboyant gestures are all part of Tollering around.

He has a great sense of context and content in everything. Watch the layout of his program and you get the feeling that the ice is a canvas he is drawing on with his feet. Every part of the ice surface is covered, with highlights at every important point. Draw the program on a piece of paper and notice that it is graphically beautiful. He's closing fast on fifty, but I would still rather watch him than almost anyone else.

Brian Pockar is not usually mentioned as a major star, but he was a fabulous skater. He was the first of our male champions to display a sense of elegance that the skaters who followed him used and built upon. He was beautifully well-rounded and consistent. He did everything well. Excellent figures, breathtaking free style, jumps, spins and a sense of line worthy of a ballet dancer. Unfortunately, he got caught in the years when Toller Cranston and John Curry were on the scene and skaters at the top had one thing they did superbly well. One would think that being well-rounded as Brian was would have meant more. Somehow it didn't.

He came on the scene in the late seventies, becoming Canadian champion in 1978 and holding the title until 1980, with Brian Orser coming up behind him. He lost the title to Brian Orser in 1981 and should have won it back in 1982, but the tide had turned. Brian Orser was identified as the guy of the future and got the backing. Brian Pockar outskated him and then went on to win the bronze medal at Worlds, which was the crowning glory of his career, but all the heads in Canada's skating world had already turned to watch Brian Orser's incredible air sense, his amazing jumps, the lightness, the feet, the footwork. Everyone said, "Here's the guy."

Brian Orser had one burst out of the bubble—jumping ability—although his talent became much more than that. He made the triple Axel part of the compulsory repertoire, but also became one of the finest lyricists this country has ever produced. He still looks the nicest in the air of any skater today. He was eight-time Canadian champion and skated to two silver Olympic medals, still the highest step Canadian men have ever reached on the Olympic podium. His performance in Calgary in the Battle of the Brians was brilliant. But it was just someone else's moment.

His reign as champion pre-figured Kurt Browning's in that Canada had two truly great skaters at the same time and didn't know what to do with the second one. Gary Beacom was a square peg who didn't fit into a round hole and didn't really care. Terrifically innovative, he was like Toller in that you could sense that he didn't feel or hear a single beat of the music, but that he heard something else, something private, unique and wonderful. He didn't set out to be deliberately different. He wasn't making a statement. He just danced to his own music and is still having an impact on audiences, performing in company with some of the greatest skaters in the world.

Gary was a hero to Kurt Browning, who changed skating by making it acceptable for men to be diverse. They no longer have to be relentlessly athletic or relentlessly balletic. A male skater can be Humphrey Bogart, rock the ice, do the can-can, be a cowboy, skate the blues. Kurt could do all those things and in doing them he expanded what was acceptable for athletes to do. He was an outstanding champion. When he successfully defended his world championship title in Halifax in 1990, there was a swell of home crowd adulation. At the end of the Parade of Champions exhibition, it took him about an hour to get off the ice. He couldn't give enough back. He let everyone know how much he appreciated their support and had time to talk to whoever wanted to speak to him. He appeared as what he was, a wonderful role model, a great promoter of the sport and a Canadian through and through, raising the flag and waving it whenever and wherever he could.

So many skaters end their programs with some hokey, bad taste gesture, either sticking their fist in the air or making as if they are in prayer, thanking God for their skate. When Kurt bows, he portrays the feeling that he is grateful he made it through his program again and grateful that the audience is being so kind. A good bow is full of humility, never taking for granted for a second that what has just happened on the ice will ever happen again. Perhaps it is only part of the act, but the idea he tries to get across has to be appreciated.

After moving to Toronto to be coached by Louis Stong, Sandra Bezic took over his choreography in her usual intensive way. In two short years, Kurt tackled many different things, performing numbers that will become classics. There should be a permanent repertoire of great classical skating pieces, not just the musical selections, but the choreography. Such things should not be allowed to die. Who could do them would be the problem. Competitive skating is all about being the best you can be and seeing if you can take it in a new direction, contributing to the list of accomplishments, not just individually, but for the sport.

Elvis Stojko was identified early as having tremendous talent, but his atypical skating looks, his proportions and style made him a target from the time he was five. Walking around with a moniker like Elvis wasn't easy either. He became used to being a loner and when he rose in the competitive ranks, never was a kid so shy. But he learned by studying the best and discovering what it is that made them the best. He's very clever, willing and eager to learn. His jumping ability is extraordinary. He just hangs up there, then he comes down, kisses the ice with his foot and the edge floats away.

It's beautiful. He can go up in a jump almost upside down and come down right. That's the way his body is structured. Kurt Browning does not have the same magnetic feet that are attracted to the ice. Kurt can wipe out, but Elvis rarely blows a jump. The landing might not be pretty, but he always gets down and has already taken the acrobatic side of skating to new heights. Time will tell what his ultimate contribution will be.

Canadian pairs skaters have not been as innovative as the men, but they have also made valuable contributions to the sport and have equalled the number of Olympic medals won by our men. Suzy Morrow and Wally Distelmeyer were the first pair to perform the death spiral in the low position common today, with the woman's hair brushing the ice. Frances Dafoe and Norris Bowden, Canada's first world champion pairs, worked with the country's most celebrated floor dancers of the era, Alan and Blanche Lund, to develop lifts no one had ever seen before. They did the first loop twist, the first throw jump and the first lasso in the air, still the most difficult of lifts from the forward entrance, as they did it.

Wagner and Paul, Otto and Maria and Guy and I all benefitted from their legacy in world competition, as did later pairs such as Sandra and Val Bezic. But it is Barb Underhill and Paul Martini who have become the epitome of what a great pair is, making more audience magic come true than almost any other couple. When they skate, I find myself sucked into the number to the point of speechlessness. That wasn't always the case. When they were amateurs, they were very good skaters, winning the Worlds in 1984. A decade later, they have become better and better. The skating world tends to confuse being a champion with being great, but they are two different things. And there is no shortcut to being great.

They have won every professional competition imaginable but have never remained stagnant. They have always pushed themselves more, with the help of Sandra Bezic, and have grown as performers. They radiate the professional aura of classiness and command. The effects of life on an artist can never be underestimated. There are child prodigies in skating as there are in every field, but they are one-dimensional. Only when life starts churning and mucking around with an individual does that individual have something to say. Barb and Paul suffered through many crises in their lives as individuals and as a team, not the least of which was their struggle to the top as amateurs. There was a time when they didn't like each other much, but they weathered that stage under the guidance of Louis Stong. The positive effects of a coach can also never be underestimated.

If Martini and Underhill are about life, Lloyd (Herbie) Eisler and Isabelle Brasseur are about skating, taking pairs back to the era of Rodnina and Zaitsev when it was breathtaking, fast and glorious, an era that was not to everyone's liking but was necessary to advance the technical edge of pairs skating. Herb and Isabelle have neither the body types nor the refined aesthetic sense to evoke emotions the way that Gordeeva and Grinkov's soft, balletic style can. But they have gymnastic daring. They're fast, innovative, creative originals who set a new standard for lifts. They are the best lifting pairs team of all time and have worked hard at integrating the better elements of ice dancing into their work so that the elements flow gracefully from one to the next, building momentum to the end.

Pairs skaters often seem to plan their programs from trick to trick, with something down in one corner, another element at centre ice, then off to the boards in another corner to pull off something else. Dancers use the whole ice surface as their canvas to put down beautiful pictures. Few did it better than Tracy Wilson and Rob McCall, although they were never given the kind of recognition they deserved. They were just beginning when Torville and Dean were ending their amateur career. Torville and Dean had incredible ice power and a variety of skills most dancers do not have. They also had a repertoire that was shocking in terms of its versatility and latitude. Tracy and Rob did not turn heads the way Torville and Dean did. They were magnificent personalities, both on and off the ice, while Jane and Chris are rather bland in the non-ice world. But dancers are supposed to be Freds and Gingers recalling Viennese waltzes of old, the elegant, majestic over-protective prince with the needy, beautifully adorned princess partner. Rob and Tracy did not have that typical look. That's just the way they were built. They were well matched, almost the same height. They were superior skaters, their material was the best, but their look worked against them.

The ragtime number they developed for the Calgary Olympics was perfectly them. The detail with which it was conceived and performed was brilliant. They only won a bronze, the only medal Canada has ever won in ice dancing, but when the ISU came to suggest to their judges what the direction of ice dancing should be, it was not the Olympic champions whose program they took as the example. It was Tracy and Rob's.

Many people, media people in particular, think that because ice dancers aren't throwing themselves into the air, twisting dozens of times and crashing to the ice like bags of potatoes that ice dancing is not a sport. Its critics think it is more akin to floor dance and does not have the athletic merit that free skating has. But at the international elite level, dancers are every bit the athletes free skaters are. It is a grave mistake, and does ice dancing a great disservice, to claim that it does not have sporting merit.

Dancers within their four-minute free program do not have one moment to rest. There is no reprieve. If they are doing a good dance, their footwork, their speed and their program development are non-stop. Free skaters can at least choreograph rest moments where they can let go for a second or two. It is much, much more difficult and athletically challenging for two people to do footwork at full speed than it is for a free skater to stroke around the ice to get ready for a jump. Great dancers like Wilson and McCall executed over three thousand coordinated, synchronized movements within their tight four-minute time frame. That takes incredible concentration and physical ability.

The kind of program attitude dancers bring to the sport has won converts. There has been great development in the artistic end of skating in recent years, with more emphasis, not just psychologically, but technically, on the artistic side of the program. In the free program, it is now the artistic mark that breaks a tie and artistry requires self-knowledge, analytical skills and courage. To become the best in the world involves a stripping down process. You become naked in your attempt to analyse, not just the athletic side of your skating, but who you are as a person, what you are willing to say and how much of yourself you are willing to share with an audience.

Competitive skaters used to only have to weave spells in show programs, but those days are over. Now they have to do it in competition too. If they don't figure out how to do it and make the leap beyond jumps and spins, their names might go into the history books, but not near the top of the list of skating greats.

Nowhere is it said that a skater has to have a new program every year, but that has become the norm. Many skaters manage to pull it off superbly, although I've always wondered whether we are seeing each skater's best. It's hard work finding a new idea and finding the appropriate music to go with it. It takes a long time to become good at every section and it can take a year of daily run-throughs before a skater starts to feel as one with a program.

An exhibition program doesn't have to have the competitive edge or detail that a free skate or short program must have. One short-cut many skaters take is to use their short program as an exhibition piece, changing the elements a little bit, maybe not doing a triple Axel or simply doing a double Axel in combination. That puts a lot of miles on a program and gives the skater the experience of doing it often in front of the public. It's one thing to do a program day after day after day in an empty rink. Once it plays in front of an audience, the program takes on a personality and a life of its own.

Many show programs come from the skaters themselves. They hear some piece of music they love and are dying to skate to or may have a message they want to convey. Skaters keep a repertoire of half a dozen numbers that can be pulled out when needed depending on the situation. One event programmer may ask for a slow number, another might want something uplifting to close the show.

The quality level in show programs is rising, with triples and other difficult moves becoming expected, paralleling the rise of yet another new generation of jumps in competition. When I was skating, we used to warm up with singles in the hope of landing a double. Now skaters warm up with doubles in the hope of doing a triple and they will soon warm up with triples in the hope of landing a quad. The level of physical achievement boggles the mind.

It takes a particular body type to reach that level. With long legs, you can have a beautiful line and very good speed, but jumping requires a lower centre of gravity. Elvis Stojko or Liz Manley, who have almost no legs, are the best jumpers, although they are not as aesthetically pleasing or pretty in the traditional sense. The explosive power in the legs provides the elevation needed to have the time to rotate. Then the body has to learn, "This is two, this is three, this is four. You're done now."

The competitive season is so long and the requirements of producing new material so great, it's hard to find time to learn something new. The pressure of competition means that skaters have to have all their ammo early. The technical requirements are now so high at such an early age that a skater is not  seriously considered without triples by about age sixteen or seventeen. A skater who hasn't learned a triple Axel by then is probably not going to learn it. You might be Mister or Ms. Personality, but the skating world won't look at you. It won't be long before everyone will have to do quads, but thankfully, it is becoming more common now for people to sit up and take notice of artistic bravery too.

Program content is fairly restricted. There are only six basic jumps—three off the edge and three launched with the toe—with everything else in a program being a variation or combination of those six. They begin as singles, then go to doubles, triples and quads.

A triple reveals itself over time. Sometimes it comes by fluke. The body knows it is something more than a double, but isn't quite sure how much more. So the skater hammers away at it. The successful landing of a triple involves months of learning one degree at a time. Reach a plateau, fall back, move ahead a bit more. No one can make it around at first. The key is to get landed on the proper foot, then worry about the rotation.

There are many stages to completing that extra rotation and many things to teach the body. Skaters work with harnesses, belted in and lifted, so they can find what the rotation feels like. It is not something that can be put into words. It has a character the body comes to know and identify. You know what the final feeling should be, so you have to do whatever it takes to get to that feeling. The technically correct position in the air is very vertical, with the body wrapped tightly around itself. The tighter the body becomes, the faster the rotation. As you pull in against the force trying to make you open up, you turn faster and faster. Some skaters such as Elvis have tremendous air sense, like a cat thrown up in the air and always landing on its feet. The best skaters will be able to land no matter what. Don Jackson always said, "Anybody can land a good jump. But it takes talent to land a bad one."

If the technique is perfect and the approach is perfect, you go into the air. The body stays perfectly perpendicular, your feet are crossed, your legs are pulled together, your arms are tucked, the rotation gets done and you get to the landing and there you are, you just settle down onto the ice. Great. That's easy to do. But how do you land when you slip off the edge on the take-off, your body starts to tilt, you're torquing out of the circle and your life is before your very eyes? Can you get landed then without killing yourself? A good skater can. A good skater has the sense and the ability to correct errors in mid-air when there is no time to think. In a blink, the jump is over and you're either hamburger on the ice or you've landed and are skating away. When you have the sense up there that you are falling out of the circle, you had better hope that your body corrects itself appropriately. Pummeling your carcass into the ice hour after hour is not fun.

For the best skaters, the jumps are not the focus, however. The program is. Everything—the elements, the music, the choreography, the costume—radiates from the concept or idea that flows from the key questions asked every summer. How am I going to look? What am I going to say? What's the message I want to get across? Who do I want to be this year? Skaters go into great detail to examine and bring their ideas to life. It is as if they were preparing a thesis for a major paper in university. The elements do not take over. At the end of the program, a viewer may not even remember what the elements were because they were woven into the fabric of the choreography, beautifully subtle, even breathtaking.

Themes, like Kurt's *Casablanca* number, are one way of unifying all the elements of a program and have become all the rage in the past few years, although skating to a theme is really an old idea dressed up in new terminology. In the late seventies, Canadian dance champions Lorna Wighton and John Dowding, coached by Marijane Stong, decided they were going to do *Swan Lake* in world dance competition. There were cries of outrage, with people citing chapter and verse that the ISU did not allow themes. But it wasn't long before everyone was skating to theme programs, even in singles. So long as the skater and the choreographer involved had talent, the programs were successful. But a theme program is hard to do well. It takes outstanding acting ability. Ice dancers have generally been better at it because they didn't have the jumps and spins to get in and have always been more dramatic. Theme programs are a challenge to free skaters who tend to be more gymnastic than theatrical.

Themes create a certain style and a portion of the free skating mark has always been given for style, although it is often not clear exactly what the term means. Even as a skater, I was never sure what it meant, but it always seemed to relate very strongly to a uniqueness, a personal quality or talent that no one else could display. But skating tends to be a fashion industry. Someone does something wonderful, so everyone else follows suit. Suddenly, people come out of the woodwork to tell skaters they have to do such and such if they want to win because that new something wonderful is what the judges are looking for this year. It takes faith, self-esteem and courage to say no to all the advice often backed by the entire weight of the sport, from the top down.

Skaters get lots of feedback. In Canada, the national team members all have mentors, national and international judges who might be judging them during the year, who are brought in at different stages over the summer to comment on the development of the program. The CFSA will send a representative to give the Association's viewpoint on whether the content of the program is a good vehicle for the skater and whether the artistic direction is impressive enough. Next to competing, this is the most nerve-wracking, pressure-filled time for both coach and skater. After spending much time and money developing a program, it is not pleasant to have someone come in and say, "Oh, we hate it. The music's not right for you." Having to go through this constant perusal and analysis can be creatively intimidating, even debilitating. Artists who are athletes ask if someone would have sat beside Renoir when he was painting and said, "I don't like that, Jean, I think the blue would be better."

What makes a great program is doing what you and your coach think is the right thing to do. When other opinions insinuate themselves, the program often seems watered down to the point where it is nothing but a bunch of different pieces. When a skater believes in an idea, whatever it might be, that's when it works. There are real tests of will, when it comes to holding off the best intentioned, positive criticism. The coach will very often say to the advisor, "Take a hike. Get out of my face. Here's what we're doing."

Occasionally, more subtle means are required. When Brian Orser was developing his programs, he always received high-level advice to change this and that. He says, "A week later he'd call to see how we were doing and I'd say, 'We changed it, it's great and we love it.' The next time he'd see it, he would say, 'Oh, they're going to love this' and we'd say, 'Thank you so much for all your help.' We didn't change a freakin' thing."

Skaters don't have to take the advice from mentors, judges, the CFSA or anyone else. But that is not to say that the advisors cannot be right. Eisler and Brasseur decided in the summer of 1993 to do a cutsie, comedic short program during the Olympic year. It was reminiscent of a clever show number where Herbie played a big buxom blonde to Isabelle's Charlie Chaplinesque character. The cross-dressing worked well with Herb, who's five-eleven, lifting Izzy, who's a tiny dot of a thing at five-foot-nothing. It was clever and cute in a show, but cute is out when it comes to competitive skating. They would not be told that they were making a mistake by doing this junior-level number. They are not cutie-pie or comedic-type skaters. They're athletic, hell-bent-for-leather skaters and the routine was inappropriate. They spent the summer getting the program organized, went to Piruetten and found that not only did everyone in Canada hate it, but every other judge in the world hated it too. In a matter of weeks, they had to come up with a new idea, new music, new costumes. It may have already been too late. First impressions are important. Their new program was a much better vehicle, gypsy sort of piece that was nothing new, but they did it well. It nicely fit their personalities on the ice, it had a bit of a romantic feel to it and well-known music that people could tap their feet to.

By the end of August, skaters should have their material organized and be starting to feel confident with any new moves. There are several international invitational events throughout the summer. The skaters assigned to them are generally the less experienced team members. National champions get their pick of international events beyond the Worlds and Olympics and usually choose events much later in the season, closer to the time when a skater wants to peak.

By Labour Day, skaters will have progressed through several of the key stages involved in having a program ready for the competitive season. The first stage is learning the elements that go into it. The second is doing the elements in the program successfully, with all the connecting steps. The third and the hardest is to get it ready for performance, but that stage lies way down the season. Technically, a skater is constantly stepping up the ladder in terms of expertise and skill, but the final push is to let the program acquire a personality, to let it become what it should be: not just a series of elements strung together, but a *Work*. That is always the most gruelling part and the most interesting. Once skaters feel comfortable and don't have to think anymore about what comes next, they are able to put something of themselves into it. Only then does the program come to life and breathe.

September is spent getting the winter season organized and continuing the training that becomes more intensive as the heat of competition gets closer. September is a key month for putting the finishing touches on things, starting the push to peak for whatever major event is scheduled for the fall. That means very hard training sessions, off-ice conditioning, aerobic and anaerobic training, stretch classes, dance classes. The three or four hours spent daily at the rink are just the tip of the iceberg.

September is the hardest time to train, a blah month when the nature and character of the athlete emerges. These are days of just plain slogging, of endless run-throughs and nit-picking. Every day is exactly the same; go to the rink, lace up the skates, wear the same clothes, see the same people, do the same thing. There is neither the joy and excitement of starting something new, nor the thrill of last-minute preparations for a competition a few weeks away. This is when athletes can either help themselves or go bananas. It takes a disciplined mind and a disciplined body to continue, both fixed on a clear goal, whether it's passing a test or heading into elite competition.

Many talented skaters can't hack it. Probably every coach has come across students who have talent coming out of their ears but who have no respect for that talent nor feel any responsibility to it. They take it for granted and feel so special that they don't think they need to work hard or set goals or develop good work habits. Their natural gifts may get them through a few tough situations, but those kinds of kids rarely make it to the highest levels. They are talked about as having had something great, but not the personal integrity, insight and courage to develop it and use it well.

For serious competitors, the incentive to sticking it out is moving along the track to the top, a tricky procedure that is always a challenge to the skaters themselves and to the coaches guiding their careers. So much of the country's great skating talent was developed by coaches whose names are never heard, young coaches often in small-town rinks who do all the hard work of developing basic skating technique. The student-coach relationship is the closest adult relationship a young child will ever have, other than the parental one, and the best coaches are caring, nurturing and trusting. But few skaters stay with the same coaches throughout their skating careers. To get into and through the maze of competition requires particular skills.

There is a lot of manipulation involved in bringing a skater into the limelight. Sometimes it begins at the club level where the members of the club executive have children skating. It is a natural and human thing to promote your own child and it takes an exceptional person in a position of power to throw off the temptation of promoting a child for, say, a solo in the club carnival. Are there not some rewards for volunteering? The other students twig to any favouritism quickly, but feel powerless. In many cases, the parents who are interested enough to devote their time to club work are also the ones with the kids who are most interested in skating, but that's not always the case. Sometimes there is a power march by people who like being president of something and will go so far as to rewrite club constitutions to make sure they stay on top. Smart clubs get rid of those kinds of people fast, especially if decisions are not backed up by good talent. Clubs fall into terrible shape when they are driven by egos rather than common sense.

Coaches may also manipulate, holding students back from trying tests so they can stay in a lower level of competition. A student who can do a double Axel and should be at novice level where everyone can do that jump may be held back to compete at the pre-novice level where maybe only two other skaters can. Coaches may also hold students back from having contact with other individuals who might help them grow as athletes. Coaching is a competitive business and coaches are always afraid of losing star pupils. Many years ago, there was a coaches' code of ethics, which was hilarious because no one paid the least bit of attention to it. Student stealing has a long tradition and so does the practice of bad-mouthing other coaches' techniques.

Ultimately, either a parent or the skater makes the decision to move on to another coach, often at the suggestion of officials, judges or the CFSA. There is always lots of free advice around and it is easily worth the price. Changing coaches can be a traumatic affair for the original coach, who may feel rejected and bitter, and for the skater. Moving on often means moving away from home. Some skaters find the move to their liking and do well with it, many are intimidated by being uprooted and suddenly finding themselves in places where life moves fast. They may be very unhappy without the special attention they felt in the town where their talent was discovered.

But everyone knows the big names in coaching. The same names keep appearing on the list of champions and they generally work in larger cities. Doug Leigh's Mariposa Skating Club, first in Orillia and now in Barrie, is the exception. Success often seems to go in waves, with schools in various cities producing champions for five years or so before the wave moves on. After the war, Ottawa was the place, then Toronto, Vancouver, Kitchener-Waterloo, Edmonton and now Montreal, where Josée Picard and Eric Gillies are producing an incredible number of good skaters.

What the big-name coaches have that younger, more inexperienced coaches do not is managing capabilities and political connections. They have reputation, impact, power and sway. They can say to the CFSA, "Hey, I am working with a new skater you should have a look at." Ding-ding-ding, the bells go off. The machine starts to function. The talent is identified, the skater is assessed psychologically, emotionally, physically, intellectually. The sport begins a file that will be maintained for years and years.

It is the great managers who get skaters to the Worlds and the Olympic Games. These days, they are helped by the CFSA and teams of teachers and consultants in everything from physiology to choreography and psychology. In the old days, they did it without any support from the CFSA or anyone else.

Sheldon Galbraith set the tone for coaching in Canada for many years. A CFSA official, Don Gilchrist, spoke to him during an appearance of Ice Follies in Montreal in 1941. Sheldon says, "He wanted some footwork that I had in our pair. It was crossing steps when the ankle stayed soft, but you stayed on the ground—you didn't swing your leg—and then you just drew it. We could slither ice. With pressure, we could make the rink move. We were strong kids. It's a wonderful feeling in skating that you can drive the rink around."

After the war, Gilchrist recommended Sheldon be hired as the professional at the Minto Club. He was not hired just to be

Barbara Ann Scott's coach, but just months after he arrived, he was asked to go with her overseas for the European and World championships. Doors opened all over Ottawa. He was an American citizen, but he was given a passport and the outdoor rink on the grounds of Rideau Hall was made available for training. Minto Club officials took him through downwind take-offs on figures and pointed out everything he would need for Barbara Ann.

Sheldon says, "I had what she needed. She had the skills in figures. She didn't have free skating, she didn't have choreography and she didn't have musicality that laid out. It took a bit, but the girl sensed 'this is where I want to go.'"

"He made me into a free skater instead of a little soldier that just marched through 'The Battered Wives'," Barbara Ann says. "He gave me this wonderful new program—*Only Make Believe* was the slow part—and he would skate with me like a silent pair partner to lengthen my stride a little bit. It was such a nice program with some showmanship in it and change of music. Oh, he worked like a demon. And he was such a good psychologist. Without him I never would have made it."

His political smarts were a great benefit. In Europe, he found that the judges were still playing favourites the way they had before 1939. The Gerschwilers from Switzerland—Arnold, Hans and Jacques—had trained most of the continent's skaters in England during the war, so it wasn't hard for them to have an influence. They were manipulating against Barbara Ann, sending people onto the ice to make disparaging comments about flats in her figures or having earnest conversations with judges in restaurants to point out other faults. Sheldon says, "Oh hell, I knew what they were doing. I was raised in California. This was street stuff."

He always spoke to other skaters at the competitions, offering his advice even to some of Barbara Ann's competitors. He says he had no agenda, but was mindful of the proverb, "Sucker thy enemy and thy shalt heap coals of fire upon their head." Some of the people he was helping let him know what the Gerschwilers were up to. He countered every move. He was also helped by Barbara Ann's mother. "Mrs. Scott could reel around the room with a drink in her hand and a cigarette hanging down and say, 'Watch this guy in the corner, he's trying to do a deal with the Belgian judge.' She was very clever at that."

When the marks for Barbara Ann's first figures were ridiculously low, he said, "Look Barbara, with this milky sky and the ice, no one can see what's going on. Can you do this thing right down on the edge in front of the audience?" With 4,200 people looking down on the judges, the marks started to change. She won every figure.

Hans Gerschwiler should have been the world champion from 1939 all through the early forties, but there were no competitions. He won in 1947 only because Dick Button had poor strategy and didn't compete in the Europeans where the judges could get a look at him. He couldn't break through the wall of judges all lined up for Hans. But in 1948, the Gerschwilers knew Hans wouldn't be Olympic champion the way Dick Button was skating unless they made some deals. In Prague that year for the Europeans, Arnold Gerschwiler said to Sheldon, "If Hans doesn't win, it's too bad for Barbara."

Sheldon said, "Shove it up your sleeve."

He traces his style and success to his service in the American Navy's air service during the war. "That helped in coaching," he says, "because it was pedagogy, methodology, psychology, training, expertise, aviation, mechanics, aerology and administration, all the things you go to school for, but it was a crash course. What makes an airplane fly? And the theory of flight is the same thing that makes a skate and a motorcycle and a bicycle work. It's resistance against the angle and the opposite effect. This is what made skating easy for me to teach, because I had the tools to do it. In flying, I learned to do it hands-on. I could take a kid through every manoeuvre I wanted him to do. I could teach him the relationship of the senses that he would get going through these manoeuvres, but I couldn't teach him the energy and the thought patterns, the sensitivity to it. That helped me get this perception of what coaching should be and how it should impart information to those who were going to wear the information, not the view from the coach or the judge or the onlooker."

After leaving the Minto Club, he taught non-stop at the Toronto Skating Club—later the Toronto Cricket, Skating and Curling Club—before retiring from the coaching scene, although he is still involved in special projects. As a competitor, I was terrified of his presence on the ice, so large and so stern. I don't recall him ever laughing or smiling, but he came to his teaching with the kind of dedication that is rare today. He brought science to skating. He was the first coach to study force and the dynamics of movement, the first to study biomechanics before it was even a term. Figures, mathematically elegant, were a strong point with him and he could make his skaters do things I only dreamt about. He found an incredible joy in learning and being on the cutting edge. He brought in the very best costume and program people at a time when any talk of team teaching was heretical. He was an incredible communicator and he loved what he did.

He was given some of the best talent imaginable in a facility that was probably unequalled in the world at the time. He seemed to have a magic bag of tricks that he could just reach into and pull out the next champion over and over again. What also made him different from many skating people was that he never rested on his laurels.

After Barbara Ann turned professional, it took him five years to get his next world champions, Frances Dafoe and Norris Bowden. After years of skating with his brother, he always was pair oriented. "It immediately opens doors when you have parallelism in things. This is really what a pair is, symmetry or counterpoint." Pairs skating was still in its infancy in the forties. There had been some good synchronized skating done in Belgium, but for competitive pairs skaters in the United States, a Lutz jump was a big night. Skating to a silver medel in the 1948 Olympics at St. Moritz, the Canadian pair of Suzanne Morrow and Wallace Distlemeyer advanced the art. "Suzy and Wally were doing double loops and double flips, but they didn't win. They should have, but you aren't going to win a grapefruit contest in Florida if you come from California. You just have to recognize what these kinds of influences are. But that's geopolitics and I learned that in the navy too."

He made good use of technology in his teaching. He filmed everything his skaters did and played the film forward and backward, in slow motion and at fast speed. In California, he could get film developed in days. In Ottawa, it took almost two weeks. In Toronto, he worked out a system to get his footage developed in hours so that his skaters could review in the afternoon what they had achieved that morning. Filming a competitor in Davos, Switzerland, at a very fast shutter speed, he even proved that the skater was doing a forward jump rather than the backward jump the skater thought he was doing.

He was also adept at music production. By 1946 in California, music could be cut on tape. In Ottawa, he had to work through the night at a radio station with three turntables to produce eight passable records with the cuts he wanted. That helped with Dafoe and Bowden. "Frannie and Norrie were timely. There were pairs who could have given them competition, but others' training wasn't as complete all the way through with music. We were integral with music. The people we were competing against had two records with a blue chalk line and a green chalk line marked on them. When they got to the spin, the guy was supposed to move the needle from one to the other. With music from showbusiness, we coordinated every step to influence the audience. Every kid as an amateur or coach should go through showbusiness first so they find out how music affects people. Because you can make them respond."

The same approach worked well with his next champions, Barbara Wagner and Robert Paul. Bob was the most talented of the pair technically. Sheldon taught him to spin and jump both ways after discovering that Bob didn't have the Axel in the way he naturally rotated. Barb's technique was not as clean, so he masked the shortcomings. "Barb was vivacious and had charm. We chose some music that exhibited the romance angle between the two of them. Up until that time, there was no real romance in a pair that was that strong. Norrie and Frannie had some, but Norrie was pretty straight. They didn't have the embodiment that Bob and Barbara had. You could tell with his superior abilities that he was nursing her along, as a man should, because this was part of the romance angle and she was playing it back. Whatever an audience responded to, we went after and worked it."

When he started working with his next two singles champions, Wendy Griner and Don Jackson, he had them x-rayed. He found that Wendy had pulled a bone loose from her ankle from forcing a double Lutz too early in her life. Donnie had curvature of the spine. "He had so many mechanisms screwed up from landings. The spine was taking the load. With the split double Lutz, the best you can do is land in a back sit spin then work your way out of it after that landing. It's easier to do a triple Lutz than a split double Lutz. Once you get your legs spread, it's awful hard to close them up again against the centrifugal force with those boots on."

Sheldon said, "Why don't you go for a triple Lutz?" It took a month before he was sure Donnie really wanted to try it. When he landed the jump in Prague to become world champion, Donnie nicely rounded out Sheldon's first sixteen years of teaching. In that time, his students had won nine World championships, five silver World medals, two Olympic silvers, an Olympic bronze and the only two Olympic gold medals Canadian skaters have ever won.

Osborne Colson skated in Ice Follies with the Galbraith brothers. He is a sprite little wisp of a man with energy coming out of every pore. Skaters on the same ice feel like they are in the presence of a light bulb at five hundred amps. He started skating in the 1920s, is still on the ice almost every day and can still kick his leg up over his head. He has worked with almost every major skater in North America at some point in their careers and to this day draws a magical artistry from his students. His best skaters have not necessarily become great champions, but have had long performance careers. Sarah Kawahara—"Ozzie's unfinished symphony," Sheldon calls her—didn't really win anything, she wasn't that great a jumper, but she became one of the world's finest choreographers for American champion Scott Hamilton, among others, and with Ice Capades.

Ozzie's unique abilities were apparent even as a competitor in the thirties. "Guy Owen, who married Maribel Vinson, had the most fantastic knees in the world for jumping," he says. "His jumping was terrifying. My jumps were average, not sensational, but my stylization, my admiration of beauty and line and colour and the colour of movement meant something. If someone told me to go a pale pink or a pale blue, I knew what they meant. I skated in colours."

Marg Hyland once told me when Ozzie was teaching, "Stand by the boards and watch." She wanted me to experience an artist at work.

"My style of teaching is done a lot with my arms and hands and feet," he says. "Some students look out on the ice and think I'm a maniac, but it's just my method of getting the thing across."

I always paid attention to him on the ice. He was generous with his opinions and expressed them in an enthusiastic and positive way. But he is a high-strung individual who works from the tradition, verbally at least, of spare the rod and spoil the child. When I was skating, all the students would come into the arena and whisper, "Who is Mr. C today?" If he was in a foul humour, we stayed out of his path. When he is disgusted with how his skater is skating, he lets them know it in no uncertain terms, a style of teaching that I would have withered under. He says, "One thing that age has done has made me mellow. But I was a tyrant and still am quite a strong tyrant in teaching. The students that have more talent I'm a little stronger with because I realize they have great potential so I'm more demanding of them. It can upset me if they don't do what I want that day, though not to the extent that it used to. But even today, they question the mood I'm in. I don't consider myself a moody person, yet I must be."

His bluntness is legendary, but sometimes the toughness seems orchestrated, as if he sensed his skater needed a verbal thwack in the head to get going. He was once asked to evaluate a young skater's potential. After watching her on the ice, he took her into the arena's office and said, "You're wasting your time, you're wasting your coach's time and you're wasting your parents' money." The poor girl fled in tears, but with someone like Ozzie you could never be sure whether his words weren't part of the evaluation. If she had said, "Well, Mr. Colson, I think you are wrong," he probably would have leapt to his feet and said, "Wonderful, let's get going."

He tries to develop the way a skater moves, increasing their depth of understanding and their vocabularies of movement. He tells his skaters, "In figures, feel your inner guts. You know what's happening inside your body. In free skating, I want the expression to pop out the end of your fingers. Your finger nails should tingle. Feel the extension right down to the end. Skating a good solo is like having a good bowel movement."

His reputation is in "finishing" skaters, giving them a show-biz gloss, but he insists on the importance of personal growth and personality. "If I have one more person call and say fix my child's arms…. It doesn't start with the arms, it has to come from inside. If you don't have a personality, you can hardly give anything to anybody. It doesn't have to be a personality you like, but it has to be a personality. It's the commital of yourself to not be yourself but to be the thing you are doing. You don't always want to be yourself. An actor varies the part each year with the music."

Ozzie was a pioneer of team teaching as co-director, with Don Jackson, of a summer skating school at the Banff School of Fine Arts for ten years. Guy Revell was on the faculty. It was a difficult process, trying to find a common denominator so that individual coaches were not working at cross-purposes. "I went about it carrying a clipboard and having meetings after the day just like a doctor would in a hospital. We had great meetings. They were most cooperative. The Banff School had the facility, the ballet was right there, the students were living in residence, no parents, they saw the opera people practicing and had meals with them. It was an expansion, a way of life. All the children who went out there grew up immediately."

Team teaching was a breakthrough because students were finally allowed to have input from someone other than their coach, although as the practice has evolved, a senior coach remains in charge and makes the decisions about who the team instructors will be. A coach still has the need for power and control. There is a lot of information to be passed on to very young minds and conflicting messages from different members of a teaching team can make the process harder. Not everyone is enamoured of team teaching, but it became a fact of life because schools were so large that one coach couldn't service all the skaters. An elite, highly motivated training staff—choreographers, fitness specialists, figure specialists, jump specialists—has become an indispensable part of the system.

Ozzie believes the evolution has not yet gone far enough. "The clubs haven't grown to the same capacity as some of the coaches. Clubs are either community minded for skating or social clubs like the Granite or Cricket. We should have people selecting skaters to go to national centres for a limited term, have funds to assist them and see how they excel after one year."

The idea of a national training centre along the lines of the National Ballet School has been championed by many coaches for over thirty years. Many others have vigorously opposed the notion, believing that the talents and egos involved in skating are far too diverse to be massaged and managed by one curriculum or one controlling intelligence. The closest Canada has come to realizing the idea is Kerry Leitch's Preston Skating Club, which in the eighties came to be recognized as a national school for pairs.

As a competitor, Kerry says his major claim to fame was competing in the junior championships the year Don Jackson won. He came last, almost, but not quite, defeating John Rodway, who had fractured his back and was skating in a brace. He figure skated so he could be a better hockey player, but his first love was baseball. He even had tryouts with the New York Yankees and St. Louis Cardinals. He started teaching skating when he didn't have the funds to continue studies at the University of Detroit to become an aeronautical engineer. He's been teaching ever since.

He always lived by his mother's dictum that "you are only as strong as your weakest link." He figured that while he had the aggressive strengths of a leader and coach, he sometimes didn't have the patience to be a great teacher, so he surrounded himself with strong people, now all ex-skaters.

His school's emphasis on pairs was a practical decision. Almost every boy who figure skates runs a gauntlet of abuse—fag, fairy, pansy, fruit, homo, queer, gay—that begins in late elementary school and becomes brutal once puberty hits. Legions of wonderful skaters have denied their talent and left the sport because of it.

Kerry's school was blessed with some very good boy skaters and he came to the conclusion that pairs skating could influence other males. "Hockey players and those people tend to look up to pairs skaters, whether it's because of the macho image or being with a girl or the fact that they're picking somebody up or throwing somebody in the air. They don't particularly have the same respect for dancers or singles skaters. Hockey teams were always next onto our ice surface, so we always put the pairs sessions at the end so the hockey players would come out and watch. I thought we could keep all these boys interested beyond the transition to high school where they'd have to fight off the criticism. We wouldn't lose them."

Having never skated a pair nor lifted anyone, he watched pairs coach Ron Ludington at several competitions in Lake Placid, then introduced himself and learned. The "national school" came about when his pairs started to have some success. There were few other pairs in Canada at the time and national championships became virtually Preston Skating Club competitions. The school's students won the novice Canadian pairs championship 14 years in a row. There were several years when they won novice and junior championships and a couple of years when they won novice, junior and senior Canadian titles. Lloyd Eisler started skating at the school as a child and, with his first partner, Lorrie Baier, came second to Underhill and Martini at the 1980 championships in Kitchener. In 1984, it was a one-two-three finish for Kerry's pairs at the Canadians in Regina, with Lloyd and his new partner, Kathy Matousek, winning the gold, followed by Melinda Kunhegyi and Lyndon Johnston and Cynthia Coull and Mark Rowson.

Young skaters from across the country, like Doug Ladret from BC, flocked to the school, the first where masses of competitors were put on outstanding programs. The skaters all worked together, many of them billeted with families that were part of the school community. Rules about skating schedules, off-ice conditioning and even eating were strict. The school stressed manners and the importance of appearance and behaviour. To this day, the kids are not allowed to wear jeans in the arena. There were classes in nutrition, time management and organization. There were specialists on hand for costuming, music recording and choreography.

Kerry schooled his students in the real world of skating, saying, "Don't ever use politics as an excuse. You knew there was politics when you got into the game. When you went to the competition, you knew that the BC judge was going to give more marks to the BC skater than the Ontario skater. I don't know the way it can be made so it's not political because it's subjective. You've got to wait, pay your dues, work hard, be dedicated."

He was good at being a PR person for his skaters, always making information available to the press and teaching his students how to work with the media. A couple of times I had the privilege of talking to his skaters about how to prepare for interviews. They were young, bright eyed, cooperative and helpful. They were like sponges, taking everything to heart. "You're trying to market a product," he says. "If you were trying to sell something, you would do the same thing. The kids have to be prepared to be nice to a hell of a lot of people they don't even particularly like because it's not to their benefit to be nasty or rude. It's a big maze and you've got to figure out which is the best way you can get through it and still be a better person when you get to the end."

Every skater had a timeline to follow and everything was produced on a schedule. This was big business, with a nucleus of outstanding people who put their psychological, emotional and physical forces behind the idea of turning out champions. It was run much like the Soviet bloc systems. Conditioning and fitness programs, planned with the help of physiologists, were and still are considered brutal. Before they are allowed to compete, the students run 55,000 stairs over eight weeks, roughly equivalent to climbing up and down the CN Tower 32 times.

As it developed, the regimented program was not to everyone's liking. The school developed a reputation for being very tough on kids, particularly young women. Kerry says, "If I were to judge myself, I would say that I'm tougher on the guys, but if you ask my kids, I think the girls would say I'm tougher on them. I never think that I'm dealing with girls or with guys. I think I'm dealing with athletes. But males love to compete. Watch guys before they go on the ice for their six-minute warmup or their competition and they're always doing something physical. Females tend to cling to other females. That's being female, so immediately I'm labelled as chauvinistic and I don't think I have a chauvinistic bone in my body. I think females are caring, touching, loving people. At the ages that we're dealing with them, I don't think males are. In our culture, they're more animals. Like hockey players or baseball players, they're so busy trying to impress all the girls around them and impress all the other guys as to how macho and cool they are, there's not much time left to be loving or caring or anything else."

He thinks girls have to be more competitive at the moment and more responsible for their own actions. He has no patience for any skater who becomes unnerved and weepy at a competition. He refuses to get out the cheerleader's pom-poms and say, "Come on, you can do it." He was one of the first coaches to use a sports psychologist, Wendy Jerome, to help the types of students he didn't have the patience for. For other girls, he believes his style wasn't a problem.

"Some of the most successful kids I taught under pressure of competition, like Melinda Kunhegyi, Cynthia Coull or Kathy Matousek, were all those things—loving, caring, whatever—until they stepped onto the ice. Melinda Kunhegyi would become a machine. She would do all these physical things, start moving her arms around like a windmill. She took on a completely different character. Take a kid who is a great skater, my own stepdaughter, Tuffy [Christine Hough]. She's a great performer who I think has left a mark in pairs skating with her style, her tremendous rappport with an audience, her personality, which is really wonderful. But she is one of the worst competitors in the world. If, just before she was to compete, the announcer said we were going to have to hold for 15 minutes, Tuffy would say, 'Thank God, what a relief. Boy, what a break.' Melinda Kunhegyi would say, 'Why do we have to wait? I'm ready to go. Why can't I get out there?' The Kunhegyis, Coulls and Matouseks I don't think would say that I was hard on them. I think they would say I was tough, but not tougher on them than I was on the guys. The ones who would find that I was tough on them would be the Tuffys."

The school produced outstanding athletes, although not necessarily great artists, Kerry's philosophy being "first we teach them how to skate, then we work on the artistic end of things." But the mass production of skaters does not always encourage the individuality that is the basis for great skating today and the idea of the national school, in Kerry's view, was doomed from the start anyway. "I said from day one, this is wonderful, but this is not what is best for pairs skating in Canada. The dream that I had was that we could produce some really great kids and they could go across the country and start teaching and Canada would be a very strong pair country because of that. There's not the need to come here and train."

Many competitors are no longer participating in large schools where they have to board close by or board within the school itself. Those arrangements don't work terribly well in this country. It takes an unusual individual to be able to cope with the stresses and strains of moving away from home. It's a crisis of belonging, a crisis of roots.

Many skaters, and I would have been one of them, fall apart when taken out of familiar surroundings. I needed the small town nurturing. I needed to know that my shoes still fit. I needed the kind of coaching I got from Marg and Bruce Hyland, who are a vanishing breed. There are few coaches today who have all the abilities they shared. They had the kind of commitment that included driving from Oakville to Unionville for a 7:00 am Saturday morning patch and teaching little babies as well as national champions. They were teachers, choreographers, lobbyists. They had vision and knew what skaters had to do to make their dreams come true. I used to feel blessed that such gifted adults would take an interest in me. It was as if they turned a key and opened a door and stood behind me saying, "That's the Olympics out there. If you want to go there, we'll help."

We depended on the personal attention, but even in those days, coaches could find themselves spread a little thin. Sometimes Guy and I felt deprived when Bruce had to referee Otto and Maria. Like any good brother and sister, they would rise to each other's defence at the slightest provocation but left to themselves, they would kill each other. Bruce would tear his hair out over their fist fights and arguments and always held them up as examples of how not to behave. He says, "In Prague, I spent 80 per cent of my time keeping these two people on a reasonably level basis to be able to compete. They laced their skates on, they became animals, both of them."

But we always sensed Bruce and Marg really cared about us and weren't there just to do a job. As we skated, Bruce would stand behind Marg on the sidelines, grab her waist and squeeze harder and harder as his heart rate soared. Marg would say, "For heaven's sakes, will you relax. You can't do anything. This is their problem out there."

Marg always maintained, "When you go over the line, kid, and you step on that ice, it's your responsibility. You're the artist. You put the picture you want people to see out there." We accepted the responsibility mainly because any nervousness on their part was never visible. They never showed a moment's doubt. It was so comforting to be on the ice, glance back at them by the boards and feel an energy coming from them like a silent roar of confidence.

They teach in Tampa–St. Petersburg today, having taught for awhile in California after leaving Canada in 1977. Team teaching is very fashionable, especially in the States, but it wasn't their style in the past and it isn't now. "These people don't understand," Bruce says, "especially in Florida. There's no point in me trying to even educate them. They know more than I do. I'm told by the mothers that I can't choreograph a show number, I've got to hire a choreographer. Figure skating is an individual sport, a one-on-one sport. Having nine people teach, I don't really agree with. We should have some sort of bonding between us. No one has a bonding now. It's like specialists in a hospital."

They both feel that the team approach lessens the rewards for both people in the student-coach relationship. Marg thinks, "If you're in one of these school systems where there's two or three national coaches, you're a number. It loses that personal depth. There has to be that closeness. I got such a pleasure out of seeing children develop. I always felt that the skating was part of it, but if they blossomed in themselves their skating would be better and everything they wanted to do would be better. I was always interested in the person."

Her approach was inspirational to me and to their other skaters like Louis Stong. He says, "To me they were the dynamic duo. I miss them in every way in skating. She was the person that I modelled myself on. Even now I think what decision would she make at this point. I always thought he was a bit of a bugger, but there was something very admirable about him. One good thing they had was the energy for sustained hard work. They never denigrated each other. And positive reinforcement? Nothing but. They just fed it to you. It was like an overwhelming force."

The best coaches are often not the people who have made it to the top, but rather skaters who have had a taste of what it is to be great, who have seen greatness brush past them. The motivation to be the greatest continues on into their coaching careers so that even though they could not be a Jackson, Orser, Browning or Stojko, they work their hardest to make sure their students might be. As a skater, Louis placed second to Don McPherson in junior and senior championships. Louis, Don McPherson and Don Jackson made up the Canadian men's team at the 1960 Worlds in Vancouver.

Louis shares with Marg and Bruce the habit of always looking on the bright side, which can be infectious. Even in the darkest times, he tries to find a light. Teaching at Toronto's Granite Club, his career as a coach has been long and productive, with a string of Canadian and international champions. He excels as a teacher and as an on-site coach, which are very different skills. He has always surrounded himself with a strong team and, since the Martini and Underhill days, has been known as a great packager. He says, "Why we've been successful is that we always really think about the music. I mean *really* think about it. We try to pick the right vehicle and dress the skaters in the right costume so that when they're out there it's a 'look'. People like Martini and Underhill have always followed that. But the thought process has always been agonizing."

The effects can be dramatic. For years, Josée Chouinard skated to music that I wouldn't want to hear while grocery shopping, let alone skate to. For the 1993–94 season, Louis had her skating her short program to *La Fille Mal Gardé* and her long to *An American in Paris*, both of which were perfect for her.

For Louis, as for other coaches, the closeness with the skater only exists within the skating world. Off-ice socializing is off-limits. On a practical level, the potential for conflicting loyalties and mis-understandings on the part of other skaters only leads to danger. A certain distance is also required emotionally. For Louis, "The results of what your kids do can't hurt personally. All it does, good or bad, is build on your own toughness and character and I mean that both ways. When Kurt won Prague, I wasn't on a high. I stayed exactly where I was and took the win. That's just part of being the coach. You don't think differently of the skater. When it goes bad, you hurt for the moment for the person, but it doesn't hurt you. It can't or you wouldn't survive."

For him, "The big question is always, did I prepare this person for the job? At least at the Olympics, you have some idea about what they're going to do. When a preliminary free skate test goes out, that's when you're really scared. You have no idea."

What keeps him going are the day to day successes at any level. It may be someone reaching a new stage, technically, artistically or psychologically, or a high point like a badly injured Karen Preston delivering two tremendously gutsy performances to win a silver medal in Lalique or even a young student landing a first Axel. "Those kinds of things make up for everything. All the little benchmarks. I live for those."

There have been many times when Louis has pretty much de-cided to call it quits with coaching, but certain characters always seem to drag him back. He had almost had enough when Gary

Beacom arrived at his door. Louis found him "a very interesting boy to teach. His mind was wonderful and his talent was phenomenal and I couldn't sleep at night waiting for his lesson at 7:30 in the morning. He was a challenge."

He had more thoughts of retiring in 1992 and was really winding down when Kurt phoned one day and said, "Is this Louie Stong?"

"This is *Louis* Stong speaking."

"Oh, I guess that kind of shows how much I don't know you."

After the disaster at Albertville, Kurt had decided he needed a new challenge. He and Louis talked, but Kurt was tentative. He had made the decision to move from Edmonton to Toronto, but found it difficult to make the break with Michael Jiranek. Kurt wanted to keep a bridge to Michael, but Louis would have no part of such a counter-productive arrangement. Paul Martini acted as a go-between to keep the dialogue going. It took a few weeks for both coach and skater to decide to go through with the relationship.

Louis had only seen Kurt at seminars and competitions and had never come to know him in a coach-student relationship. The first summer they worked together, Louis tried out a battery of musical suggestions to see what music Kurt could interpret. As Kurt moved around the ice showing what blues, rock 'n roll, jazz, classical, ballet and everything else said to him, Louis just kept stepping further and further back, thinking, "Oh my God, he can do that too."

It is unusual to see someone after many years in the sport be so inspired, refreshed and enthused. Louis could not stop talking about Kurt and his immense untapped talent.

"You have to personalize each skater. To improve Kurt Browning the skater, we had to improve Kurt Browning the person, in his living style and how he looked at his own body and how he treated his body. He was really lucky to come out standing up. Pretty wild kid. It's like a musician spending thousands of dollars on a wonderful violin. With a skater, this is it, this is your instrument and what we had to do was teach him a respect for it and not to injure it and not to do it harm in any way. So we had to very subtly change his lifestyle, the parties. It didn't enter my mind whether he'd be willing or not. It had to be done so that he didn't even realize it. We introduced him to the right people, a physiotherapist who is more than a physiotherapist, a magnificent person who, as she was applying her therapy, also worked on his head and gave him a new insight into what he had. That's an extraordinary body, but I don't think he ever looked at it and thought, 'This is my life. Without this, there's nothing.'"

During Kurt's first year with Louis, Marijane Stong suggested music from *Casablanca* for the long program. They wanted something completely different for the short and started working with a floor dancer who suggested a Led Zeppelin piece. Every drum beat, every note had something to it. It was brilliant. It was skating like we had never seen before. For the 1993–94 season, the short program music was switched to *St. Louis Blues*, with amazing footwork all created by Kurt himself. Louis found the footwork sequences "scary to watch." The other steps and program elements were devised by Louis and Sandra Bezic.

The collaborative approach to program creation is a fact of life in skating now, but the expansion of the coaching and production staffs has led to some problems for the sport that are only now being addressed. Louis says, "The coaching fraternity hasn't decided who is what yet, because when a skater is allowed to take one person to a competition, who do you take? It's too late for the stylist, it's too late for the choreographer, so you take the coach and this is where there's a problem with people like Uschi Keszler. We don't accredit choreographers and stylists. Is she a coach? My short definition of a coach is the one who's in control of the whole situation. Then someone like Eric Gillies will say, 'Then I'm not a coach. I'm never in control of the situation. Josée Picard is.' That's where we are in the coaching scenario. We're confused."

Sandra Bezic, who has worked closely with Louis, among other coaches, since the early eighties, is recognized around the world as a great choreographer, but she says, "I don't think I'm a choreographer. I think I'm more a director, although that's not true because I do the steps. I don't know what I am. Sometimes I'm a choreographer and sometimes I'm a director and sometimes I'm a shrink. I wear different hats and I like the variety. What I do is give every skater what they need or what I think they need."

She and her brother, Val, were Canadian pairs champions from 1970 to 1974. Their own choreography was always a collaboration. Along with their coach, Ellen Burka, they worked with floor dance choreographers, Ice Capades choreographers if the show was in town and a National Ballet dancer brought in to fix their positions. When Sandra retired from competition, she knew she had something to offer the sport she loves, but didn't want to be involved in any traditional sense. She says she wouldn't know what to do with beginners. She had only been working for about a year when Louis called to say Barb Underhill and Paul Martini had come to him and he didn't feel comfortable handling them on his own. They were basically her first clients. She and Louis decided, she says, "To share fifty per cent of the responsibility, whatever that was. It just evolved into what it evolved into."

There is no one with more talent and skill than Sandra for finding the little golden kernel in the middle of a skater's soul, the key discovery in a complex creative process. Requirements for the Olympics, a pro competition or a show are all different, so she looks at the market, the event, the venue, what the public wants, what the judges want and what common feelings and ideas are out there. But most important is what the skater wants to say and feels the need to do. "When I'm working with my skaters, they're people and I care about them and what makes them tick. In the dance world, the choreographer is god and the dancers are the instruments. It's the opposite in the skating world. There is something magical about the performance and the performer and that's what you've got to find."

Barb and Paul posed particular challenges beyond the obvious height difference. They could do all the tricks, but had no line and no identity. Sandra spent the first summer working with them playing with line to find something that worked for them. Louis zeroed in on a classical feel, which Sandra thinks is always the best place to start, and over the years they kept punching that out. "My style is very much about character and about life and honesty and simplicity and romance and sexuality. Very basic, very simple. And it works with Barb and Paul. There's lots wrong with them, but they somehow transcend it because of their personalities and their strength of character and their relationship, the respect they have for each other and the caring they have for each other. The true love they have is then delivered in their performance. It's about their lives and the pain and the happiness."

She took on Brian Boitano after she saw him lose the world championship in Cincinnati. Watching him skate, she thought, "He is incredible. The program's a very poor fit, but he is incredible. His strength and his technique and his power, just the way he did his back cross-overs around the rink and the position and the angle of his body. Yeah, I'd like this challenge."

Over the years, people had told Brian, "Do this, do that. Smile more. Look into the audience. Get some music that makes the audience clap with the beat." The more he tried to make everyone happy, the more uncomfortable he was and the worse the work became. Sandra started by just watching him on the ice and soon realized, "This guy doesn't want to look into the audience and smile or shimmy. I wanted to find something that he could really, truly believe in. Marijane Stong came up with the Napoleon music, but the whole Napolean thing was a way of giving Brian a character that he could hide behind, but a character that was actually him." She took him from being an outstanding skater to being an Olympic champion.

She has worked the same magic with Katarina Witt, Kristi Yamaguchi, Kurt Browning and many other skaters over the years, but finds it harder and harder to keep going back to the competitive level and be inspired. "Every time I choreograph another program I break into a cold sweat. I'm always scared to death that I won't have an idea and I'm always fearful that I'm not going to be good enough or it isn't going to be good enough. I've got the pressure of their careers on my shoulders all the time and that gets really hard."

Sandra is an original who has carved out a unique role for herself as the director of the Stars on Ice touring show and as both choreographer and director of brilliant television specials, including Katarina Witt's award-winning *Carmen on Ice*. She is leaning more and more to the showbusiness side of skating, just as the line between showbusiness and competition, always fuzzy over the past fifty years, is becoming even more blurred.

The overlap is troubling to many people, usually sports writers who only come into contact with figure skating at one or two events a year or even once every four years and really don't know what to make of it. Is it athletics? Is it theatre? What seems to irritate such critics most is the costuming, which seems to them a frivolous part of the sport. There have even been suggestions that all competitors should skate in generic costumes if they want to be taken seriously as athletes. But figure skating isn't short track or barrel jumping. Costumes are a critical element in programs that involve emotion and the interpretation of music and designers are key people on the team preparing skaters to face competition.

Skating fashion provides one of the more cheerful moments at an event. Some of the ugliest costumes imaginable have been put on the worst bodies imaginable. Some of the most exquisitely designed and executed clothes ever seen have also appeared on the ice. For women, a sequin fetish took over the sport for many years, the thought being that if one sequin was great, a million must be a million times better. But for all the recent excesses, today's skating costumes are a vast improvement over those in the old days. Before science came up with lycra and other fabrics that are lightweight, breathe and move nicely, everything was very formal, unfussy and boring. The man wore a one piece tuxedo-type outfit that came to be called a monkey suit, almost always in black, navy blue or maybe dark brown. The woman always wore the perfect little dress. Thick beige tights were *de rigeur*—this was the pre-pantyhose era—with skating pants that matched the skirt over the tights. Fancy fabrics like chiffon, satin and lamé couldn't withstand the physical requirements. Costumes would rip under the arms, pull out at the sleeves and come apart at the seams. Flexibility is important for a pairs skater. Death spirals and the like demand maximum reach, without the need to be yanking the dress down during the rest of the performance.

The requirements of the sport pose a particular challenge in how to make the pants so they stay down under the bum cheeks. So many women skaters do a move—perhaps lifting a leg up in a spiral—then find themselves eating their shorts. It may appeal to some men in the audience, but it is not an attractive look. The question becomes how to design the pant to cover everything properly, allow movement and have style. What is important is the design, shape and cut. There is no need to go overboard, although walking around in a $10,000 costume does something to the level of performance.

Frances Dafoe is a master at looking at a skater, assessing the body and defining what kind of design is needed. She designed her own costumes during her skating career and, when she retired from competition, landed a job in the CBC wardrobe department and was soon promoted to designer. Petra Burka was her first skating client to become champion. Brian Orser, Liz Manley, Katarina Witt, Kristy Yamaguchi and many others followed. She understands their problems and never forces anyone to wear anything that doesn't give them a lift or make them feel happy.

She has many simple ideas about what makes a good costume. She loves to use colour and fabric, always with the idea that it has to be something that moves, not only in terms of flexibility, but in the sense that it enhances speed. When skaters are travelling over the ice, a rippling costume makes them look as if they're moving twice as quickly. She has a wonderful eye for colour and balance and is never gimmicky.

"When in doubt, simplicity wins out," she says. "A costume is only part of a whole. If all you see when a skater is skating is the costume, then the costume is not well-designed. If it becomes part of the skater—and I like to have a slight reflection of the music—that's wonderful."

Body line is the first thing she considers. "Is the costume complementing the line, because there are a lot of people out there with really bad figures and if you're careful, you can camouflage that. Second is the colour, usually. People forget about the philosophy of colour and the emotions evoked by colour. Half the time it's a subliminal influence, but if you are skating to something that's intense and hot, then the colours have to be that way. And who would skate to *Rhapsody in Blue* in pink or green?"

Her perspective is unique because not only does she look at costumes with a skater's and designer's eye, but also a judge's eye. She has judged national and international events for years. When Brian Orser was skating to lesser-known tunes from *Cats*, she dressed him in a tiger costume that not only reflected the music, but helped make sense of his cat-like motions, letting the judges, to her mind, settle down and listen.

One year when she was not judging pairs, she saw Christine Hough and Doug Ladret skating to music from *Les Miserables*. Doug was dressed in Elizabethan sleeves, Tuffy wore blue and black. After the performance, she said to Kerry Leitch, "You can shoot me down in flames, but I have to say something: *Les Miserables* is a story about death and blood and it's patriotic and it's from the poor part of France. When your pair stands on the ice, you've got to give the judges some inkling of what it is they're expecting to see."

Kerry asked her to re-design the outfits. Attention is evenly divided by having pairs dressed alike, which with some types of pairs skaters can be a mistake, so she suggested that Tuffy have a blood red skirt. "Every time she went up in the air, the eye would follow this brilliant blood. I also suggested we break it down, dressing her as the peasants dressed in the Revolution, but simplified. Doug has a strong face, so I wanted to pull his hair back and tie it the way they did in the period. I wanted to use a shirt the way they would have worn on the battlement, have him wear pretty tight pants, dark blue, and have a brilliant sash at his waist. I wanted the judges sitting there to think, 'Oh, that's French Revolution.' The costumes prepared them for it."

For the skaters, the final fitting of the costume is the finishing touch, the icing on the cake, that rounds out the summer's training.

All the hard work of developing an idea, choosing music, learning elements, putting soul into performance and getting all dressed up for the part prepares them to head out of the safety of local rinks and arenas. Out in the competitive skating world with their coaches by their side, they find judgement, politics, celebrity, thrills and maybe even some glory.

The first competition of the year is a shock, no matter how experienced the skater. The experience is rather like the labour of giving birth for the second time. You know what it is, you've been there before, it's starting to happen again and all you can say is, "Oh, God, I was wrong, this is not what I remembered at all." There is always something new, something that catches a skater off guard. Competition has a tingle and pain about it that is quite exceptional. It is the sort of thing you hate doing but love having done.

For a skater, the common dream—some would say nightmare—of walking naked through a crowd is no dream. It's real. Elite competition requires total vulnerability. Five to nine judges are looking, assessing, analysing and deciding whether they really like you. Thousands of people in the building are doing exactly the same thing. Hundreds of thousands or even millions of people in their homes may also be watching this baring of the soul, the most courageous and most debilitating thing an athlete or artist can do. It involves showing what all artists are afraid of showing: themselves. For many, it's a Pandora's Box. Some don't want to open it because they are afraid of what they might find.

This is the struggle every time you put yourself on the line and face the challenge of being the best that you can be. What you might find will undoubtedly be you, but will it be a you that the rest of the skating world is willing to accept? Will it be a you that says something memorable? You have to believe in the product, but may doubt that you have all the ammunition to win. A backlog of successes should inspire confidence, but what happened yesterday doesn't matter. The only thing that matters is what you do right now. In four or four and a half minutes, everyone will know whether you've got the goods or if you've been faking it. So much self-esteem is packed into so few minutes. The pressure is only increased by knowing that all the years of training, all the money spent by parents and others, all the expectations of family, friends and coaches are riding on what you do in this tiny sliver of time.

Preparing for those few minutes takes effort. Experiencing the building before an event is important to test the quality of the ice, the colour, feel and temperature. Skaters know the second they walk into a building whether it is a friendly building for them. Not every building is the same for everyone and not every ice surface is the same. The ISU has strict requirements about venue locations that do not fall within Olympic standards. Exhibition events may be held in places where arenas are square or half-size, but never a competition. But the length and width of a rink can still vary and that can require some adjustment. Going from a large to a small surface, skaters almost walk through the program instead of really skating it, but it is essential to be going full-tilt. Adjustment is even harder when skating a pair. Unless both skaters have the same picture in their minds, they end up banging into each other.

For skaters who train on rinks with hockey lines, there may also be adjustments if they suddenly find themselves on a pure white sheet of ice. Those skaters have to develop other cues outside the ice surface in the audience or on the boards—flags, signs, banners—that subconsciously become part of the choreography. Visual cues are essential when laying out a program. There has to be some system to figure out where you are on the rink.

Preparation can also involve adjusting the body clock. Jet lag and other travel factors have to be taken into consideration. After flying all night, anyone would be zonked on the first day at the site of the event. Day Two is probably not bad, but things get worse and worse until Day Five when everything seems to fall apart. Any athlete knows moments when you are really in tune with your body. You hear it. It talks and you listen. But with jet lag, your body goes absolutely silent. Dead. Nothing. No communication at all. Your legs are numb. Your brain won't function. When your body has been so finely tuned and expertly organized, you panic when it goes dead on you. Once you've been through the experience, you know that the phenomenon is short-lived, but for first timers it is a really dreadful feeling.

The most critical part of preparing for competition is finding a way to deal with nerves. Under pressure, it is not all that uncommon for younger skaters to black out and forget what they are supposed to be doing. Hysteria sets in. They get totally lost, don't know where they are or what the next step is, don't recognize the music and can't remember when to get off the ice.

Everybody gets nervous. Some people like the feeling, some don't. The anguish you feel when nervousness is part of the vibration of your body is horrible. The moments when your nerves start backing up on you are not cleansing ones or moments when you feel glad to be alive. You dread the next second. But to this day I like a good case of nerves. I never viewed nervousness as a bad thing. It is an appropriate and logical response to a bizarre situation. Nerves sabotaged me once in a while, but that was more a result of attitude and not doing enough homework.

The worst response to nerves is pretending they aren't there, listening to people who say, "Oh don't be silly, what are you scared of? There's nothing to be afraid of." Well, yes there is. The times I tried to squish the nerves down into my stomach so I could think that I was in control of them were the times when under the pressure of the moment they would rise up like a tidal wave and bite me from inside. I could feel them gnawing at my muscles, at my psyche and self-control. The only thing I could feel was fear and the certain knowledge that I was not doing the job required. My legs were dead, my feet were numb, the music was playing, but I couldn't hear it. It was like living in a dream.

Marg used to tell me, "Look, you don't have to worry about the judging or anything else. All you have to do is go out and show them what you show me every day. Don't even let a doubt enter your mind because your subconcious will try to live up to it. Eighty-five per cent of everything is up here in the head. What you think is what you get. What you think is what you are."

Sheldon once photographed trap shooters so he could study them when they put the gun up and see their posture, their attitude and their eyes. He spoke to the best trap shooter the US has ever produced, a man who won over 60 tournaments without a miss. "I wanted to find out what do skills count for and what the philosophy is of the guys that have those skills. He told me, 'I know this. If I break every target, I'm tied for first place. It's the other shooters who make me the winner.' It's easy. You win by not taking the load on your back."

Nerves can also make a skater do well, push hard, skate fast and think a little more. But experience, energy and desire have to be channelled into where they can be helpful. Everyone has something that they use. Superstition plays a big part in all sports. Skaters often have a certain routine or ritual they consider lucky. I used to think that if I skated well in practice and had put my guards at a certain place on the boards, hell would freeze over before I would be stopped from putting them there again. If they weren't in that place every day, I was done for. Some skaters have to do certain activities before they go on the ice. Some carry mascots, stuffed animals festooned with skating pins, or the stuffed animals often named after skating moves like a spread eagle or a flying camel.

The key is to have a support system in place. The CFSA once suggested that coaches didn't have to be at international events, but coaches are part of a skater's everyday environment. The coach is always there whenever the skates get laced up and should be at the competition even if not much actual coaching is going on. Many coaches are just there to observe and refresh a few things. If they still have to coach at a championship, they are in big trouble.

"Coaches take themselves far too seriously at those times at competitions," Kerry Leitch says. "I wish somebody would video the insanity that goes on in a coaching area during a six-minute warmup. The coaches look like water boys and hold the guards. I would love to say to a coach, 'When else do you hold your kid's guards? In your entire life?' What's important is the kid can come off the ice after a disastrous warmup and say that was terrible and I'll say yeah, but you found out what the ice was like. The ice is a little harder and we talked about what we have to do with hard ice. You were a little bit uptight, so what does Dr. Jensen tell you to do? Then they put it all into the right perspective. But when the kid is hysterical and the coach is hysterical and the people around them are hysterical, there's absolutely no chance."

Around the mid-eighties, it became quite fashionable to have a sports psychologist in tow, although they are not as visible around the competitive scene as they once were. The practice became a little ridiculous, with skaters walking around trying to get in touch with their inner selves. I mean, it is just skating. But many found the psychologists useful to deal with the stresses of competing or other problems. Michael Slipchuck went to a sports psychologist for quite a long time because, being on the ice with a name like *Slip-* chuck, he had a sense of impending doom.

The best known psychologist is Peter Jensen, who worked with seventeen of the Canadian athletes at the Calgary Olympics. His approach involves deep relaxation, mental imagery, vision and other techniques to achieve consistent high performance. Many skaters use off-ice exercises as stress reducers. Others have developed or been taught a variety of strategies and tactics for dealing with stress such as breathing techniques, finding a sound or a letter or a word to repeat like a mantra, finding a spot in the brain that is peaceful, a special spot to go to when you need to calm down. Many skaters find such techniques helpful, so long as they are committed to them and don't think them stupid.

In Ozzie Colson's day, no one tried to correct the nervous system. "There's no real way to stop a choke," he says, "but the sports psychologists are rather nice to have. At first, I was opposed to introducing something that seemed not totally connected to such a virgin sport. But when you see children losing their focus and you know you can refer them to the gentleman on your right or the lady to the left, it's wonderful."

In Cincinnati in 1987, Hough and Ladret were making an impression with their practices for their first world championships, but on the night of the short program, Tuffy looked nervous as they were doing some lifts a few hours before the event. Kerry said to Peter Jensen, "It's all yours. I'm not going to be patient, so you handle it."

He took Tuffy out into the audience to look at the 18,000 people in the stands. Kerry thought, "Oh, this is bright, Jensen. She's going to pass out." But he took her up through the seats and introduced her around. "I'd like you to meet Christine Hough. She's going to be skating for you tonight. She's in the pairs, the seventh team to skate." Tuffy would shake hands. After meeting half a dozen or so people, he told her, "They're human beings just like you. What are you nervous about? You like performing. These are nice people."

Kerry says, "He got her right down so that she was as calm as I have ever seen her. They skated the best they ever skated. Never missed a thing."

Whatever tricks people use, facing an unknown mass of judgement is frightening. Many people are watching and making their own private judgements, accepting or rejecting. The performance is not a race against a clock. As a sport, some people have compared skating to golf where you have no contact with your opponent. You just play against yourself, your own mentality and your faults. But by the words common to the sport, skating seems to be more like horse racing. People talk about skaters being like horses in the gate, chomping at the bit to get out there and do what they have to do. Like trainers, coaches have a stable of skaters and like to look into their charges' eyes to see how they are going to perform or wonder whether they have the heart to make a good run in the field of skaters at the event.

Skating also has its touts. They can be seen at every competition. I always thought they were kind of like groupies, turned on by Kurt or Elvis or Josée or Herb and Isabel, just in love with the people participating. Wrong. With this one large section of the audience, personalities are not what it's about at all. They are turned on strictly by the sport. If they become too close to the skaters involved, they are unable to maintain any kind of perspective on who is skating well. Everyone finds Kurt adorable, but that doesn't enter in to where he should end up.

A friend, Barb Strain, set me straight. She and her "skating friends" all travel to the Canadians and even the Worlds. Every one of the group can tell the difference between a double Axel, triple Lutz or double flip, which is astounding for non-skaters because it is very hard to tell the difference. It took Barb about a year to do it. She recorded all the competitions, put together a compilation of every jump with commentary about what the jump was, then studied each jump frame by frame so she could distinguish whether it was a forward or backward entrance, inside or outside edge, pick or no pick.

She and her group—made up of mostly women and gay men—study placements at the international competitions, check the protocols, read and gossip about everything, discuss the pedigree and respective strong points and weaknesses of both coaches and skaters, talk about their programs, costumes, practice sessions, everything but the skaters themselves. They only discuss the personality of skaters with respect to what makes them great or also-rans. They check up on things through skating magazines, newsletters and telephone hotlines that dispense the latest skating news, with the content changed weekly. A racetrack tout doesn't have to worry about whether the horse will run well to the right piece of music or make the oh-so-elegant move rounding the clubhouse turn. But the group will debate whether *Hungarian Rhapsody* is wrong for a particular skater. They have definite opinions about what each skater should be skating to. They even often suggest music to skaters.

All the discussion serves to give skaters a handicap. Every year the group does "podium picks," chipping into a pool covering several events. There is a hierarchy in the group, determined by how many years they have been involved, how many competitions they have been to and how accurate their predictions have been on placings.

For them, there is a brutality to the sport that makes it addictive. The brutality is in the skaters being used like pawns, with little regard in the long term to who they are or what toll the sport takes on them. There is brutality in the fact that most skaters have to put in their time, pay their dues and take their turn before eventually, if they are good enough and consistent enough, making it to the top. The sport has a certain predictability. Skaters can be watched growing from the grass roots up. Depending on how many and the calibre of competitions attended, they can begin to tell who in the next wave of talent has the magic.

They are active in the sport. Some have become guardian angels, helping to supplement the CFSA's living and training allowance that doesn't begin to cover the $20,000 to $50,000 a year often required for skating instruction. There are many cases where people have given money anonymously or through the parents so that talented skaters could continue skating.

The ultimate for Barb and her group is that everyone skates his or her best, all personalities aside. Judges have to work the same way. If they become personally involved with the skater they may find themselves self-conscious about a mark or even about where they want the skater to finish. Yet the CFSA has judges acting as monitors and mentors. It is done to benefit the skater, to take away the sense of an ominous presence and make a young and impressionable skater realize that the judge is just a person without any miraculous power trying to do a job just like anyone else. That has been good for competitors, but I don't know if it's the right thing for the credibility of the mark that that judge puts up. If there is one thing judges and the sport need, it's credibility.

The shorter the amount of time a person is involved in or watching the sport, the less the understanding of judging. Even many skaters feel that the judges are out to get them. As a former competitor, I still have a prejudice against judges. They are not perfect and goodness knows on many, many occasions I thought some of them were out to lunch. But in terms of a panel, rarely does the wrong person become champion.

Depending on the event, judges have four or four and a half minutes to watch and take notes, then maybe 30 seconds to make up their minds before punching in a number that may make a difference in skating history. That takes experience, and these are an experienced and professional group of people.

Judges train for years, mastering a complex set of requirements. Many of them have been former national and international competitors. They have gone through a test system that takes them through low, medium, then high-level judging. Within Canada, at least, these are not people who don't know what they are doing. They have been schooled, have worked with all the top skaters and have judged extensively to maintain their rating. They do not take their job lightly, nor are they out to screw the skaters and the system.

In some parts of the world people become international judges who, through lack of experience and opportunity, have no right to be on a panel. They have not been schooled properly and don't have the experience. But if a member country of the ISU has competitors in the world championship, that country is allowed a judge in the mix of "possibles" when a panel is being put together. The only time a country is guaranteed a judge is when that country has a skater in the top three from the previous year's Worlds.

The CFSA trains and certifies national judges through seminars, conferences, practical training and apprenticeships with more experienced judges. The aspiring judges have to put in so many test days and come out of them with a certain percentage correct before they are allowed to advance to the next level. The process doesn't happen overnight. For international judges the training process is even longer. International judges have to judge at a low-level international event and have to have a lot of international experience before they would be named to a World or Olympic panel. They are carefully monitored. A judge has to have a certain percentage of success in terms of placements. A judge's protocol at the end of an event lists every skater in order of their finish. Sometimes, the judges are uncanny in their protocols, with ordinals reading 1-2-3-4-5-6 all the way down. Other judges are 6-4-1-3-2-5, which is not good at all.

It is not unusual to not get a unanimous decision when there are seven or nine people on the panels, each of whom comes to the judging table with a set of preconceived ideas based on their culture and their personal likes and dislikes. It's hard enough to get a majority decision.

Many people, especially infrequent observers, still don't realize that the winner is determined by the majority and that what matters is not the numerical value of the mark—whether a judge gives a 5.8

or a 5.2—but what that mark represents. A 5.8 on one judge's board might not be a first place if it isn't the highest mark given that day. A 5.2 may be another judge's highest mark, a first place, in which case the 5.2 becomes a better mark than the 5.8. Instead of looking at the marks as they go across the board, each judge's card should be examined to see who the judge placed first, second and third. One advantage of the system is that one judge does not skew the panel. Officially, the high and low marks are not eliminated, but if one judge placed a skater fifth when all the others placed the same skater first, that one judge is so far out of the running that the placement is not a factor.

The judging structure doesn't please many people, especially the media, who are always hounding the ISU. Part of the problem is that sportswriters who only cover the Olympics or maybe a world championship once in a blue moon do not really grasp the complexities of the system. But admittedly, there are real problems in the system.

Part of the problem is that some judges have never been skaters themselves. They are textbook judges, so they miss the element of being able to feel with the skater when something exceptional is happening. Judges can learn from a book what is right and wrong, but unless they have jumped themselves they have no appreciation for what a "good one" feels like. For a judge judging by the book, there is only right and wrong and black and white. There is no shading. The skater did it or didn't. For a judge who has a feeling for how to do it, there are myriad possibilities.

A jump has a certain look, a certain movement and feels a certain way that cannot be put into words. Looking at a double Axel, a textbook judge can see that the take-off is on the right edge, the jump has the right number of rotations, the skater travels across the ice so far at a certain height and lands correctly on a back outside edge. Any non-skater can understand that. A spectator or TV viewer can understand that. But only a former skater can understand the depth of the edge on the takeoff, the force, the momentum and the feel of the body in the air. Is the tuck good? Is it a tight tuck that keeps the skater balanced? Does the body settle gently onto the ice or does it fall to the the ice like a sack of potatoes? Does the flow continue through the landing? Is the speed still there? These elements can only be judged well through experience. A skater might get the jump done, but not with the quality that a good judge with a skating background is able to appreciate. Every judge does not need to have been able to do a triple Axel—not bloody likely—but the essence of a good triple jump is every bit the same as a good double.

Even in figures a skating background is essential. With young skaters who think they're ready to try the test, I will often say, "No, no. You've learned the figures, but you haven't learned how to do the test. I have to see it. It has to look right." They look at me as if I have horns. When I see a certain consistency, when I see the figure—all of the figure—done at the same speed, with control and with a visual understanding of what it is the skater is trying to do, then the figure has 'the look'.

When an experienced judge comes out to judge a skater's test, they may see imperfections in the print, but they will give value for the way it looks. That's simply appreciating the skater's ability to move across the ice in a controlled manner, which is what the sport is all about. Skating is about learning how to control the movement of the body under the most bizarre circumstances.

When I tried my driver's test, I made mistakes. I didn't stop properly at a stop street and didn't parallel park very well, but the examiner passed me, saying, "You did this wrong and you made this and that mistake. But you know, I like the way you handled the car." There is a flow, movement, control, confidence and comfort level that comes with the skill. A judge who has been a skater can reward that. A judge who has not been a skater cannot possibly understand.

The credibility of the judging system has also been compromised by the fact, or perhaps the legend, of national bias. The practice of national bias has been promoted on one hand but disdained on the other. Let a Russian judge place a Canadian skater well below a Russian skater and the howls of protest are deafening. But a Canadian judge place a Canadian skater well below a Russian skater and the howls are about how unpatriotic the judge is for not supporting our skaters. We can't have it both ways.

Support comes in many forms, however. It does not always mean placing the compatriot skater first. Louis Stong criticized a Canadian judge for not supporting Karen Preston's performance at an international event. He didn't expect the judge to place Karen first, but he did expect the judge to at least put her where everybody else did.

"She put Karen at least two to three places lower than the average and then said, 'I goofed up on that, but don't worry, the short program's only worth 30 per cent, I'll make it up tomorrow night.' Then she had Karen even lower the next night. I wrote and said I had a couple of problems. If this was an independent incident, I wouldn't bother. But I look at the protocols when Karen was in Europe and won a silver medal and this same judge had her fourth in the short program, where she came second, and fifth in the long program, where she came third. She got her silver medal in spite of our judge. Then this same judge was sent to another international event with the same skater. Why? It creates a negative feeling in the air. It eroded Karen's self-confidence and it eroded the panel's confidence in her. They see she came sixth in NHK and got a silver last year, so they say, 'Oh, obviously she's going down.' This was a big decision, a very big influence that this judge had on my star."

What is sometimes perceived as bias can also be a reflection of real differences, both internationally and within Canada. Politics starts down in the provinces, with the eastern section against the western and central sections. Ozzie believes not just politics is involved. "The styles vary in different sections of the country. In the mosaic of skating in Canada, the colour lies in Quebec and the skill is equally as good if not better. The French association has done wonders for supporting their skaters and their rinks. They bring a colour to skating. Their clothes aren't right, they're overdone, but that's the way they are. They're more flamboyant. We have to be stylized to the hilt because flamboyant people can attract your attention without you knowing it. The judging is sound. The western section has a certain style of program. The programs are a little different. The judges are used to that and they're not sure they like the ones from other sections."

All that said, there have been enough scandals over the years to confirm that national bias has been a factor in judging for a long time, although the practice has noticeably declined. We used to think that all the Eastern bloc countries would judge together and that Canada, the US and Japan would judge together, but that perception is changing. The ISU frowns upon it and does its damnedest to eliminate it by disqualifying judges after an event, which is rather fruitless because no guts are involved in that kind of decision. The judge gets thrown off the panel for two years, but the damage is done. They should be yanked up on the carpet at that very moment.

After the 1993 Worlds, six of the nine judges on the panel were reprimanded and disqualified from judging because they didn't deduct enough marks for illegal moves by the Russian dance team of Gritchuk and Platov, who eventually finished second. There was also a question over the third-place team, Krylova and Federova. The suspension was revoked because the referee had not gone through the proper channels in notifying the judges, so the judges' respective national associations put pressure on the ISU and the decision was reversed, but at the same time the six-month suspension was up anyway. What nonsense.

The media have done a disservice to the process, yet have also helped clean it up. Judges used to feel somewhat protected. The only person they had to answer to was the referee. They are still insular, but judges are now fair game. They have to be prepared to back up their mark with a reasonable explanation. They must be able to tell a person in the media, a non-skater, why they judged the way they did. As the profile and money-making potential of skating have increased, the sport has to be sure that everything is clean and that the right people are winning. The ISU cannot account for every situation or for every individual who may have ulterior motives, but they police the process strictly.

One of the earliest celebrated controversies resulted in a rule change on the composition of panels. At the 1927 Worlds, Sonja Henie won her first championship at the age of 15 from a panel with three of its five members coming from Norway. After that, the rule became: one country, one judge. At other competitions early in the century, judges spent several hours consulting, acting more like a jury than judges, before announcing their results. At the 1952 Olympics in Oslo, an Austrian skater won the silver when almost everyone believed he should not have been placed higher than fourth. That result, the ISU's official history says, "brought into the open a problem that had been seen in the judging of figure skating since the post-War revival of competition, of active efforts on the part of certain associations and individuals to influence the results by external means."

There are still many people in Europe who remember the results of the 1956 pairs competition at the Olympics and the Worlds as *the* scandal of figure skating. Frances Dafoe and Norris Bowden were the two-time defending world champions and were expected to win the gold at the Games in Cortina. The challengers were Sissy Schwarz and Kurt Oppelt from Austria. At the time, there was some suspicion that the directors of the Austrian figure skating federation, who were also the directors of a professional ice show in Vienna, were determined to have a world title to sell.

At the Olympics, the result was almost a tie. Both pairs had four firsts, but the German and Swiss judges had Frannie and Norrie in third place. The German judge had the German pair of Marika Kilius— she was twelve then—and Franz Ningel in second place. Schwarz and Oppelt won the gold. The result was, at best, questionable.

At the Worlds in Garmisch, there was no question at all. After the draw for the judges panel, the Canadian judge went to Frannie and Norrie and said, "Everything's great, kids. There are seven judges and the neutral judge is going to be Switzerland. You'll get a fair competition this time."

A few hours later as they were practicing on the ice, Frannie said, "Norrie, how many judges do you count out there?"

"I count nine."

"I count nine too. What happened to seven?"

The result was a given. Frannie and Norrie lost the title. The audience was outraged. Even Schwarz and Oppelt's coach, Arnold Gerschwiler, came over after the competition and said, "I am here to shake the hands of the true champions. I am so ashamed I don't know what to say to you."

The coaches met and asked the ISU to declare the competition null and void, but the ISU couldn't agree. At a closing banquet, a speaker made a reference to the fact that the pairs medals were going to the wrong people. The Austrian team rose *en masse* and marched out of the dining room. In Prague, on the first stop of the following tour of champions, the headlines in the local newspapers tore a few strips off the Austrian pair. After one night, they pulled out of the show, refusing to skate with the Canadians.

The ISU's history says, "It is hard to imagine today (in 1992) the depth of feeling and animosity which the two 1956 pairs competitions generated, which to some extent soured the normally friendly relations between Europe and North America. It would take some time and the Council action against the Austrian officials in 1957 to clear the air." Three judges were given lifetime suspensions from the sport.

Even in more recent times, Austrian judges have been observed quietly sitting at their desks during a competition, looking up maybe once or twice during a performance, but generally being intent on working out mathematical equations that produce the result they want.

Such blatant bias has almost disappeared. Frannie, now a judge herself, says, "I really don't see much of it today. I don't see any chatting. I really don't see any collaboration." But the perception remains among the public. David Dore suggests, "Having judges more anonymous might help. Do we care which judges put which people where? Don't give them an identity. They've been picked from the International Skating Union because they're good judges. There are nine of them sitting there and up come the results. Who cares that the Russian put the Russian first and the Canadian put the Canadian first? That's what makes it so controversial."

Frannie even says that judges should take off their markings and slip on an ISU blazer as soon as they arrive at the competition. "Then you're an ISU member, period. End of game. Mentally they would become a member of the ISU, answerable only to the ISU and not their country. I don't think the judges should perhaps be appointed by their country. Maybe it should come from the ISU and if they feel that there are certain judges that are very knowledgeable in certain aspects of skating, they should use them."

The identification of judges also creates opportunities for soliciting a judge's favour. Louis has been approached to do a number on a Canadian judge in return for certain considerations when it came to marking one of his skaters. He says, "They introduce the panel. The judge from Russia stands up and bows, the judge from Canada stands up and bows. Rather than having nine ISU judges from whatever country they happen to be drawn from. Canadians who work on the panels become well known. It becomes part of the charisma. 'I had dinner with the Germans last night and we've got the Germans sewn up and they can control Central Europe, so all we need is the Japanese and we're in.' People buy this shit. First of all, I wouldn't trust anybody from anywhere to give me anything. I figure if my skaters do it, they'll get what they deserve. If they don't, they'll get what they deserve."

At least one source of suspicion about the judging system was removed with the death of figures. When figures were involved, a major portion of the event was completed before the television audience could tune in. Even when their value was reduced, they were still the first element of the competition and a skater ranking lower than third after the figures was almost out of the running. It took a miracle to win. Viewers could understand why skaters who landed on their butts four or five times in a program lost. They could not understand why those same skaters, because of these strange school figures, could win. That was bad for the sport, giving the media the ammunition to get the public riled over how skating was being judged.

Even the judges have been let off the hook because school figures are also open to interpretation. What is a beautiful turn? What makes a perfect circle? Is it the way the edge moves across the ice? Their elimination of figures puts pressure not only on the judges to be more careful in their evaluation of free skating, but also on the free skaters themselves who now more than ever have to land the jumps.

One other source of suspicion remains. The public sees judges at practices taking notes and thinks they are deciding on their marks. But watching practices is necessary. Singles have to do three jumps, three spins and two sets of footwork, more or less, a triple jump and a combination that includes a prescribed jump. That allows the skater to tailor-make the program with only the things they can do, making it difficult to compare the technical content. Singles have to put most of the jumps in the long program, so discrepancies can be caught, but until 1994, pair skaters could do the same death spiral in both programs. They can also have the same short program for their entire careers as long as they cover the vague descriptions of what they are supposed to do and can then use all the same elements in their long program. That kind of doubling up makes sense in terms of training, but it does not develop skating talent. The better the variety, the higher the technical content mark.

Frannie says she has to do homework to familiarize herself with the program, the music and the kind of skater she is seeing, as well as to guard against a one-shot wonder. "You'll never see me in the arena the day of the competition and rarely the day before. I go a couple of days in advance, have my look, then get away from skating, so that when I go back I've got fresh eyes. The level of their basic skating ability is what I look at. I put them in units of A, B, C and D. Those skaters can move up and down or all over the place, but I also have to leave enough space that if somebody from the A unit falls all over the ice and moves down to a C and somebody from a C unit is absolutely brilliant and moves up to the A, there's a spread to take care of all these eventualities. All you'll see on my sheet is 'A–AB–C?–maybe D.' What it does is familiarize my own head with the level of skating ability. I know those programs so well that I know the difficulty of the elements. The top skaters have the most difficult elements. The only thing I'm looking at is the difficulty. I'll make notes of what the elements are and where the critical breakdown factors could occur. Those are their futures out there and you want to make damn sure you know what they're doing."

Skaters themselves believe in the system and the need for homework. Brian Orser had his problems with judges during his career, but he says, "Being a judge myself, it was always nice to sit on a panel and watch some skaters come out for a warmup and know you can count on him, him and him to skate well. Automatically, you're putting them in the top five or top three. I think the system itself was pretty fair, as fair as it possibly could be. There's no way getting around it. In a judgement sport, there's obviously going to be some politics. There is never going to be a perfect way of judging. After every event, not everybody's going to be happy, period. But in the amateur world they do the best they can."

What gives credibility to the system is when skaters like Rodnina and Zaitsev or Oksana Baiul can come into a world championship out of nowhere and win.

The system is still in need of reform and one aspect that will have to be looked at soon is the fact that judges are the only amateurs left in the sport where the services of trained professionals are needed. Judges doing several international competitions give up three weeks to a month of their time each year, either using up their holiday time or prevailing on unusually understanding employers, all without any remuneration except direct expenses. Only people of certain means can be judges. Besides, if the judges don't measure up and do their job well, it's hard to fire volunteers.

The CFSA is willing to look at alternatives and, as in other areas of the sport, is promoting new thinking about how to improve the judging process. David Dore says, "The sport tells them that they have ultimate power and tells them to stand apart and render a decision, not do a lot of talking and not hound rinks. How do you criticize someone for doing a job the way the job is defined? The sport hasn't changed the job and then we get mad because they're doing the job the way we told them to do it. The big problem in the judges is that they are not knowledgeable about how the sport is changing and they are unwilling to step out of their own little world. There must be a thousand different ways to judge a competition and I don't understand why we aren't looking at some of them. I was kind of taken with the freestyle version which is, somebody throws up some marks and they all get tallied together and you get told that so and so has a collective mark accumulation and is in this place. Go by numbers, not names or countries. Feed the numbers into a computer and out comes the result. Some of the judges say, 'My decision is important.' But the result is what we're interested in. Some people are still living in that fantasy world where they think they should be interviewed at great length and have their protocol examined in detail. I want to say, 'I don't really care. The majority decided this and as far as I'm concerned, your job is over, go home, thank you very much and here's a lovely gift. I don't want to know who you are. I want to know who won.'"

Who wins an event is decided not only by how the winner skates or how the losers lose, but by a complicated equation of talent, personality, temperament, body type and a range of other attributes. The secret is, as Sheldon says, "the development of talent so that the people in the judgement position don't have a choice of who is going to be the winner. Be so superb in what you do that there is no opportunity to have a choice."

Skate Canada is usually held the first week of November, preceded a week or two by Skate America. Most major skaters are involved in those events. They provide an opportunity to try out new programs in front of big crowds, get a feel for how judges respond and see how some of the younger skaters react to the pressure of high-level competition, although the youngest go to invitational events during the summer to gain experience and become known.

The Canadian Figure Skating Association hands out the international assignments during the summer, always avoiding having two contenders competing in the same event. In 1993, it was Kurt who went to Skate Canada, along with Marcus Christensen, Karen Preston, Susan Humphries, Sargeant and Wirtz and Bourne and Kraatz. Elvis, Josée Chouinard and Eisler and Brasseur skated at Piruetten in Hamar, Norway. The assignments are worked out in consultation with skaters and coaches according to a rough formula based on placings in the national championships.

Skate Canada is a key event for the CFSA. Along with the Canadian championships, it generates revenue to help keep the Association's programs afloat. It has to be professionally run and it is.

At every competition under ISU rules, a technical representative is in charge of running the event. One of the best in the world is Joyce Hisey, now Canada's representative on the ISU. She has played an integral role in the development of figure skating in Canada and abroad. A very sharp, bright, kind woman, she is sort of everybody's mother. No problem is too big for her to tackle, but ask for something out of the question and she'll give a blunt, "Nope. Can't do it." She was a skater and a national and international judge before going into the organizational end of things. She can pull a team together fast, making sure that the local organizing committee, made up entirely of volunteers, is on board so the event can run smoothly.

She is the person who gets feedback about ice conditions, flooding or the temperature of the surface. She hears what TV needs. All the players—skaters, coaches, organizing committees, television—work through this one person who has to come up with the answers to keep everybody happy. People pay attention to Joyce, but she seems to stay out of the political firing range. No one ever has a sense that she is on 'their' side. That takes real skill. Skaters think they're artists and have an overly sensitive side to them. They have very thin skin, but Joyce dances through all the vanity.

She also has a presence internationally, following in the footsteps of another excellent and long-term ISU representative, Donald Gilchrist. Canada has contributed many talented skaters and champions to the international scene over the years, but sometimes we're considered sort of a poor relation to the US. This naturally makes us extremely irritable, even hostile, but because we have such nice manners, we are rarely openly hostile. We make our views known, but always go about it through the back door. Joyce has taken us into the spotlight. She speaks up about us, tooting our horn, something Canadians always find hard to do.

Canada has become a world leader in the sport not only because of our skaters, but because of the CFSA. Over the past fifteen years, it has become a model for the rest of the world, even though some of the old guard associations still wonder who the upstart Canadians think they are. We've had to keep hammering champions at them for them to pay attention to us at all. But now that skating has become such big business, international associations have to look at Canada. Figure skating is one of the only sports in the country that is almost totally self-supporting, with very little government money in comparison to other amateur sports, yet the CFSA has created a support system for our athletes and clubs that is second to none. That has taken real nerve and courage.

Volunteers play a major part in the Association's success. There are many of them, all committed and often professionally educated. The CFSA couldn't function without them. They give the office in Ottawa regional input and take part in one of the major activities of any national skating federation: lobbying for their skaters. All the representatives of the CFSA have a certain kind of marketing talent. They are people people, with gifts in terms of handling others and communication skills they come to naturally. They love the sport, have probably been in it for years as skaters or skating parents and have found pleasure in staying involved.

The process is ongoing throughout the year as our teams are represented at international events. The scuttlebutt and conversation goes around. Every country has something at stake. The more favourably they can impress the ISU and the judges with their particular skater, the better the chances are of that skater doing well.

There are days when a skater needs to be forgiven or needs a little help. An inspiring performance that no one can put down might happen two or three times in a career. Most skaters skate to maybe 70 per cent of their potential and hope that their training has been so good and so thorough that they won't skate at 40 or 50 per cent. A reduction in absolute best is inevitable, and that is when lobbying comes in handy. If you maybe haven't done your triple Lutz that day but your federation has been talking about how breathtaking your spins are or how your choreography is in a class by itself, the judges have a guideline, a benchmark to use.

But the bottom line is still, do an outstanding job and you win. When Oxsana Baiul won her first world championship, no one expected her to do it. She was a nobody, she was nothing, but she was so phenomenal and so much better than everybody else, she had to win. Where she came from or what her federation said on her behalf didn't matter at all.

It has often seemed that Canada has only been able to lobby for one skater, Kurt, for example, even though Elvis was right behind him. The former Soviet Union could bring a full team to an event and if the defending world champion was part of the team, the second and third skaters would somehow be automatically in the top ten, in many instances because they deserved to be there. If their world champion went down to defeat in their own national championships, that seemed to enhance the reputations of the other members of the team so that they would automatically finish higher, rather than diminish the importance of the defending champion. But if Elvis had beaten Kurt several years ago, it would not have meant that Elvis was automatically ranked higher in the world. It would have meant that the two of them were further down the pack.

In any sport or any other activity, whenever there are organizers or "bosses" like the national associations and the ISU, the people actually doing the work—the competitors on the ice—naturally have a paranoid notion that they are being manipulated and used. It's not just paranoia. It is every national federation's job to ensure that their skaters get as high as they possibly can because that gives the federation more power—the power of more athletic representation in an event and more representation on the judges panel and, therefore, more power within the ISU. No one wants to be on the bottom rung in any organization and the only way to climb up is by improving the placings.

The lobbying campaign is not professional in the sense of being carried out by professional lobbyists, but the Association's representatives can certainly work a room. It is considered necessary and normal to do it. Skaters not backed by their association won't be backed by the ISU. That does not imply some kind of conspiracy or unfair advantage. Tell friends that you love a movie and if they respect your opinion, they'll naturally view it in a more positive frame of mind. It's just human. Many people in skating have risen through the ranks together, whether from Europe or North America. Close friendships develop and a lot of information is shared. There is certainly a "you scratch my back, I'll scratch yours" dynamic at work and everybody wants to be first on the street with any new information, but the process is not as orchestrated and organized as many people think. It is something that is done very subtly and very nicely, with all the right sort of people.

Although it is amazing how "middle class" skating has become, it still retains a genteel quality that reflects its roots. Just as in other countries, skating in Canada developed as a recreational pastime of the well to do. No one could skate without a lot of money or guardian angels. Few people had either. Only people from wealthy families could ever compete for any length of time. For twenty years after 1947, the CFSA was essentially one man, the secretary, Charlie Cumming, sitting in a little office in Ottawa granting sanctions for skaters' performances. The power structure of the sport was based on the private clubs of Ottawa and Toronto. Club executives easily slid onto the CFSA executive and back again.

The style and tone of the organization was clubby and, instead of seeing themselves as stewards or caretakers of the sport, the powers that be seemed to think they owned it. Private money and internal club agendas often drove the process of awarding the CFSA's blessing to competitors. Some of the country's finest skaters had to succeed despite the CFSA, none more so than Frances Dafoe and Norris Bowden.

Before the 1952 Olympics in Oslo, they were told they weren't good enough to represent Canada, the CFSA having already anointed Suzy Morrow, who was training in Europe, as the bearer of Canada's hopes for a medal. When Frannie and Norrie won both the pairs and dance events at the Canadians in Oshawa, the Association reluctantly named them to the team, but refused to recognize their coach, Sheldon Galbraith, in any official capacity. Frannie's father paid Sheldon's way to Europe and even had to buy him tickets so he could attend practice events. They ended up training on a tiny village rink and had to buy shovels so they could clear the snow every morning. At precisely eight o'clock, a girl with an empty milk can would drive her sleigh across the ice. When she passed, Sheldon would say, "Okay, kids, you've got fifteen minutes." Fifteen minutes later, the girl would drive back with her milk can full. Frannie and Norrie had their revenge, placing fifth, higher than anyone else on the team.

Before the 1956 Games, they were defending world champions and Herbert "Hobo" Crispo, president of their own Toronto Skating Club, was president of the CFSA. They wanted to go to Cortina early for altitude training. The CFSA told them the whole notion was ridiculous and the ISU had to intervene to get the CFSA to release them. Then Crispo told them they couldn't have their airline tickets unless they signed a paper promising to come back and skate in the Club carnival. Frannie told him, "We've always come back for the carnival and will continue to do so. I won't sign. You'll have to take my word."

Sheldon says, "There was going to be a suit right then, but I didn't have to run into him. The pupils ran into him through their fathers. They were intelligent people. Dr. Dafoe? You're not going to scare these guys."

After the Olympics, Sheldon was called back to do the Skating Club carnival, leaving Frannie and Norrie to compete in the Worlds without any coach at all. Sheldon's problems with Crispo continued after his term as CFSA president was over. The rules for pairs skating were always changing and Sheldon always had to modify programs when he and his skaters got to the scene of the event. Before Wagner and Paul skated to their second world championship, Crispo went to the ISU meeting with a dictaphone to record all the rule changes. Sheldon says, "We didn't find out what the content of the meeting was until after Bob and Barbara had skated their summer. Crispo may have thought his job was to record the meeting rather than transfer information that was pertinent to our needs. With [CFSA executives] Donald Cruikshank and Don Gilchrist, it was an interplay of information each one needed, complementing the other. It was an association of who was needed to accomplish a task. Later on it started to be who would get credit for the task. Pretty soon, there started being distance. But that doesn't happen at the start when the workload's there. It happens after there has been some recognition for successes."

After the scandal at the 1956 Olympics and Worlds, Norrie asked to appear at the CFSA's annual meeting to explain the facts of life in Europe. The CFSA, insisting that there were no politics in figure skating and the best skater always won, refused. He then wrote a long letter to the Association, with recommendations to help team members in the future. Frannie says, "All Norrie was concerned about was that the skaters had proper support and backup and weren't just left out there to fend for themselves. Of course, the Association took it that we were being very critical of them, which, in effect, we were, and they suspended us. But we had already announced our retirement, saying we weren't going to turn professional because we wanted to become judges. So the only way they could effectively hurt us was deny us the right to be judges."

The Association did precisely that. The banishment from the sport lasted for about five years before emissaries from the CFSA started arriving, suggesting that Frannie and Norrie would be reinstated if they wrote a letter of apology. They refused, saying they had done nothing wrong. Finally, they did sign letters promising "to abide by the rules and regulations of the Canadian Figure Skating Association, as we have always done in the past."

Back they went, but they had to start at the preliminary level. They were only allowed to move up two test levels at a time and, since they were not allowed to judge on the same panel, Norrie would judge one year and Frannie the next. Eventually, she told him, "This is ridiculous. Neither of us is going to get there, so I'll wait and you work your way up first. When you're up in the international level, I'll start."

When both became qualified judges, they were still not allowed to judge even at the same competition, let alone on the same panel. Frannie said, "Why? We've never agreed about anything in our lives. Why should we start now?"

She says, "It became absurd. Finally, I think even the CFSA realized how stupid it was and we ended up at the same competition on different panels, then finally on the same panel together." She judged her first World championships in 1984, almost thirty years after the controversy. She doesn't feel angry or bitter about it. "I just feel maybe Norrie and I were the catalysts that had to happen to make our Association wake up. Our Association today, I have nothing but the highest regard for them. They're fabulous, but maybe all this had to happen first. It was part of the evolution of the sport and we just happened to be there."

The change in organization and attitude within the CFSA since those days has been stunning. From an establishment clique playing petty games with skaters' lives, the Association is now broadly based and is the most powerful amateur sports organization in the country. It is so powerful that there is a perception within the skating community that it is an organization solely dedicated to creating champions, that it's greedy, purposeful, direct and tough. Talk to people in the skating world and the CFSA's director general, David Dore, is described, often by the same people, as visionary, catty, brilliant, stubborn, manipulative, energetic, powerful and on and on and on. Many see him as the omnipotent one. He says, "There are a thousand perceptions out there about how I do this job and what I perceive my power to be and what I perceive I can do. I live with perceptions all the time. Some are hurtful, some are quizzical and some are just downright untrue, but that's life."

What everyone can agree on is that he is a very effective man who has probably been 99 per cent responsible for the tremendous success of skating in Canada over the past two decades and for the way the CFSA has become a model for associations around the world. He is a wonderful friend of skating. He loves it. But he sometimes seems to have retained a touch of the capriciousness of the skating old guard he worked so long and so hard to overthrow. Young skaters find it hard to understand his duality. One moment, he's your best friend, the next minute, you say, "What did I do, what did I do?"

David's in a no-win job. He has to keep a line between himself and the athletes and the coaches or he'll be accused of playing favourites. He often has to tell people what they don't want to hear and he tells them bluntly. He can tell skaters they will never make it, that they have no artistic element in their program, that they don't look right. There is always an element of truth, but it's horribly painful for young kids to swallow. It takes a special type of person to be able to take a brutally frank message and not want to shoot the messenger.

When he started skating himself, he had fought a battle with polio and couldn't walk at all. He skated competitively—he was in the junior men's division in Rouyn-Noranda back in 1959, where Don McPherson and Louis Stong finished in the top two spots—but his aspirations were always individual. Wally Distlemeyer called his progress a series of "personal achievements." Where he ranked in comparison with anyone else didn't concern him. He developed a knack for setting ambitious goals, working diligently toward them and passing off any pain as best he could.

He finished skating competitively in 1962 and went into club administration and judging. What he saw of the sport from those perspectives he didn't particularly like and he eventually decided to do something about it. The turning point was the 1969 Canadian championships in Toronto's Maple Leaf Gardens, which he co-chaired with Norrie Bowden. "It was the phoniest thing I had ever been involved in. They wore tuxedos to judge and sat on the ice and there was no recognition that what they were doing had anything to with anybody else on the ice. I was horrified at the whole thing."

Three years later, he managed to get himself elected to the CFSA. There he found that the one subject that almost never came up in meetings was skaters. In 1976, he became technical vice president. It was the power base he needed. The association was never known for its activists, but David loves doing things, so he changed the figure tests, established competitive tests, started the skater development committee, ran seminars and set up a system of judge's exams and promotions. "I was all skater. The beauty of that was I didn't have to deal with finances and all the craziness."

He was soon seen to be the person who could get things done for the sport and by 1980 he was president, probably the first person without money or social position to hold the post. For the next four years, he had virtual carte blanche. He attributes his rise to "Luck and timing and probably cleverness on my part without my really realizing it. I think I manoeuvred myself so that they had no choice. I didn't even quite realize that I'd done that. I didn't really want the job. I wanted the opportunity to make changes which I perceived went with the job."

He made changes to everything. He sent very clear messages to skaters, the skating establishment and the coaches that there was a new regime in town. The message to the skaters came in the form of Tracey Wainman. She was a wonderfully talented skater, but in 1980 she suddenly became more than that. She was the saviour who would lead Canada back to the world podium. She was the second coming. She was also a child.

Heather Kemkaran had won the Canadian championship in 1978, had lost to Janet Morissey in 1979 and battled in Kitchener in 1980 to win the title back. Twelve-year-old Tracey also skated in Kitchener, giving a performance that was exquisite far beyond her years. Men were crying in the stands. She placed third. A week later, the CFSA chose her to represent Canada at the Worlds while Heather would go to the Olympics. The age of eligibility for skating in seniors competition was about to be raised to 14, but anyone who skated in world competition under the existing age rule would be allowed to compete again. The CFSA decided to make Tracey eligible to skate in 1981.

The effect on Tracey was long term. There is a widespread view in the skating world that the CFSA took one of the most talented skaters the country has ever produced and destroyed her. Tracey could do beautiful double Axels and triple Salchows until she hit puberty. Then she just couldn't tough them out. Triple jumps were becoming important for women and every serious competitor had to have at least two triples, the Sal and the toe. She kept up for a bit because the rest of her skating was so wonderful, but ultimately the triple jumps beat her. She won the Canadian championship in 1981, then dropped to third. At fourteen, she was washed up and not taking it well. There were enough people on the Tracey bandwagon to spread the blame around, but the CFSA was driving.

In David's view, "The decision was right. The CFSA opened the door of opportunity, along with warnings to please proceed slowly and with advice. They didn't. The CFSA got used as a whipping boy to obscure the family's mistakes."

The effect of the Tracey decision on skaters was to let them know that the CFSA was willing to jettison the "deadwood" in its quest for medals. Everyone started to realize that the CFSA was no longer just a bunch of old folks floundering around in a mickey mouse organization. Even the skating establishment got the message.

Early in his presidency, David organized a retreat at the Milcroft Inn. Among the twenty or so people there were Chris Lang, a brilliant marketing man, along with CFSA officials, including a couple of "old guards." There was paper all over the walls with charts and graphs and ideas. They talked about marketing and deals with CTV, about having something to sell and about a national team and money. In the midst of all the excitement about possibilities, the old guard realized their time was over. At the same time, the dedication to winning medals was born. David says, "In that room, you'd say what is it you want? What is it that will make this tick? What is it that will make people be attracted to you? It's medals. I've been quoted as saying 'medals, medals, medals' and I don't deny it. In those days, that's what you said because what did we have in 1980? Janet Morrisey, nineteenth in the world. Toller was our last one in 1976 and Karen Magnussen before that and they were singular people. There was nothing behind them."

He set out to build a system where champions would not come out of the blue or be anointed by the powers that be in the skating world. The idea was to build a system where skating ability would decide. The goal was striking a balance between finding the talent, letting it develop with some spontaneity, throwing resources behind a group of contenders, then letting the randomness of competition take over. It took a long, long time to do it. The key ingredient was money.

At a competition in Lake Placid in 1982, Barb Underhill and Paul Martini defeated Kitty and Peter Carruthers, an American team, but were thinking of retiring because they had no money to go on. David met them for lunch at the Howard Johnsons and said, "If you stay until the '84 Olympics, I'll make sure that every one of your bills is paid."

Afterward, he went out into the Lake Placid streets thinking, "Now what on earth did you just do? You don't have any money. How are you going to do this?"

He went to the board of directors with a plan for an Athlete's Trust fund. He worked with CTV's Johnny Esaw to develop corporate funding for the fund, looking for long-term commitments. But those depended on successes. In those days, companies might spend $10,000 one year and then be gone the next because they weren't really getting anything special for their money. There was no return for companies when there was no momentum in the development of a successful Canadian team. Wherever David looked, the need was for medals, medals, medals.

The CFSA had never had a two-term president before, but in 1982 the board told him to just keep going. He was driven by a vision.

"I could see Paul and Barbara on the podium. I could see the whole thing. Always I could see it. I can't explain it, but I could see it."

In 1982, the Athlete's Trust funded nine skaters. The objective then was for the Trust to have a capital fund of $300,000 within ten years. In 1994, the Trust has a capital fund of $3.2 million and funds about 750 skaters every year.

David's single-minded drive to change the sport ran into a few roadblocks, the major one being the coaches organization. Sheldon, Bruce, Ozzie and Hellmut May had started the Professional Skating Association of Canada in 1965. Marg and Bruce had belonged to a similar organization in the States in the fifties. The founders thought Canadian coaches needed an association where they could work together on common problems. Sheldon says he just wanted "to move the world of coaching away from camel-haired coats and pearl buttons." The PSAC wasn't formed easily. The coaches were wild and woolly roughriders who jealously guarded their students, went their own way and communicated as little as possible. When the organization was set up, Hellmut May was president of the British Columbia Skaters Association. Sheldon and Bruce didn't know that organization even existed. The PSAC was an amateur association of professionals working in an amateur sport. It eventually developed educational and certification programs, dealt with employment and insurance issues, had seminars and generally acted as a clearinghouse for any information relevant to coaching.

It was the first forum for coaching interaction. Entrepreneurial coaches like Bruce used it to promote new ideas. He tried to broaden the market for coaches by developing a method of teaching boys figure skating without the boys feeling threatened. He called it Power Skating and started selling the idea to hockey organizations. Many other coaches, however, thought the PSAC was too much like a union and refused to join. By 1978, there were an estimated 2,000 coaches in Canada and only about 1,100 were PSAC members.

Tension between the PSAC and the CFSA existed right from the start. The CFSA didn't want to cede any power of influence over figure skating to an independent group and the coaches were very suspicious of any CFSA sympathies among their members. Ozzie says he was shifted out of the presidency because of it. "Some of the coaches thought I was wearing two hats, one for the CFSA and one for myself. I was trying to get our association to be stronger. I had wonderful liaison with the CFSA, with no thought of exalting myself to another height. It was just for the gang, for the coaches."

By 1976, there were talks and proposals about a PSAC–CFSA affiliation, with a "congenial working agreement with the CFSA on certain committees" as a first step. Also in the late seventies, Sport Canada studied all sports and identified coaching weaknesses as a major problem in many of them, including figure skating. The federal government decided to devote some resources to improved training in the latest teaching techniques and in related sciences like biomechanics, physiology and nutrition. The catch was that any money had to go through the amateur sport governing bodies. The PSAC's educational programs would not receive any funding from Ottawa unless a new relationship was established between the coaches and the CFSA.

Some coaches in the organization, eventually renamed the Figure Skating Coaches of Canada, fought to keep as much distance as possible between the two organizations. Ron Vincent from Vancouver, a former vice-president and president of the FSCC, was a leader of the group. Others, like Sheldon, thought they saw the writing on the wall and should use any connection with the CFSA to the coaches' advantage. When the CFSA offered to do the educating, Sheldon said to Kerry Leitch, "Capitulate. They're doing what we want. We formed our association to get education to help all of our coaches develop. The communication they're giving to us and all the teaching organizations are doing it for us. That's it. All you have to give up is, yes, sir, three bags full, sir. They can't teach. They're not going to do your job, so join them. Let them do the communications for us."

Push came to shove in 1981 when David decided that the CFSA would enforce the Sport Canada edict and "bring coaches under the CFSA umbrella." The relationship turned bitter and vicious. For over 18 months, the two organizations wrangled and almost went to court. In David's view, "The whole thing came down to a group of people who thought that they weren't going to be told what to do and thought it was quite possible that if they folded into the CFSA, they would lose their so-called power base, which they weren't using effectively anyway. They didn't have a vision of the sport. They just wanted to keep it the same. They didn't understand where it was all going and that it was never going to be the same. My objective was not restraint of trade, as I was accused of at the time. What I was trying to say was, 'You're an integral part of the sport. As a matter of fact, you're the most important part. But you can't operate outside it. You can't be out there somewhere, you've got to be in it and if we all believe in the rightness of coaches to do the job, then you have to conform to some set standards.' We've got to give assurances to all of our clubs that everyone has had at least some basic training and has knowledge of the system and knowledge of the sport."

He was also concerned that the coaches were outside the decision-making process in the Association. When he was changing the test and other systems, every decision was made by six or seven judges. He says, "Judges know how to rank people, up to a point. They can be taught how to rank someone using a system to make deductions and so forth. But can the same people say how someone should learn a skating skill? Absolutely not. I would be in meetings where judges were creating skating skill programs and I'd wonder, where are the coaches? Where's Louis Stong? Where's Sheldon Galbraith? They know how to do an edge and a three turn. They know what a child should be taught. Who better to tell us what we should be doing on ice? That was my point in 1981. I was not trying to destroy the coaches, but I had to allow that perception to go on because we were in a big legal case. Ron Vincent put his heart and soul into that thing and I think he took it the hardest. In order to move them over here, he had to go down the tubes and that was the shame of it. They convinced him to stay outside and he should have said, 'To hell with it, I'm moving the thing in.' He was just so stubborn."

When the dust had settled, a Coaching Committee met in the spring of 1983 and elected Kerry Leitch as chairman. The new structure of coaching in the form of the Coaching Department of the CFSA was set up the same year to direct and standardize educational programs through a National Coaching Certification Program. Coaches now must contend with theoretical, technical and practical courses at all levels.

The wounds still haven't healed. Ozzie believes, "We could have stayed with our own identity, like the Americans stayed with their own identity and we would have been respected the same way. But now they've bought us out."

From his vantage point in Florida, Bruce says, "Yes, we have our own association, the Professional Skaters Guild of America, but they're going to be swallowed up very soon by the USFSA and the government."

"It was blackmail, the way the CFSA took over," Marg says. "It was so dictatorial that everybody loses their identity, which is not good for anybody in any kind of business. Unfortunately, right now the USFSA is exactly as Canada was ten or fifteen years ago. The USFSA and the PSGA work very closely together and everything is just coming along. But a man from the Olympic committee came to our meeting this year and informed everybody that the United States should do better in skating and that all the coaches throughout the country would be amalgamated and overseen and given so much money through the USFSA. Everybody was walking around saying, 'Isn't that wonderful.' Bruce and I were dying, thinking, oh, oh, Canada all over again."

David recognizes that the CFSA still hasn't won the war. "We're getting there slowly but I think the end of that story is, and I can say with great pride, that there isn't a technical committee that doesn't have a coach on it and now *the* technical committee is run by a coach, Louis Stong. Bravo, I say, nothing but bravo."

The coaches were not the only ones to react to David's sometimes abrasive style. CFSA muscle flexing bordering on the dictatorial soured some relations between the Association and skaters in the early eighties. Brian Orser was one of the first children of David's system, but there was often tension between them. Brian says, "He did do a lot of great things, but he also tried to control some people. His only downfall was that sometimes he didn't trust everyone's judgement. Sometimes we would decide things that he didn't agree with and that's when things would maybe get a little ugly. He was famous for letters. We all got them."

Brian's attitude toward the CFSA was shaped by an incident while he was still a junior just getting on the fast track. In 1979, a letter from the CFSA suggested that if he was going to succeed, he would have to leave Doug Leigh and Orillia and move to Toronto to study with Louis Stong. Brian decided he was quite happy where he was.

David says, "When the skaters started to become successful—Brian Pockar, Martini and Underhill, Orser, Manley—there was a group in the Association that started to take ownership and part of the ownership was to say 'let's own where they go and how they do this.' There were people issuing those kind of dictums. I didn't feel completely comfortable, but the time wasn't right to counter-balance. You can't change everything overnight. I had to let that one go and pretend that I didn't know anything about it when I clearly did. Brian wasn't the only one that was done to and I give all due credit to Brian and Doug Leigh for standing up to it."

Brian was also one of the pioneering amateur skaters to become more involved in their own careers. Along with Tracy Wilson and Rob McCall, he was the first to establish a personal trust fund and to pursue a relationship with an agent. He says, "I always worked very closely with the CFSA. They were always well informed, but I thought the CFSA felt threatened. There was some tension between them and the agents. That was always pretty evident. But as an athlete at that level, I had to have a manager and an agent. In a perfect world, the CFSA would like to have some control and manage the athlete. You have to work with the CFSA because a lot of funds come your way and they've done a lot of great things for athletes. They've done a lot of great things for me. But the CFSA is a big umbrella and there's room for agents as long as they cooperate with the Association. My manager, Jay Ogden, did."

Like Brian Pockar, Tracy and Rob and Paul Martini and Barb Underhill, Brian was informed that the CFSA expected a return on its investment. "Where I always had a hard time was, I was working hard for myself and also making the CFSA look good, so that's the payback. I always felt, yes, they were giving me money, but my reputation was helping them. If I was just taking the money and having a great time and not working hard, not producing and not getting the medals, then I can see their point. But unfortunately, there's a payoff and you just have to work it and that's part of the politcs as well. Everybody wants something back, not just the CFSA. There's always a period when any amateur skater who retires from skating and goes into the professional world has to go through something with the CFSA. Then it comes full circle and you get back together. Kiss and make up and away you go."

Having wrought enormous changes during his presidency, when David's second term was over, a job called "program director" was created for him in Ottawa, which was partially his idea. Within a year, he was filling the new position of director general. It was the opportunity he needed to launch Phase Two of his revolution. He redesigned the administrative structure, leaving the volunteers as the front people for the Association while expanding and professionalizing the office of director general. One of the criticisms of the coaches in the eighties had been that the Association was "amateurish" and that they didn't like to be beholden to people who were voted in and out. They never knew who was in charge. David set out to create a business and create a relationship between all the people in it.

At one of his yearly retreats, members of the CFSA executive kept referring to the people within his office as "the paid staff." After hearing the phrase repeatedly for a couple of days, he went nuts. He told them, "We're in a relationship here. We're professional people. We're in the business of sport as professionals. You set the policy and we execute it for you, but we work together. Paid staff is a clerk, it's a stock boy in IGA, it's somebody who doesn't care. The people that work for you at CANSKATE care. They're not just doing a job. It's very important to them. They're committed."

He got approval for changes that allowed his staff to be more creative and have more leeway in the direction of the Association and for changes that entrenched his reforms. "We're the constant now. The people can change but the system isn't going to change and I think that has created confidence among our skaters and our parents and among our corporate community. They'll consider, 'Okay there's a new president and that might change the perspective on the direction of the Association, but we know the Association won't change in its business practices and its focus and function.' A new president can't come in and say the national team is gone."

One way of forging a relationship is through communications directed at various CFSA constituencies, including parents and skaters, such as a National Team Guide. Skaters are encouraged to contact the Association with any questions at all. Many do, which is quite a change. In my day, I wouldn't have thought to call the CFSA about anything, assuming I could have even found a number. He says, "We get a lot of mail. We get a lot of cries for help, we get people saying I'm not sure and we get a lot of people who simply say, 'I just really have to say this.' I've had skaters phone with questions about choreography or phone to say, 'Just wanted to let you know that I've got a new apartment.' There's always the ten per cent who say I'm not talking to them or giving them any information, but 90 per cent of our skaters know they can call."

Over 50 people now operate out of the director general's office, all within a structure designed so that David knows exactly what everyone is doing all the time even if he is often out on the road. Marketing is run out of the office, not so much to find new corporate clients for skating but to service long-term supporters like SunLife, the Royal Bank and Centrum. Many sports get into problems with sponsorship because they take the money and run. The CFSA now tries to analyse what each company wants to accomplish with their sponsorship and make sure they get a return on their investment.

Developing the corporate sector is looked at as a business that has to be professionally run. "We cannot depend upon a volunteer. We're dealing with contracts and clauses and hard-nosed people employed by hard-nosed people who want hard-nosed decisions. You can't have a new person every year."

He takes the same attitude with events. In the old days, volunteers would meet at someone's house, piece together the advertising, sell the tickets, do what they could with what passed for customer service and hope for a good turnout to fill the arena. The emphasis on professionalization was a practical decision. "Our money used to be in the television and patch test fee and membership, but we're in the business of children and the trend in membership is not children, so we have to diversify. The company has to look at other ways of making money. We're in the business of Canadian championships. We're not running Canadian championships to make everything all wonderful, we're running them to make the money we need for programs. We've changed our focus here. It's a rock concert we're selling and you don't sell a rock concert by hoping that Mrs. McGillicuddy sells tickets out of her kitchen. It doesn't work."

The Calgary Olympics convinced him that Canadians wanted to see figure skating competitions, but not the small-time affairs that drew a few thousand spectators and usually didn't even tell them who won at the end of the night. Starting with the 1992 Canadians in Hamilton, the championships have become glittering affairs with fanfares and skating stars from Barbara Ann to the present happily working the crowd. Ozzie says, "It's quite funny that our director general fancies himself a Cecil B. DeMille. He always comes up with an extravaganza."

The CFSA's transformation is not yet complete, but David has already decided the date when it will be time for him to go and has started moving his successors into place. The Association now numbers over 180,000 members in about 1,400 clubs, and they are increasingly the focus as the skating world enters a period of turmoil. But that doesn't mean the hunt for medals is pursued any less energetically. At the top of the sport, the perception of the CFSA as a medal-hungry powerhouse is likely to remain.

That's another one of the perceptions that David is prepared to live with. "That perception is driven by the media because what you see is the end product and it is flashy and it is nice and at that level when you're down to the last competitors for the Olympic

Games, you don't mess around. Those people have made a commitment and done all those years and there is a lot at stake. But that's only for thirteen people and there is enough money generated from the marketing and television for that to become self-funding. But that is less than two per cent of our business. The big income generator is the children, all the little people who send us seven dollars and try their preliminary, first and second test. That's where the money comes from. And we spend a lot of time on developing programs and club relationships and communication and training methods, teaching children to skate, teaching adults to skate. There's a lot of just the business of skating and recreation and fun."

In December, skaters keep working through their routines to prepare for the national championships coming up in January. There are often exhibitions to perform and Christmas commitments to keep. This is also the time when television starts priming the audience for the big events ahead. Children's shows with cartoon characters on ice and specials featuring the more celebrated skaters have become a staple of the pre-Christmas fare.

But the range of skating in December is just the beginning. Whether it's from CTV, CBC, TSN or the American networks, there is a skating event on television almost every weekend throughout the winter. Everybody's getting into the game.

Modern figure skating is a creature of television, as every other big sport is. Just as Hollywood made a star of Sonja Henie, television has made stars of several generations of skaters. It has packaged them as heroes, with the odd villain thrown in. It has influenced the way the sport operates. The demise of compulsory figures in competition was partly driven by the fact that no one could figure out a way of televising them without putting audiences to sleep. The remaining national bias in international judging is in at least moderate retreat under the glare of television coverage and analysis. Figure skating events are consistently among the most highly rated programs on North American television.

The Calgary Olympic Games in 1988 was a turning point, the beginning of the current relationship between skating and TV. The spotlight was intense and the ratings astronomical. TV noticed that figure skating was hot and change began to accelerate. Now the sport has been radically transformed and has found a new and growing audience in a sports-happy world.

Doug Beeforth, long-time CTV executive producer for sports and now a network vice president, explains it by saying, "Figure skating is one of the few sports that isn't just a sport. It has all the elements that other sports have—the competition, the thrill of victory, the agony of defeat, teamwork and all this stuff—but what it also has that other sports don't is elements of life, like the relationship between man and woman. People watch a pair or a dance team and everybody sees the performance in a different way. There's something out there they can identify with that there isn't in any other sport. There's the romance, as well as the athleticism. It brings back a memory. It crosses the line from sport to entertainment."

As executive producer, Beeforth would start thinking about the upcoming season the previous March, choosing which events to cover and deciding what times the network would like the events to take place. TV has a tendency to dictate how things should happen, in the same way that judges and associations used to do before TV manoeuvred itself into a position with clout. The two anchor events in CTV's coverage are Skate Canada and the national championships, with four or five other shows that fit into the season chosen from an increasing number of available events. Audiences prefer competitions by far. Ratings are much higher for them than they are for exhibitions.

An Olympic year is a different year for television. TV always tries to make sense of a season, figuring out what the story of the year is to help viewers grasp the significance of why something is happening. In an Olympic year, the big story is obvious. Every skater is out there for the Games, so season planning works backward. The Olympics is where the story ends, despite the Worlds coming soon afterwards. Nationals is where the Olympic team is built. Other competitions are pre-Olympic skates. Ratings are generally better in an Olympic year and stay higher than normal the next year in the Olympic afterglow.

The schedule is locked in by the beginning of June, the same month the production people survey the venues and decide where the cameras and announcer positions will be. Once the site survey is done, things begin to happen. In the 1993–94 season, CTV's first major event was Skate Canada in Edmonton at the beginning of November, followed by a couple of pro events before Christmas. For several other competitions, such as Piruetten in Hamar or Germany's Nation's Cup, the network bought tapes from the host broadcaster and a producer edited them into a package to air

Saturday afternoon on *CTV Sports Presents*. After Christmas, we covered the Canadians in January, which was the final tune-up for the Olympic crews, went on to Lillehammer, did a few exhibition performances, then ended the season with the Canadian precision championships in Montreal on the Easter Weekend.

For each of the major events, CTV's Toronto office sends a skeleton production staff—producer, director, all the associate producers, maybe 10 people in all—to direct the 30 or 40 technicians who get the telecast done. Usually, the technical staff come from the closest affiliate with a mobile unit large enough and sophisticated enough to handle the setup for the network feed and the complex computer-generated graphics. For broadcasting live Friday, Saturday and Sunday, the crews usually come in Wednesday to begin the setup, so that we are in place to record Thursday night any stories or segments that could be used during the live coverage.

The scheduling is planned far ahead of time, in close cooperation with the CFSA. At a live event, the competition cannot be one minute late; television does not have one extra minute. Organization, timing and execution are the most important production criteria. We have to know that if TV is coming to the event live at 12:07 on a Saturday afternoon, a certain skater must be on the ice or waiting for his or her name to be called.

The producer has to get the modular bits—features on skaters, graphics—and so many commercial units into the show while the ice is being flooded. Commercial content usually gets plugged together during the icing and viewers often complain about so many commercials at a time, but without them there would be no show. The alternative would be to call a pause at the event, but organizers are becoming much more strict about holding up the proceedings at inappropriate moments, feeling that it's unfair to the competitors to delay a warm-up. TV has to figure out how to get its commercial content in without disrupting the flow in the building. A major difficulty is that TV doesn't see the order of who skates when until the draw the day before.

Jeff Mather, the producer for live figure skating events, knows to the second what he has booked via satellite and when he must be at a certain point in the program. What goes where is ultimately his decision. He works closely with his associate producers who come up with ideas as to what stories might make better television.

A tremendous amount of organization goes into it, forcing television into an ever-closer relationship with the organizations governing the sport. CTV and the CFSA agreed some years ago not to stage events in crummy buildings where the lighting or camera angles are bad. The learning experience was the Canadian championships in the Victoria Gardens, an old building with a low roof. The intense heat from the TV lights melted the ice, the arena staff cranked up the brine and the ice became very sluggish on top, but crunchy and brittle below. Skaters would dig their picks in for a triple jump and huge chunks of ice would fly across the surface. They'd land on a top so spongy that it was as if a hand had come out from below the rink to grab their blades and hold them tight. It's not uncommon, especially at lower levels, to see lots of falls, but even big guns like Brian Orser, who never falls, were flopping around like fish out of water.

The CFSA also realized that an event held in a 4,500-seat cinder block arena exudes "small time." Holding the Canadians in a sold-out Northlands Coliseum feels like the big time.

The current contract between CTV and the CFSA calls their relationship a partnership, and says they will work together to develop new concepts and ideas. The relationship wasn't always so solid; it took several years for a hide-bound sport like figure skating to come to terms with television. In this country, coming to terms meant it had to work with Johnny Esaw, the head of sports for CTV, who was the one with the vision of what TV and figure skating could do for each other. Johnny worked tirelessly and brought skating coverage of age. He made the world sit up and take notice. Sports kept the fledgling CTV network alive for many years and figure skating became the crown jewel of CTV sports. It is still one of the only North American networks to broadcast multiple skating events live on a regular basis. There is the occasional live broadcast from the States, but for the most part, event coverage is taped and tidied up before it is sent out on air.

Johnny never figure skated a day in his life, although everyone thinks he must have because of his enthusiasm for the sport. As a radio man, he loved covering hockey and football. In his second year as a broadcaster, he did the play-by-play for the 1951 Grey Cup. But figure skating became his baby, the sport he truly loved.

The Wascana Winter Club in Regina, where he began his broadcasting career, was an active organization in the fifties, with several skaters moving on from local competition to ice shows, but Johnny never even saw an ice show himself until 1950, when Father Murray of Notre Dame organized a fundraising event at the local arena featuring people from Hollywood and popular radio shows of the day. The major star was Clarence B. Nash, the voice of Donald Duck. The guest artists did their voices and the skaters skated.

The North American championships were held in Regina in 1955, and the line-up of skaters was filled with Hall of Fame material—Dafoe and Bowden, Wagner and Paul, the Jelineks, Charles Snelling and, from the US, skaters like Carole Heiss, Tenley Albright and the Jenkins brothers, David and Hayes Alan, who between them were world champions for seven years. Bert Penfold, a Regina representative on the CFSA and later president of the association, told Johnny he just had to broadcast the competition. Johnny knew that interest was building after Dafoe and Bowden won the world championship in 1954, but his response to Penfold was, "How do you broadcast skating on radio? I'll put it on the air, but you'll have to tell them what's happening." He says we might have had the quad and the triple Axel back in 1955 if he was doing the analysis himself. Audience response was good and when Frannie and Norrie retained their World title a few weeks later, interest in skating grew. When they had their title "stolen" in Cortina the next year, the public became even more interested.

Johnny moved to a station in Winnipeg, where nothing much had happened in figure skating since Rose Mary Thacker beat Barbara Ann in 1942, but he noticed the press play given to Wagner and Paul during the lead up to the Squaw Valley Olympics and to the world championships in Vancouver following the Games.

In 1960, he made the move to Toronto and to television. TV was still in its infancy and the CBC had only completed its full national network a few years before. Johnny was going to be in charge of sports at the first privately owned station licensed in Canada, CFTO, which aimed to be the base for a new network.

He soon got a call from Roone Arledge, a sports producer at ABC who was about to revolutionize both sports and television to a greater degree than anyone else in the last 35 years. Arledge wanted to cover the championships in Vancouver, but he said to Johnny, "If an American network bids for them, they'll be charged an awful lot of money. But if you bid for North American rights, you can get them for me and can have them yourself if you want them."

Johnny said "sure" and bought the rights for $10,000. CFTO was not yet on the air and CBC had no interest in skating in those days, so despite owning the broadcast rights for the entire continent, Canadians outside the rink and beyond the reach of US signals never got the chance to see Wagner and Paul and the Jelineks win their gold and silver medals.

The experience shaped his plans for sports on the new station and on the proposed new network. "I was now dealing at the world championship level and ABC in New York was asking me for help. That kind of piqued my interest in skating."

One of the station's owners, John Bassett, who also owned the Toronto Argonauts at the time, asked him, "What are you going to do in sports that's exciting?"

"I'm going to put on some figure skating."

"What? You mean that damn fancy skating?" Bassett laughed. He thought it was a joke.

CFTO went on the air in January of 1961, with a big party at its Agincourt studios in suburban Toronto. Skating was part of the station from the beginning. On a postage stamp-sized rink between the parking lot and the highway, those aspiring champions from the Unionville Skating Club just up the road, Wilkes and Revell, put on an exhibition for the guests.

For years, Johnny was a one-man show, negotiating rights, booking the crews, hiring commentators and doing everything else needed to get sports programs on the air. And he kept forging the relationship with ABC, which was starting a new kind of sports program that Johnny thought had potential. He said to Roone Arledge, "Okay, you owe me one. I want to buy *Wide World of Sports*."

The next year, ABC's team of Dick Button and Jim McKay were in Prague for the world championships and Johnny got the feed from ABC. It was the first time the Worlds had been televised in Canada. What the viewers saw was Don Jackson's thrilling championship performance, Wendy Griner skating to silver and the Jelineks winning the gold.

"I was lucky as hell. I won the jackpot with this *Wide World of Sports* show. So I figured, let's get active and see what's happening in Canada."

He bought the rights to the 1963 Canadians in Edmonton and covered every major event over the next few years—Don MacPherson winning the world title in 1963, Petra Burka and Guy and me on the Olympic and world podiums in 1964, Petra taking the world championship in Colorado in 1965, the win being broadcast live. People were starting to notice that world medals were coming home with skaters and the TV ratings increased. The CFSA was getting some response about the coverage too, from skaters' parents complaining. Still known for decisions that were at best arbitrary and at worst downright silly, the CFSA told Johnny that if he was going to interview any skaters, he had to interview them all. That was a *rule*. At a loss for questions to ask the junior skater in twelfth place, he dispatched Sheldon Galbraith, Frannie Dafoe and Bruce Hyland out onto the ice with mikes. The rule didn't last.

During the "dry spell" in skating, CTV started following Karen Magnussen as she moved up the rankings. Her match against Linda Carbonetto at Maple Leaf Gardens in 1969 generated better ratings than any event in years. Johnny also expanded the broadcast team for that event. Otto and Maria retired from Ice Capades in 1968 and Otto had been bugging Johnny about joining him. Everything was against it. Otto had an accent and couldn't speak. Johnny worked for hours with him before deciding it was no go. He arranged to meet Otto at Maple Leaf Gardens' Hot Stove Lounge to tell him the news, but on his way over, he thought, "I don't have anybody else. He was a world champion, a hero." Otto became a fixture.

Karen's fight back after recovering from stress fractures in both legs made for good TV through the early seventies. Trixie Shuba's triumph over Karen at the Sapporo Olympics and Calgary Worlds in 1972 made for heart-wrenching moments, but at least made it obvious to everyone that something was terribly wrong in a system that awarded 60 per cent of the mark to figures and made a champion of someone who couldn't free skate worth a damn.

All the years of tracking Karen came to fruition at the Worlds in Bratislava in 1973, with some extra excitement added to the competition from Dick Button's relentless push for Janet Lynn to win. For the final night of the competition, Johnny booked the sole transatlantic satellite from nine to eleven o'clock. By the luck of the draw, Karen was to skate at nine. But the afternoon of the competition, one skater dropped out, meaning Karen would skate before the satellite was on-line. He went to the ISU organizer of the competition to try and get the skate delayed.

"We cried and tried to bribe him with all sorts of promises, but he wouldn't change anything. Coming up to nine o'clock, we could see we weren't getting any breaks. There were no delays. I told [production manager] Oliver Babirad, who was Slovak, and Otto, who was Czech, 'Get out on the ice and stall that Zamboni driver.' The officials were patching the worst holes in the ice while Oliver and Otto were giving the driver pins, American money and anything else they had, saying, 'Stay in there.'"

As the delay stretched out, Johnny asked the CFSA's president, Billie Mitchell, and other members of the association sitting behind the broadcast booth to work out a few numbers. Janet Lynn was skating last and until she skated no one would know whether Karen had won.

Billie Mitchell gave him the word. "She'll be skating at eleven."

Johnny thought, "Oh God, we're going to miss it. I sent word out to Jelinek and Babirad to tell the driver to hurry up with that damn Zamboni and get the ice done so we can get this thing started."

Karen skated at nine and skated well. Coming up to eleven, he went to his pals at ABC and asked them for some satellite time. "No." "I was going to lose it. Janet didn't skate that well, but we got her on and just as we were getting the countdown to leave the satellite, Mitchell had worked out the numbers and gave me the word. So I hollered, 'Yes, Karen has won the world championship' as I heard, 'Three, two, one, the satellite's dead.'"

Karen's win was a media sensation in Canada and the CFSA began to recognize the value of television to the sport. Skate Canada began the same year and CFSA president George Blundun, and the secretary, Hugh Glynn, went to Johnny to ask him to televise the event.

He said, "Sure, I'll give you a three-year contract on one condition. That I get the rights to the boards."

They didn't like the idea. The Board of Broadcast Governors had never allowed board advertising at hockey games or any other event anyway. But the ISU had signed a deal with a Swiss marketing company, Gloria Transparente, to sell board ads at events beginning with the 1973 Worlds. CTV president Murray Chercover wrote the BBG to explain the problem of selling ads in Canada that might compete with the board ads coming from Europe. The BBG agreed to change its policy, as long as the boards were sold to the same companies sponsoring the telecast. Blundun and Glynn had no choice but to put the boards into the package, where they have stayed ever since.

The first Skate Canada was successful TV, especially since Canadians—Toller Cranston and Lynn Nightingale—won two of the three events (there was no pairs competition because George Blundun, an ice dancer, thought pairs skating was "kick boxing on skates"). CTV now had rights to Skate Canada, the Canadians and Worlds. Then the sport went through a period where the only skater to make a splash internationally was Toller Cranston and he was, at best, unpredictable.

I became part of Johnny's team in these years. After graduating in psychology from York University, I had gone off to Michigan State for a Masters degree in television and radio arts. By the usual circuitous route —childhood friend of my mother's who contacted a photographer who knew Johnny F. Bassett who arranged a meeting with CFTO vice-president Ted Delaney—I was offered a job. CFTO was negotiating with Metromedia, the owner of Ice Capades, to produce a variety show called *The Crystal Ice Palace*. I would be the CFTO person consulting on the show. It was perfect timing. I graduated at Christmas and started work January 3. Not long after, the deal with Metromedia fell through and the station was stuck with a skater with some broadcasting education, but who really knew nothing about TV. The thinking was, "She's an athlete, put her in sports."

Degree in hand and never having typed a letter in my life, I became Johnny's secretary. It was a wonderful education. He was splitting his time between CFTO and the network and the small sports department, with only a couple of full-time producers, was doing quite a lot of original production. One show was a magazine-style weekly hour for the network, so I would meet all the sports people from the affiliates who came to be guest contributors.

I had never done anything on air, nor did I particularly want to. But the "big break" came in 1973. When Karen Magnussen won the world championship, she signed a $300,000 contract to join Ice Capades. The show happened to be in Buffalo, so Johnny wanted Fergie Olver to zip across the border to do a *Sportsbeat* story. Fergie didn't take well to the suggestion. He said, "I'm not doing a story on some damn figure skater. She's the figure skater, send her."

Johnny thought, "Why not?" I could think of plenty of reasons why not, but he said, "Don't worry, Tommy will look after you." Tommy Rupple, still one of the best news cameramen in the business, told me what to do—stand here, say this, do that. He saved me. Karen was a great interview, bubbly, enthusiastic and excited about where her life was going. The editor made the piece look good, it aired on *Sportsbeat* and everyone seemed to like it, so I continued with more stories, including an item on Unionville's skating carnival, still one of the best in the country. Johnny liked that story quite a bit, so I branched out to other sports and started to contribute more to the on-air production.

After about a year, we both came to the conclusion that I wasn't being paid for the kind of work I was doing, so he went to Ted Delaney to get me a raise. Delaney said, "No." Johnny told me that the best thing for me was to quit. After much discussion, I took his advice. He was encouraging and very supportive, giving me a list of contacts and some wonderful suggestions about what I might do to get experience and learn more than I ever could at CFTO. For the next year I worked freelance, doing some writing for the *Toronto Star* and stringer stuff for radio station CFRB. With Johnny's help and guidance, I managed to find enough work to pay my way to the 1974 World Championships in Munich to see Dorothy Hamill win.

Later that year, I called and said, "How about my coming onto the team with you and Otto?"

Nobody had ever used three people before—the Dick Button and Jim McKay duo was still the gold standard—and certainly nobody had ever used a woman. Much to my surprise, he said, "Yeah, we'll try it, but just for the Canadian championships to see if it works." The championships in Quebec City worked out well, so he asked me to stay on to do the Worlds in Colorado Springs. That went well too and we just kept going.

These were years of invigorating work and travel with a wonderful group of people. Working with Otto was quite a change. He and Maria were always around when Guy and I were training, but I saw them as real old farts—I mean, they were 19—and was rather intimidated by them. Covering events, Otto, his wife Leeta and I were a regular threesome, getting into lots trouble all innocent enough. They were very generous and sharing of their time, taking me under their wing and off to trips that always turned into great adventures.

Johnny was incredibly driven and productive and came from the old school of doing business. He was the boss. He was autocratic and could say terrible things to people. Many were terrified of him, but that was part of his power. He was very loyal, keeping the same people around him, perhaps because he knew he could get them to do what he wanted. Everybody thought he was an ogre. I thought he was a cream puff. I loved him and had no problems at all.

The only uncomfortable moment was after I left briefly in 1983 to work for the CBC. I was there only a few months when big changes were made and many people, me included, got the axe. Brian Pockar had replaced me on the team, so there was no room back at CTV. But then Otto went to Ottawa in the Conservative sweep of 1984 and became a cabinet minister. I asked Johnny if I could come back.

He said, "No, I don't ever take anybody back who leaves me."

The person who lobbied for me and got him to change his mind was Brian Pockar, who was an absolute delight to work with. Brian loved life and had an appreciation of the surreal that took us into many strange places. In Tokyo for the Worlds in 1985, we ended up in a transvestite bar where all the drag queens were on roller skates. They would serve the drinks and nibblies, then don their Carol Channing outfits and come out on stage to sing *Horrow, Dorry*. We had a blast.

But seeing Johnny at work was the best education. He was always very quiet about it, but he personally helped finance many skaters. As his secretary, I sent out the cheques. He didn't always sponsor the number one people. More often, it would be someone showing skill and ambition, but whose family could not manage the costs. He didn't only operate out of personal generosity. He knew from his involvement with other sports that he needed to get associations on side and make the coverage lucrative for them so they could help more skaters. Many associations struggle just to make it through to tomorrow, but once TV is involved, the potential for corporate funding becomes much greater. Funding tends to dry up without television. There is no point for a corporation to stick its name on an event if the event isn't seen by the public.

Johnny developed corporate funding and was instrumental in setting up the Athletes Trust to make it more feasible for skaters to stay in the sport longer. He got company chairmen and presidents to donate $10,000 each on air during events. His own bursury, the Johnny Esaw Trust Fund, still hands out $10,000 a year to members of the Junior Team. And he was always willing to do just a little more for skaters he believed in. Before the Worlds in Ottawa in 1978, Vern Taylor went to see him and said he had run into some trouble and might not be able to compete. Johnny called Imperial Tobacco, which used to give spending money to the kids in the Worlds, and got $2,000. A tennis promoter happened to be in his office the same day to finalize a deal to broadcast a tournament. Johnny said, "I'm tacking $1,000 onto your contract and you're going to donate it to a skater."

The Toronto Cricket Club allowed Vern to skate. No one knew, except Vern himself, that the performance was intended to be the final one of his career. He threw in the tiple Axel in desperation, knowing he'd never get another chance. There was some argument about whether his hand touched the ice when he came down, so Johnny called ISU president Jacques Favart, and Sonja Biencetti, the referee at the event. "I want you to come back to the truck. I'll put the tape up and you judge whether he was successful." After watching the tape, they officially declared the jump as the first triple Axel to be landed in competition.

In his more than thirty years as a champion of the sport, Johnny contributed to figure skating in many different ways. He placed the cameras low to give people at home a view of the sport from rinkside. He argued with judges he thought had been unfair to our skaters. He started many standing ovations by applauding like mad in the last 30 seconds of a program. "I never was afraid of letting them know what colour is on my sleeve. I'm Canadian and the rest of them can go to hell."

And the old sportsman in him would bristle if viewers questioned whether skaters were really "real athletes." He'd say, 'Real athletes? I'll tell you, if a hockey player in the NHL does a 45-second shift, he's rushing to the bench sucking for air. You can take any young skater going for a championship and he has to go for four and a half minutes, really going, not just pushing. He can't take a rest and he doesn't have anybody pumping oxygen in him. This sport is tough. These kids have got to be good athletes."

He developed skating to the point where, in Canada at least, it could compete with hockey and football. He was so excited after the 1980 Lake Placid Games when the men's final drew better ratings than the Grey Cup. The CFL was still big time then, but skating was bigger. Nothing made him happier.

The 1988 Olympics were the highlight of his career. As soon as the decision to award the Games to Calgary was announced in Baden-Baden in 1982, he started assembling the people he would need to get the rights. From then on it was hustle, hustle, hustle.

For several years, he had had a deal with the CBC where the two networks negotiated rights together to keep the bids down, with a sharing arrangement for airing highlights. This consortium seemed to work well. In 1984, by "sweating and saving a lot of money" he was ready to make a run for a deal on Calgary. He met with the CBC's new English division vice president, Dennis Harvey, at La Scala, a popular restaurant in midtown Toronto.

He told Harvey, "The consortium has worked beautifully for us, but because the Games are in Calgary, we should give you a little more time than we normally would in our sharing arrangement."

Harvey said, "There is no more sharing arrangement. The consortium is finished. This is going to be a CBC production and you're not in it."

"He told me to go to hell," Johnny says. "I went to [CTV vice president Murray Chercover. He said, 'Don't waste my time and don't worry about it. You'll never get them.' He had said the same thing when I went after the rights to the Canada-Russia hockey series in '72. Just as I did then, I called John Bassett—I always had Bassett to fall back on—and he also said the same thing he had said about the Canada Cup rights: 'You get them'."

He targeted the nine people on the Calgary Olympic Development Association's board, chaired by the Calgary Stampede's Bill Pratt, for intensive lobbying and decided to use the CBC's record at the 1976 Montreal Olympics against the public network. CTV wasn't set up to handle Summer Games, so CBC had essentially been handed the rights. The CBC had then gone back to the organizing committee and several times to the government for more money, which it used to buy mobile studio trucks that were sent to CBC stations across the country after the Games. In effect, they had stuck it to the organizing committee to re-equip their stations.

Johnny laid this all out at a private meeting with Pratt. "This is the way they do business," he said. "The sky's the limit, you have no control, you have no vote, you have nothing. Here's how we'll do it. We'll share one set of books. I'll put a price out there to do the host broadcasting and guarantee you the best broadcasters in the world. I'll bring in the cross-country skiing guy from Norway, the speed-skating guy from Holland, Doug Wilson from ABC to direct the skating, all the top professionals. All of this will be done and here's the price and everything we spend over that price will be approved by you and our comptroller together. There's bound to be increases, but not one nickel will be spent without your permission. When the Games are over, we'll stop paying rent on all this equipment. We will not buy equipment and give it to our stations."

Being a western free enterpriser, Pratt loved the idea of having a say in CTV's costs. Johnny worked on the other board members too, getting to know them, selling them. When the Committee's marketing vice president was unsure of how to sell television time, Johnny invited him and his people to come down to the office, look around, ask anything, learn anything. With good relationships with the members of the board and "a pretty good contact" in the government, he knew exactly what was going on in the bidding.

He put in his price as the host broadcaster, building the Canadian rights into the package. The vote was 8–0 in CTV's favour, with one abstention, a federal representative, who wanted a guarantee about the French language feed. Once Johnny provided it, the vote was 9–0. When the word got out, even Canada's Minister of Sport, Otto Jelinek, seemed pleased.

The day the committee was to reveal which network was the winner, CBC had arranged to do an episode of *Front Page Challenge* live from Calgary. At the end of the show, it would be announced that CBC had won the rights. Johnny was in an office at Labatt's signing a Blue Jays baseball contract that day when Bill Pratt called.

"Bill said, 'Hey, you lucky son of a bitch, you stole one from me. You got the rights. They're all yours, let's get out the champagne.' We all went nuts. I told Dennis Harvey later, 'Thanks very much.' Then the CBC came back on their knees and wanted to get in. So I gave them an hour a night for a million bucks."

The buildup to the Games was a TV executive's dream. Boitano and Orser both falling in Geneva in 1986. Orser beating Boitano for the World title in Cincinnati in 1987. Skate Canada at the Saddledome in the fall of '87, an Olympic preview where Orser beat Boitano again. Then the skating at the Games themselves. "It was civilization bearing fruit at that competition," Toller Cranston says. No skating audience has ever been so galvanized.

Brian Boitano winning the gold by one-tenth of a point. Liz Manley coming out in the battle between Katarina Witt and Debi Thomas and getting by her first triple combination, her winning of the silver more significant than not winning the gold. And most of all, for Johnny, Tracy Wilson and Rob McCall skating the best they had ever skated. "The others got marks like ballet-type skaters. The Russians were good at what they did, but Wilson and McCall *danced*. The greatest individual performance of the whole Games. I didn't know how we could ever top that. But then we didn't really notice the kid sitting back in sixth place, Kurt Browning."

The way Johnny handled the Calgary coverage started a trend. Before Calgary, the American networks always had their own camera crews because they never trusted local broadcasters to deliver the quality they required. Calgary was the first place the Americans didn't do that. Johnny's approach of taking off the flags and bringing in the best people anywhere made ABC feel comfortable. Ever since Calgary, the move in television sport has been to collaborate on major international events. It is recognized that some countries are better at certain kinds of sports coverage because they do more of it. Canadian cameramen at a hockey game will point their cameras where they know the puck might be passed because they have played the game and know it in their bones. American cameramen still occasionally lose the puck on a simple up-ice rush. Since Calgary, it has become more common for the Swiss to do downhill, the Dutch to do speed skating and the Canadians to do hockey and figure skating.

The Calgary Olympics were also something of a turning point for Doug Beeforth. Like many people, he thought of figure skating as a sport that sort of wasn't a sport, one that he might watch one or two days a year. It was something he knew Canadians did very well in, yet still seemed somehow foreign. Most of his early television career was spent working with Ralph Mellanby, Canada's legendary hockey producer. In 1986, he was hired to work with Mellanby on "host" broadcasting of the Olympics. Mellanby outlined the plan and told Beeforth to meet with all the sports federations and "make it work."

Figure skating was the last sport he dealt with. He was working closely with ABC, which considered figure skating a keystone of their Olympic coverage. A session with figure skating's representative had been triggered by ABC's insistance that the skating events be scheduled to end at ten to eleven. Together, they worked out a plan to tell the sport how to do it.

Beeforth and the high level executives from ABC were sitting in the stands at the Saddledome when Joyce Hisey walked in. "She was very nice," Beeforth says. "She listened to what we had to say and said 'Just tell me where you want to be and I'll get you there. It'll work.' That was it. All our plans of telling them how to do it didn't matter. I didn't know whether to believe her or not. That meeting had an impact in that it opened my eyes to something different in figure skating. It is the one sport that runs so efficiently. The Joyce Hiseys of the world seem to have an inordinate amount of common sense and also seem to have inordinate ability to get rid of the chaff and get to what's important. It's the same with the staging of the events. Maybe it's because they are generally run by women, but the events run like clockwork. They run so well you don't worry anymore. In other sports, you have to keep sending letters and having meetings."

Not everyone in skating on the international scene has the same understanding of how important it is to have TV onside, but common sense can still win out. CTV served as the "host" broadcaster for all ice events at Lillehammer—the American network went back to their "dueling cranes" double camera setup in Albertville, but again were comfortable with Canadians being in charge in Norway—and since CTV had so much success with backstage cameras showing skaters limbering up or fooling around, the network requested cameras backstage in Lillehammer. Word came from the ISU that this was not possible. The rights holder in the US, CBS, said they would take a crack at it. They sent a delegation to meet with ISU president Olaf Poulsen, who took the request under advisement. At Piruetten in November, the final word came down from the ISU Council: No.

Beeforth asked for a meeting on camera positions with the ISU's two technical delegates, Charles Moore and Lawrence Demmy. Before the meeting, he spoke with Joyce Hisey who told him not to give up, to keep pushing and call if he needed her help. The two sides met in the hallway in the amphitheatre between events at Piruetten.

Beeforth was passionate about how seeing the skaters backstage gives the sport a personality that people can get a hold of and lets the skaters touch people's hearts. "The meeting started with both saying no. In ten minutes, they were saying is one camera back here enough? They understood. When they brought up their problems, we gave them solutions. Their concern emerged as cables that skaters might trip on. We said we'd build tracks so the cables would come off the ceiling, then everything was fine. Other sports would have just said no."

CTV's approach to coverage is very story-oriented. The richness of stories in skating and the well-spoken qualities of the athletes almost demand it. We try to determine at the beginning of the season what the major stories are, then follow them throughout all events so that at the end of the year the whole package hangs together with some common threads running through. Our philosophy is to try to have the viewers, generally not skaters, understand in a clear and concise way what is happening at an event, why it is important and why they should bother watching.

In the 1993–94 season, everything was done with an eye toward the Olympic Games, with the big story being the pros coming back. Stories build from the beginning of the season, so in July and August CTV's research department started supplying volumes of information. In September, the network hosted a three-day seminar in Toronto, which for the first time brought together all the 200 or so people who would be involved in the Olympic coverage. We were given a fairly extensive introduction to Norway, the facilities and distances between venues, our living accommodations, work situations and who we would be working with. We had small group sessions to talk about how we wanted to make our particular unit special.

We always spend a lot of time talking about the usual challenges TV faces in covering figure skating, especially the annual judging controversy that often overshadows everything else. We have to do more to make judging less a mystery to people. CTV was the first network to show the ordinals along with the marks and we often wonder whether we should bother showing individual marks at all since they don't mean anything and upset people.

We also talk about new camera angles or innovations that could overcome TV limitations in covering every sport, namely how to take a three-dimensional activity, reduce it to two dimensions and put in on a flat piece of glass. Anything to enhance the feeling is worth exploring, without getting gimmicky just to show off what we can do.

TV does not fully capture what skating is. Skating is a language of movement that tells a story. I want the audience to understand what it is like to do it and I see my job as helping them understand. But understanding it intellectually through words and explanation is one thing. At the top of my wish list is a way for them to experience through the picture itself how the music affects a skater's movement, how it feels for a skater to glide through space and what it feels like to be airborne and soaring.

TV gives it a good shot and there have been moments when, as a skater, I look at the monitor and say, "Yes! That's it. That is what it's like. That's beautiful. That's why I love it." We have some very clever people on the skating team. The director, Michael Lansbury, a veteran of baseball and hockey games, will every once in a while do a shot that grabs me somewhere in the solar plexus. One that sticks in my mind was a very simple one. The skater was doing a series of footwork steps in a straight line down the ice, but with lots of movement—backward, forward, twisting, hopping—and the camera travelled with him, conveying a sense of speed I had never seen before.

A camera on a crane helps, although in Canada its use is usually restricted by the building. The crane can only move up and down. In buildings where the boards are out, the crane can also do some beautiful sweeping movements that convey the fact that skaters are not just kicking off and landing in the same spot in a jump, they're covering twenty feet in the air. Putting a box around skaters and panning with them, keeping them dead centre in the frame, doesn't give viewers the sense that the quality of the jump depends not just on how high or how many rotations it has, but how far it goes. They never get the chance to judge for themselves and say, "That was a nice, neat, clean jump with good rotation and height, but it really didn't go anywhere."

One setup for precision skating conveyed movement by having a camera on tracks going down one side of the rink. It worked well, but precision groups mostly move in straight lines while singles, pairs and dancers rarely do, using much different patterns on the ice. Having a track on a curve around the rink has been suggested, moving, in hockey terms, from the red line to behind the centre of the net, but there are always limitations in most buildings.

It's a struggle to define different perspectives that might provide the missing dimension to the coverage, but the elusive "better camera angle" may not exist. At Skate Canada in Victoria in 1993, the Norwegian Olympic organizers informed Doug Beeforth that there was some extra money available for any technical innovations CTV could come up with. In hockey, the result was the "net cam" that gave viewers—and game officials—a new way of seeing the play. In figure skating, there was nothing much anyone could come up with that would improve on getting cameras in the corners, getting them low and hiring cameramen who understand what they are doing. Beeforth figured, "Embedding a camera in the ice or putting one on a skate blade is not going to do anything for anybody."

The audience has to rely on the broadcast team for an insight into things, and everyone involved has to do a lot of research. I go through stacks of research material and talk to lots of people. I still coach so I hear the gossip that keeps me feeling on top of many stories. At an event, doing homework means sitting from eight o'clock in the morning until eight o'clock at night, getting "judges' calluses"—blisters on the rear end—watching the practices and the skaters coming and going, getting a feel of what's happening in the building, picking up on the scuttlebutt and taking reams of notes. How are people skating? Are they living up to their advance press? Sometimes the most insignificant little details will be what makes the big difference.

The competition begins the moment the first skater steps on

the ice at the first practice. What unfolds is more a psychological game than anything else. At the first practice for an event—and all skaters practice a couple of times a day—the skaters could come out with bags over their heads and it would be clear from the body language who the champions were and whether they might be champions again. Experienced skaters, or ones who have an enormous belief in themselves, display a sense of power, a sense of command, even in the way they take their guards off and where they put them on the ice. They show it in the way they interact with their coach. The best skaters show little anxiety and their coaches usually seem at ease, despite the turmoil often going on inside them. Over a week of practices, someone can take command, then unravel and lose it. Someone else can have a tough first practice then battle hard until a strength emerges.

In commenting on a skater's prospects or performance, there's always a debate about what is legitimate to talk about and whether some spin should be put on things. Johnny always used to say, "Be positive, be positive, we're trying to make this a positive event." But at events where no one can stand up or skate half-decently, it's pretty hard to find interesting and positive things to say.

The people in the skating world also expect only positive support. They go nuts over anything critical. I decided long ago that I will call it as I see it. If I think the judges have robbed a skater, I'll say so. Some people object, some applaud. I've become more outspoken about a lot of things over the years, while trying to remember that these are amateurs, young people who are there out of love for the sport. I try to avoid making personal remarks about things no one has any control over, like body shape or leg length. The tiniest criticism about personal things can be devastating to a skater. But anything that affects a performance is fair game.

Toller has had his share of criticism for remarks on air too. He says, "I had never really thought about it until I was fired by the CBC, but being very truthful about anything is very controversial."

Everyone in skating would expect some comment if a skater was competing with a pulled muscle, a broken foot, the flu or even a head cold. Other medical problems seem to be taboo. I got into trouble when Lisa Sargeant was trying to make her comeback. She was just skin and bone and it was common knowledge why. In the pre-season setup for *Wide World of Sports* I listed the women contenders as Karen Preston, Josée Chouinard and Lisa Sargeant "if she can keep her anorexia under control." Whoo, the shit hit the fan. It was a very pertinent fact, but it was one of those things you're not supposed to talk about.

Of all the people I've worked with over the years, Dan Matheson was a favourite because he called it exactly as he saw it. After Elvis skated brilliantly in Sudbury and was beaten by Kurt who couldn't stand up, Dan delivered one of his all-time great lines, "This is worse than WWF wrestling. It's like the roller derby, it's so fake." The skating world gasped that someone would be so blunt.

After Skate Canada in November of '93, Lloyd Eisler wrote a scathing letter to CTV about Brian Orser and me not giving him and Isabelle enough support. My crime, apparently, was to talk about Gordeeva and Grinkov as if they were shoo-ins for the Olympics. Well, they were. My credibility was on the line and nothing I could say would suddenly bestow the title on Lloyd and Isabelle. A commentator or analyst does not have that kind of power, despite what some skaters think.

I have always felt that the athletes look at me with a bit of fear, though I could never understand why. The younger ones see me in what they think is a powerful position and feel I have some influence over their careers. But I just give my impressions, always trying to think of things from their standpoint. A double Axel is a double Axel. Everybody's going to try one. Some will do it, some won't and whether it is a good or bad one is obvious. I can be fairly direct about the elements I like, whether it's a good program, the choreography or music I think is suitable. But those are just my opinions and they are not going to affect an event or sway a judge's mark.

Where I may have some influence is in helping shape how the public sees the skaters not as athletes, but as personalities. To do it requires building relationships with individual skaters, which is hard to do when they are intimidated or hostile to the media. I make a point of speaking with the younger skaters at every event. I try to speak to them right away if they have had a memorable performance, good or bad, particularly a bad one. After a bad performance, you just want the ground to open up and swallow you. But no one ever skates poorly on purpose so I try to give the kids some emotional support. The media are only too happy to speak to those who win and the Kurts and Elvises of the world are well taken care of even if they're losing. The media will soothe their wounds and give them enough accolades. The people who need a kind word and understanding are the ones struggling to gain some ground on the front-runners. Of course, I also hope that when they become champions themselves a few years down the road they remember the support.

What the athletes can do to build the relationship is to realize that the media are just trying to do a job. The kind of help I need from skaters is in finding out who they are so I can share that with the audience—a Jamie Salé chatting about herself and what her challenges have been, an Isabelle Brasseur explaining how her boyfriend Jean-Luc Brassard helped her family through their grief over her father's death. I want to bring them to the public not just as jumpers or performers moving around an ice surface, but as living, breathing human beings. I want to tell the people at home who they are, what makes them tick and why skating is important to them. What kind of people are they?

That makes it difficult to understand Herbie Eisler's approach of refusing to speak to me for years. Even allowing for his reputation as a whiner and a crybaby—he's still throwing chairs around when he's thirty, for heaven's sakes—it makes no sense to ignore or offend people whose support and respect might be useful.

Skaters have to be able to play politics. They always have and they always will, but the powers that be are no longer the clubmen nor just the judges and associations. For good or ill, TV is the star-making machinery, not through what some analyst may say but through the power of the medium itself. TV has been responsible for creating a huge audience for figure skating and TV is the connection between the skaters and the public they ultimately depend on for success. It took decades for the rest of the sport to come to terms with television and it is long past time that all the skaters came to terms with it too.

C hristmas doesn't exist for competitive skaters. Sectional and divisional competitions follow fast and furious upon one another, with the national championships coming close behind. By early January, time speeds up. Skaters start wishing they had done all the things they were supposed to have been doing since September. They become self-conscious to the point of examining carefully the tips of their toes. Things taken for granted seem to require great thought. The combinations they've been landing nine times out of ten suddenly only succeed five times out of ten. Costumes don't fit or feel truly right. Everything seems to fall apart.

For competitive skaters, only three of these events are key during a season, four in an Olympic year. The invitational in the fall is an important tune-up and the Worlds are a major focus for the highest-ranking competitors. But to make it to the Worlds or Olympics, everyone has to make it through their national championships first.

The Canadian championships in Edmonton in 1994 were expected to be thrilling, with world and long-time Canadian champions Eisler and Brasseur making their last appearance, a field of strong women competing for the two spots on the world and Olympic teams and yet one more replay of the seemingly perennial Kurt vs. Elvis showdown. The competition lived up to its billing.

For some of the main players, the event was a testing ground that could validate tough decisions they had made about their careers, such as Kurt's determination to carry on after his sixth place finish in the 1992 Olympics and after regaining his world championship in Prague in 1993. For Herbie Eisler, his decision to stay in the sport despite much advice to the contrary had been validated years ago. These were his seventeenth national championships. He has an aura about him, a star quality that comes from his longevity and the many wonderful contributions he has made to skating with his three partners. Right from the earliest days with Sherri Baier he showed himself to be a tremendously motivated young man who had a sense of his greatness, the determination to follow through and the ability to convince others to believe in him too. He has a quality of power about him, a strength of character. The power of personality just blasts out of him.

For Josée, these Canadians would show whether she had made the right decision in the spring of 1993 to move away from her hometown of Laval, where she had trained with the same coach, Johanne Barbeau, all her life. She had been very successful there, winning two national titles. But when she fell apart at the 1993 Worlds, she made the decision to train with Louis at the Granite Club in Toronto, sharing the ice with his other students, including Kurt and Josée's long-time rival, Karen Preston.

"My old coach, she got a shock," Josée says. "She wasn't expecting that. We were getting along pretty well together. It wasn't a fight. It was nothing like that. It was just that I felt if I was keeping the same routine, the same training or even doing a little bit more than that, I wouldn't go higher or improve. I'd reached a certain level and I needed something else. The most important thing is that I never had to really work for skating. It always seemed to be easy. I thought people maybe were doing more than me, so I thought I needed to make a sacrifice for skating. I thought if I left my friends and my family and Jean-Michel and everybody that was close to me, maybe I'd prove to myself that I'm really determined. And it worked. It showed in my training. I was missing home most of the time during the weekends and at night when my training was over. But I was really happy on the ice."

Josée is a beautiful skater and has a sweet-natured presence that is enchanting. When she is well-trained and well-prepared, there is a pacing to her programs that gives viewers time to pause and breathe. She can do all the tricks well, up to and including the triple Lutz, now the cut-off point for women, and is equally good at spinning and jumping. She always had limited scope artistically, but that was something she imposed on herself, mainly out of shyness. She has amazing motivation, perseverance and dedication to doing what has to be done. Even in the face of disappointment, she can pick herself up, push forward and learn from her mistakes. She has a vision about herself as all the best athletes do, particularly these days when artistry is such an important facet of what makes a skater great.

Karen was quite upset at first about Josée coming to Louis. Skaters do have a sense of ownership about their coaches and it is always hard to train with someone you know is your major competition. There was a big period of adjustment for both of them. But for Josée, the opportunity was too great to pass up. The best part was working both with Kurt and with Louis and his captains like Sandra Bezic to get the right kind of vehicle for her. They nailed it. Both the music from *La Fille Mal Garde* for the short and *An American in Paris* for the long have that lovely sweetness so characteristic of Josée, the sauciness and naiveté that turn into personal power.

For Elvis, the competition would be an opportunity to test yet one more time the rightness of his stubborn refusal to be anything but himself and to test how successful he had been in exploring his artistic side, with Uschi Keszler as his guide. When he first met Uschi, she asked him, "What do you want out of this? What do you search for?"

He said that it was something "out there," though he wasn't sure what.

She said, "Why are you searching out there? It's not out there. It's here, inside you."

Like Sandra Bezic, Uschi has an ability to strip the skater down past all the technical details and past the body to see into their souls and discover who they are. She knows her skaters in a way that few people do, even their coaches. They tell her their secrets. She connects with them as a friend and in an almost motherly way, becoming part of them. The skaters have complete trust in what she says. In competition, they rely on her tremendously, but she encourages independence and free-thinking. She asks the questions, waits for the skater to answer, then molds herself around them.

The process was very hard for him. "The reason it's so difficult to look inside is because you cannot fool yourself," he says. "As soon as you look inside, you can't play games anymore. You've got to see yourself for who you really are and see the positives and the negatives. That's the hardest thing, coming to terms with who you are and not hiding from it. You've got to deal with that first before you can go on. Once you're comfortable with it, you can take anything that comes your way because you know what's true."

Who he was, how and what he was and how he went about his work had been criticized for years. All skaters get told again and again what they simply have to do if they expect to win. With very talented skaters, the advice comes thick and fast. "I got lots of it because I was so different from everyone else. They thought I should fit a particular bill. How am I going to fit in? If I'm a square, how am I supposed to fit into a circular frame? How's it going to work? I've got to make my own frame, even though that can make things difficult. It makes it easy when everyone goes out there and skates as oranges, if you want to look at it that way. But as soon as someone throws in an apple, they wonder how to compare. But it's nice to see. It's variety. Who wants to see fifty thousand oranges on the ice?"

There was a real buzz around Edmonton as the event got underway. Even in the coffee shop at the Northern Alberta Institute of Technology, students were talking about the men's competition. There was an inkling of the unexpected about to happen.

The results of the pairs competition, however, were entirely expected. The young pairs of Kristy Sargeant and Kris Wirtz and Jamie Salé and Jason Turner showed their fabulous technical skills. Each pair has a look and both girls are outstanding. Jamie is also an excellent singles skater. She does the triples and is over the hump of puberty so will likely retain them. She's not afraid to be whoever she wants to be and has a presence that bubbles out of her. Jamie and Jason had a rough short program, but came back to win the bronze medal and a place on the Olympic team. Kristy and Kris gelled in their second year together, cleaning up some technical problems. They feed off each other and are very supportive of each other in practice and in competition. They have a magic and fire on the ice that earned them the silver medal.

But the night was Eisler and Brasseur's. Herb was gracious both on and off the ice. Isabelle was radiant, with none of the little girl doubt she had sometimes shown in the past. She had control of the situation and she knew it. She looked like a woman who had something to say and was going to be heard. The pair balanced at last and skated with an ease and confidence that elevated them into a class all by themselves. They were superb.

In the dance competition, Jennifer Boyce and Michel Brunet, skating to the Celtic music of the Chieftains, were absolutely charming, capturing the imagination of many, including me, for the first time. Their performance put them ahead of the very promising couple of Martine Patenaude and Eric Masse. The defending champions, Shae-Lynn Bourne and Victor Kraatz, fell in their first dance, but had no trouble coming back to hold onto the title. Both have faces and figures to die for and are so easy to look at. In their skating, they have the most perfect edge quality, simple and lovely with no apparent effort in their upper bodies. They perform with an elegant and refined style I haven't seen for a long time.

But what everybody was waiting for was the men's event. Kurt skated first not only out of the warmup, his least favourite position, but first in the entire competition. The nervousness he felt was made worse by a feeling of hostility in the air from the Edmonton fans, as if he had deserted them by leaving the Royal Glenora Club and moving to Toronto. It was not a nice feeling. He and Louis had gone over what the reaction of the audience might be and were expecting some negative reaction, some positive. But they weren't expecting what they got. When he went out on the ice, Louis says, "I don't think he was there. He was overwhelmed at the response."

It showed. He made a mistake on his double Axel, a ludicrously simple jump for him, then put his hand down on his triple Axel-triple toe combination. After Elvis skated to a first place finish and the other men completed their programs, Kurt was in fourth place, not only almost out of the running for retaining the title, but in danger of not making the team at all. He was in shock.

The defeat of a champion usually makes everyone at an event uncomfortable. Backstage, people turn and walk away rather than talk to the skater. No one knows what to say or do. It's like being at a funeral where the mourners say, "He looks good. Doesn't he look good?" No, he looks dead. What can you say when the moment is so painful? Audiences in the fickle skating world also respond when there is even the slightest hint of a champion's loss. There is no loyalty. Everyone hops on the nearest bandwagon, saying who's next? But when Kurt blew the short, the entire building seemed like it had banged its head and was reeling around in a daze. There seemed to be a feeling of, "Yes, we wanted him to hurt, but we didn't want him to hurt that badly. Not him. Not Kurt."

Fortunately, they found their generous spirit again by the end of the competition. In the long program, he skated first out of the warmup again, this time at least in the top group, but Louis worked to take the sting out of the situation. "Peter Jensen said, 'This boy really does not like being first and since you're stuck with first, we have to do something to make him think he's not first. So get him off the ice and sit him down, loosen his skates, take his skates off and do all the things he would do if he wasn't first. Talk to him, joke with him, say funny stuff to him.' Which we did. He was standing there going, 'This is really neat. All those other guys are out there working their buns off and I'm sitting here having a rest.' It worked. When they called him, he said, 'It's my turn now.' It was as though he was called from sitting down. He wasn't first any more."

He showed what a true champion is. He didn't even seem to be hot that day, but he bit down and did what he knew he had to do. He was brilliant and fought his way back to the silver medal.

Elvis was just as brilliant, even though he fell on his quad toe loop. He got five marks of 5.9 for artistic impression and easily became Canada's new champion. I asked how he felt now that he had finally beaten Kurt. He said, "You know, I feel like at last I've been validated. All of this work, all of this trying to be what I am, all of this trying to get accepted. I feel like the weight of the world has been lifted off my shoulders. I can be who I am."

Over the years, I had asked him many times why he didn't do an Elvis Presley number. He would say, "No it's not time yet. Not yet," never indicating what the right moment would be. At Canadians, I realized he had on a leather jacket as he came out to do the exhibition and I leaned over to Brian Orser and said, "Ooh, he's going to do Elvis." He did and it was a blast. How clever. That's patience.

The women's event was also exceptional. In championship events, there are days when no one can stand up and other days when there are half a dozen brilliant skates. In Edmonton, all the top six or seven skated their best, maybe even better than their best. But there's not much room at the top.

The first surprise was Susan Humphreys, who has all the tricks plus youth on her side, so her look was fresh and new. In only her second year in seniors, she came fourth in the short program, just one place behind Karen Preston, despite botching her triple flip-double toe combination. That set up a fascinating fight for the long.

Susan fought a battle against Karen that was inspired. She had a week of very good skating, as had Karen, who was not a poor competitor. She could fight like crazy, had experience and when the chips were down, could squeak the jumps out over anyone else at any time on any given day. But her package was traditional, skating to classical music with a typical ballet presentation which, for many in the audience, seemed too tame and predictable. She had done some great show material over the previous few years that had a different look to it, but when it came to competitive material, she became bland, dull and, therefore, disappointing.

For inexperienced competitors, being sandwiched between two big guns can be a terrifying situation. Rather than just going out and doing the job, many skaters would have fallen apart with the force of Karen coming up strongly from behind. Susan went out in the long program and looked like she was going to fall apart. She did not do the first element well. Then something took over. She seemed in her mind to be saying to herself, "This is a struggle and I'm not going down without a good fight." As the program went along, instead of deteriorating, it got better and better. As she continued more and more strongly to the end, a light seemed to shine on her, becoming brighter and brighter. By the time it was over, no one remembered that she had started badly.

For Karen, it was a skate of desperation. She started strongly, but the light on her got smaller and smaller. It wasn't that she ran out of gas with her speed or her jumps, although she fell on her triple flip, and it wasn't that she gave up. Her program simply lost its lustre. Susan glowed. Karen didn't.

Josée, perfectly packaged and far superior, ran away with the event. For once, her famous nerves didn't do her in. "I'm that kind of person that they say I'm always smiling, but it's not true. When I'm backstage waiting for my program, I can't smile, I can't feel that I have arms still. I can't do anything. I have no muscles anymore. The only thing I can do is just walk back and forth, that's it. Sometimes Louis would tell me, 'Bend your knees or do something.' I can't. I just can't. But once the music starts, it's just magic."

It was magic in Edmonton, as she struck the perfect little coy positions demanded by the music and landed a triple Lutz-double toe loop combination as if it was the easiest thing in the world. She knew she had it in the bag. All she had to do was stand up and put in a credible performance and the competition was hers, but she did much more than that. She was poised, confident and had become the skater she wanted to be.

With the Canadian team decided, the members could start preparing for the Olympics in Lillehammer and the Worlds in Chiba, Japan. They could also look to see if there were any surprises at the other national competitions around the world. Figure skating always has been an international sport and is becoming more global all the time. As a spectator sport, it has been making inroads in Brazil, of all places, and the Games in Norway featured competitors from such unlikely countries as Korea, Israel, Australia and South Africa. The Chinese are throwing huge sums of money at skating, sending Lu Chen wherever she wants to train or get other help she needs to develop. The Japanese have been active since early in the century, although it took many years before they produced a gold medal winner, Midori Ito, who became world champion in 1989. In the absence of skating resources, many Asians have learned to skate by watching videotape. Some of the greatest footwork sequences ever seen have been performed by Japanese skaters who have played videotaped performances frontwards and backwards. The skating world is now much larger, but there are traditional attitudes about where the major competition is going to come from.

For Canadians, who the competition is depends on the category. Dancers and pairs usually only have to look at the Russians to see who they will be battling against. Men and women tend to look at the Americans. There were a few years when Soviets were quite good in the men's competition, but that was back in the technical days, not since the great freeskaters have emerged. The action has been swinging back to North America since 1980, a process that accelerated after compulsory figures disappeared in 1990. With the odd exception, such as Robin Cousins or Viktor Petrenko, Europe has been pretty quiet. Everything has come from the States or Canada since the days of Orser and Boitano.

The Americans have had an enormous profile in skating despite the fact that the number of skaters registered in their clubs compared to their population is relatively tiny in comparison to ours. The US has had a very long and successful history on the podium at Worlds and Olympics, particularly in women's skating. They have for years and years had at least one woman at the top or threatening, right from the time of Tenley Albright and Carol Heiss in the fifties, through to Peggy Fleming, Dorothy Hamill, Jill Trenary and Kristi Yamaguchi. Jill was the real American princess with an exquisite, yet girl-next-door look. Kristi had consistency, and in women's skating if you can consistently put two good programs back to back, you're on the way to the podium. Kristi was beautiful and very precise, although I found her rather flat and one dimensional, pretty, but without much passion. Being professional has been good for her, sparking some imagination and bringing out some character in her skating. But women's skating has been a rather predictable "best of a bad lot" sort of competition of late. Katarina Witt made it so colourful and controversial and was such a star that no one since measured up, until Oksana.

In 1991, American women had a clean sweep of the world medals—the first time women from any one country had done so—with Kristi winning the championship, folllowed by Tonya Harding and Nancy Kerrigan. When Kristi retired, Nancy was ready to take over, as was Tonya, but beneath that group was a dip in the valley. Those immediately behind the big three realized that they were never going to make it, so decided to go in other directions. Some high-ranking skaters switched to other disciplines, like Jenny Meno, who became a pairs skater and won the national championship. Some others joined shows, leaving very young kids in the ranks of the top five, all with good skills, but without the experience and maturity that comes with having competed at the highest level for a few years.

Nancy Kerrigan is a very good all around skater. There is nothing breathtaking about her, but she does everything well, plus she has a beautiful look on the ice, very elegant and aristocratic, appearing to be quite tall because of her leg length, despite being only five-foot-four. She is a good jumper, solid, classic and clean in that her skating is not cluttered. There's no need for flourishes of the arms or any hiding of things. Her jumps can be appreciated for their speed, rotation, position in the air, position in landing and control across the ice.

Her coaches, Evy and Mary Scotvold, long-standing stars in the coaching world, nurtured her through the pain of growing up and competing at a high level. She was in the shadow behind Yama, but came up quickly. She always had a kind of unreality about her, a typically American princess with fairy tale costumes designed by a fancy New York designer. She brought simplicity, elegance and style back into women's skating. She is the best dressed skater on the ice and that, coupled with her beautiful appearance, despite the toothiness, can capture the imagination of any photographer.

Tonya Harding, on the other hand, does look like a weightlifter. There is too much muscle, the body is not pretty and nor is the face, the hair is bad and the costumes are always in the worst taste imaginable, looking as if they were bought in a second-hand store. If skating was only jumps, given a good skate, she would have had championships locked up. She is the best jumper in the world, the only woman besides Midori Ito to complete a triple Axel successfully in competition. The bulging muscles give her the strength she needs to catapult herself into the air. But the rest of her skating is mediocre. She never rose to the challenge in the choreographic end of things. Either her trainers were stuck with thinking that all she needed was jumps, or—as is often the case with skaters—the programs may have been very well choreographed but Tonya refused to do them. In pressure situations, skaters often revert to their worst habits, leaving out the connecting steps because they think they are not important. But even in practice, Tonya's programs were nothing but skate, skate, skate, jump, trick, trick, trick.

Coming up behind Nancy and Tonya in the 1993-94 season were thirteen-year-old Michelle Kwan and Nicole Bobek, both of whom have the sparkle of youth in their eye. The magic is still real for them. Skating hasn't become a job where the aim is to finish in the top five in Worlds. Their places in the rankings are one indication of why Canadian skaters have their work cut out for them to compete.

Kerry says, "The Americans have been beating us all over the place with female skating because the conservative Canadian way is, you don't do a double Salchow until you've got your Axel so you can land it, then you don't do your double toe loop until you've got your double Salchow. In California, nine and ten-year-old girls are doing double Axels, triple Sals, triple toe loops. They're not landing them, but they're working towards them. We always held people back and I was the worst offender. I came through the old school of Mr. Gold that you never went on until you had perfected a particular skill. Canadians are very slow learners sometimes. By the time we've got our kids to the point where they're ready to learn the new skills, they're at that age where girls have discovered that their hips have grown and they've found out that boys aren't the jerks they thought they were when they were ten years old. So now, coming into a female's most critical time in their whole life, we're trying to teach them double Axels and triple jumps and, in pairs skating, trying to do the difficult throws. We've got a lot better and some of the coaches have started pushing more difficult things earlier on. That doesn't necessarily mean they're going to have them after puberty, but it's going to give them the best chance."

But there is more to American predominance in singles skating than the early acquisition of skills. With a few notable exceptions like Tonya and Nancy, American skaters usually have the money to belong to private clubs. Local community clubs barely exist. That gave Americans a big edge before the CFSA started funding our skaters. Before funding, Canadian skaters, who usually do not have money these days, couldn't afford to stay in the sport long enough to reach their potential. American coaches often find that they can't get their skaters to quit. The Calla Urbanski syndrome—named after a pairs skater who, with various partners, has been competing for years and years without really going anywhere—is common in the US when the private financial resources are there to support that kind of longevity.

There's a certain attitude that goes along with having money. The recurring joke at the Olympic Games is that if there are seventeen members on the American team, they'll need seventeen taxis for transportation. Ozzie has seen generations of American skaters over the past sixty years. He says, "Americans are aggressive to the nth degree. They think they're good even if they are not and they wear the stars and stripes on their jock straps."

"American skaters are better competitors than Canadian skaters," Kerry says, "because they have an ego within them that wants to be first. Canadian skaters are like Canadian people, wonderful to know, but very conservative, very well-mannered. The American kids are rude, loud, obnoxious, although I respect their skating. Maybe it's just the fact that we do everything as a team and put so much onus on being great people that we lose out on that competitive spirit. Our kids aren't the dressing room talkers like the American kids. I don't see loyalty amongst their own athletes, amongst the child and the parent. I don't even see loyalty amongst the child and the coach. But at competitions, I sit there and wish our kids could be just a little more American. My kids were always the type who would go right over and shake hands and wish everybody the best of luck because we teach them the only real credit in winning is when all the kids who skated against us skated their best. That's a true victory. I'm being facetious, because I do respect the kids for that, but I sometimes wish they didn't wish them that much of a great performance all the time."

American skating often shows its roots in old-style showbiz, more in terms of vaudeville or the circus than Broadway or Hollywood. The Europeans have always had a greater sense of class and style, the former Soviets particularly because they had a manufacturing machine that identified body types and looks. With such a large population to draw from, they rarely produced people who weren't absolutely perfect. In the North American system, particularly the United States, it is more catch as catch can. Whoever rises identifies more with talent than looks. In the old Soviet system, talent and looks were everything.

Success for all Eastern bloc skaters meant such a difference in their lives from the moment they were identified as having talent and put into the system wherever they fit. Every step upward was rewarded. It became very clear that progress meant success and any skater not tough enough to deal with the training was out. The Soviets never took very long to decide who wasn't producing and, therefore, should be summarily dismissed from the team. Even to qualify to represent the Soviet Union was like having to go through a mini world championship. Very young children were pawns in a vicious game where success was total. The rest of the skating world began to see the machine from the Eastern bloc as something formidable, intimidating, even terrifying. That perception worked its way into the psychology of every competitor who ever had to share the ice with the products of that machine.

The image was built all out of proportion through a fantastic PR campaign directed not only at the western press but also at the kids themselves through their day to day education as they were plucked from their coaches and taken to national training centres, fed information on the great traditions, taught by the cream of the crop and costumed by the Bolshoi Ballet. They believed.

When Soviet skaters first arrived on the scene in the early sixties, outward appearances belied the image. The men's costumes looked as if they had never been cleaned, the women's costumes were always riding up the crotch, they didn't have boots or blades with any kind of quality. They couldn't afford equipment from outside their country and what they were using inside was substandard. Yet, at a time when North Americans always whined and felt slighted if they didn't have at least one pair of new boots every year, the Eastern skaters could do miraculous things skating on boots they had worn for ten years. But the externals didn't matter. There was always an incredible aura about the Soviet team. They came in as if they were wearing silk underwear. They had a take-charge attitude that was awesome.

The vaunted training system was a patchwork. Marg says, "When you really get down to it, when they did this there were very few coaches and very few places to skate, so the only way that they could develop skating in Russia, because they wanted it politically to be known, was to create this one training centre. People like Ellen Burka went over to help teach them how to teach and

*Debbi Wilkes and Guy Revell:  Canadian Junior Pair Champions 1959*
*Canadian Champions 1963, 1964*
*North American Champions 1963*
*Bronze Medalists – Worlds 1964*
*Bronze and/or Silver Medalists – Olympics 1964*

*Louis Stong, Maryjane Lennie, Guy Revell, Debbi Wilkes 1959*

*Bruce and Marg Hyland*

*Johnny Esaw*

*With Brian Orser*

*Chris, John, Debbi, Jilly, sister Susan*

*Katarina Witt as Carmen*

*U.S. figure skaters sweep the medals at the 1991 Worlds:*
*Tonya Harding, Silver; Kristi Yamaguchi, Gold; Nancy Kerrigan, Bronze*

*Josée Chouinard
Canadian Champion
1991, 1993*

*Karen Preston
Canadian Champion
1989, 1992*

*Lloyd Eisler and Isabelle Brasseur*
*Canadian Pair Champions 1990, 1991, 1992, 1993, 1994*
*World Champions 1993*

*Shae-Lynn Bourne and Victor Kraatz*
*Canadian Dance Champions 1993, 1994*

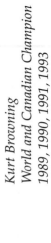

*Kurt Browning*
*World and Canadian Champion*
*1989, 1990, 1991, 1993*

*Elvis Stojko*
*World and Canadian Champion, 1994*

World Champions
Back row L-R:
Brian Orser,
Donald McPherson,
Paul Martini,
Kurt Browning,
Robert Paul,
Otto Jelinek,
Donald Jackson
Front row L-R:
Petra Burka,
Barbara Underhill,
Barbara Ann Scott,
Barbara Wagner,
Frances Dafoe
Absent:
Maria Jelinek,
Karen Magnussen,
Elvis Stojko,
the late Norris Bowden

Claus Anderson

what to do. Otto and Maria were skating in Davos when the Protopopovs came in and they couldn't even do an overhead. It was Otto and Maria and Bruce that gave them that and then they became successful. But when the Russians first came, what did we all think? They had no expressions on their faces, they had no feeling. They were just there to do a job. It was just a big machine."

It was an attitude borne of a mentality about sport and participation that took them far beyond anything seen in North America. The best of the Eastern bloc skaters showed a ruthless commitment to what had to be done. It was part of a lifestyle, an attitude that emerged from their sociocultural milieu. For them, skating success was an answer. It was their whole life. For North Americans, skating was something that was fun to do and maybe you could make a few bucks off it if you were lucky. It almost seemed ridiculous, considering that our society is based on ruthless competition and theirs was officially non-competitive, but their competitors would go to any lengths to win.

The Soviets took over, with their greatest influence being felt in pairs competition. The Protopopovs did the man-woman thing better than anyone. When they retired from amateur competition after 1968, pairs skating deteriorated, becoming cookie cutter stuff. With a few exceptions, pairs lost the man-woman dimension and became essentially athletic. There was some great skating and good tricks, but no soul, no artistry, no love on the ice. Irina Rodnina, who went on to win three Olympic gold medals with a series of partners, took pairs skating away from the artistic side and into the technical end of things. It was an important stage for pairs to go through—it had to have more athletic innovation—and she and her partners did amazing things at terrific speeds, but she was like a wind-up doll that just kept pumping it out. Rodnina and her partners marked the beginning of the "rag-doll" pairs of tiny girls with great big guys. It was hard to see any connection between them on the ice.

That was the direction pairs went in for many years. There was the odd breakthrough. The American team of Tai Babilonia and Randy Gardner, evenly matched in height and skating ability, won the Worlds in 1979, the year Rodnina took off to have a baby. They had some beautiful moves, very different in style from the Soviet pair. But Rodnina came back with Aleksandr Zaitsev and won again in 1980. Their successors as pairs champions, Elena Valova and Oleg Vasiliev, also a rag-doll pair, came along in 1984. Their successors in turn, Katarina Gordeeva and Sergei Grinkov, also began as a rag-doll pair, but gelled into something else entirely, something exquisite, silent and beautiful. Even when they don't look at each other during their skate, electricity seems to shoot down their arms as they reach out for one another's hands. Watching them, it is easy to get lost in the emotion. They are the true heirs, not of Rodnina and Zaitsev or Valova and Vasiliev, but of Liudmila and Oleg Protopopov.

Eastern European skaters are still a formidable presence, but the political and geographic changes over the past few years have caused enough lurches in the process that the rest of the skating world has come to think, "Hey, these people are human too. We can compete against them." Competitors coming out of Lithuania, Ukraine, Kazikstan and so on are just as bad as many others, ending up at the bottom of the list. The system, much different now, is still working by virtue of the numbers of children available and the talent that can be identified at such an early age. The system can still produce, but can no longer be seen as the be-all and end-all of skating. The machine that once was is no more and the best Eastern skaters now spend much time training in the West.

The transition to the new world didn't take more than a few years, and bridging both the period and the different styles of east and west was the most notable women's skater to emerge from the Eastern bloc, Katarina Witt. She was one of the toughest competitors I have ever seen. There was no question when she competed that she was out to win or die in the process. She could take command of a practice session, stepping out onto the ice and sending out vibes that said, "Stay out of my way because if you don't, you'll be sorry." That kind of power often comes with experience, but Katarina was like that from the moment she entered the scene. She wasn't a braggart or outspoken. She was just extremely aware of her magnetism and always seemed to be suppressing a little chuckle over what she could do. From the beginning, the only thing Katarina was interested in was Katarina.

In the early 1980s, when Mel Matthews and I were working with ice shows, we needed some promotional pictures done at an event in Ottawa. We hired Dino Safari, an outstanding rock 'n roll photographer from Toronto who photographed many groups, including the Rolling Stones, becoming best buddies with them in the process. He knew absolutely nothing about skating, but he knew star quality and charisma. When he saw the teen-age Katarina, who had yet to make much of an impression on the skating world, he said, "You've got to get this girl. See if you can talk her into defecting. She's going to be the best."

Her personality and charisma were the foundations of her success. She was powerful in a way that was a different look for women's skating. She could throw her body around and do anything she wanted with it. When Sandra Bezic got hold of her, she became sexy. Her sensuality was a wonderful diversion from actually watching her skate. She did not have a neat foot. Everything was kind of sloppy. The line was poor, she didn't point her toe, she skated with her feet wide apart somewhat like a hockey player. Figure skaters, male or female, in the classic sense should be more like ballet dancers, with the feet perfectly pointed and extended. Katarina never had that touch. While she would get her stuff done on the ice, there was a sense that if she managed to find a beautiful position, it was not something she felt, but something she had been taught. With a skater like Oksana Baiul, the feeling of where the body is, what it should look like and what feels good and appropriate just drips off her. If Katarina struck a similar pose, a viewer got the sense that someone had told her "Your hands should be at a 35 degree angle, point your toe this way and your leg should be in this direction."

That she could land the combinations without the finesse of a figure skater  bridged beautifully into the sexy persona she developed because it had a rawness to it that was quite shocking to the staid, puritanical skating world. She played the thoroughly modern woman, never succumbing to the classic Cinderella-little-girl-tutu-stuff. She displayed some women's predilection for being powerful but also feminine, if she so chose at the moment. If she didn't so choose, she would be out there digging in the elbows along with everyone else. She was perfect for her time.

She knows her effect on people. There is nothing like a powerfully sexy woman to get men pawing the ground and when Katarina walks into a room, even today, men fall down on their faces, saying the stupidest, most idiotic things to her. It's hilarious. Women hate her, of course, a reaction driven partly by jealousy, partly by envy and partly by the exasperation all women feel when they see their men acting like fools. Yet she is not the femme fatale type at all. You are not only aware of her sexuality but you're also aware that she ain't dumb. She displays none of the poor helpless little female thing. She does not want a protector. She seems to say,

"If you've got the balls to come and meet me half way, let's see how it goes." Her attitude is a dare, a taunt. In 1988, there was much press nonsense about a relationship between her and Alberto Tomba, the Italian alpine skiier, her counterpart in a world outside of skating, and probably someone in the eyes of the world who had charisma, talent and sexuality in quantities to match hers. She met in front of the press with Tomba and said, "What sport is it you're in?" Boom, she levelled him. It was her way of saying, "Let's just get it straight who's in charge." We all loved it.

She always knew her limitations and refused to accept them. Even on a bad day she could force herself to be great. For all the talk in skating about the importance of choreography and concept, when push comes to shove, you gotta land the jumps. It doesn't matter how brilliant, new wave, theatrical or adventuresome your program may be. If you don't do the tricks, it's "see ya chum." The good part is, you can also, these days, land your tricks and if you don't have a program, you might make the top ten, but you are never going to be a champion. Katarina knew what had to be done.

She was at the right place at the right time, a great moment when women's skating was beginning to change. You knew from her body language that she had every intention of taking over and she did so, repeatedly. Many skaters have an attitude and expression on the ice like a rookie pitcher who feels he can't make a mistake. People will accept that in skating for a year. The skating world will allow a Katarina a year of success, forgiving a bad performance now and then, but she had to live up to the attitude or get smacked. She always lived up to the attitude.

She does not play the glamour-puss when it comes to practice. Many women competitors, particularly young women, feel that unless they are totally done up they are not fit for show. Some will wear sequins and beads for days on end. Katarina would come to practices in black tights and an old T-shirt, with no make-up and her hair pulled back matter-of-factly in a ponytail. That takes the self-confidence and self-assurance that is one of her most refreshing and endearing qualities. She is exactly who she is and if people have other expectations, that's their problem. She is unique, delightful and very special.

She approached reinstatement to compete at the Lillehammer Games with her eyes open and with much more realistic goals than some other returning professionals. Women's skating had changed direction since 1988, with women doing almost every kind of triple men do. Katarina, even in her best days, never had all the triple jumps. She was coming back to stretch out a career that was pretty much over. She was getting another two years out of the competitive circuit through reinstatement. She didn't pretend that she was going to be the best, but she knew without a doubt that she would be Katarina and that's what the world still loves to see. She entered her national championships against two 16 year olds and lo and behold if she didn't come out part of the German team. She was thrilled. Her public statement was that she was going to compete for another gold medal, which if she won would have tied her with Sonja Henie, but that was just good press. She never really believed she could do it.

In the European championships before the Games, she came in eighth, well behind the defending world champion, Oksana Baiul who, surprisingly, placed second to Surya Bonaly, the French competitor who was the world tumbling champion at age eleven and brought her jumping ability to skating. She has struggled for years to try to match that athletic side with something more and thinks she is being artistic by hitting a nice position or doing something exotic, but has yet to get the right idea. When Oksana, this waif, this little doe-like thing, skates across the ice, you have a sense of presence, a sense of theatre, yet she does all of the triples, except the Axel. Comparing Surya with Oksana raises the typical apples vs. oranges problem in skating. Surya is like a machine while Oksana is a living, breathing thing.

The other surprise at the Europeans was the first place finish of Viktor Petrenko. It had been only two years since he won the Olympic gold medal. Many people, me included, felt the win in Albertville was a "gimmie." He was the best of a bad lot that day, except for American skater Paul Wylie, who blew himself and everyone else away with the performance of his life. He was outstanding and should have won the title, but was never seriously considered. By 1994, Viktor displayed a kind of "what am I doing here" feel. A skater can stand on the ice, flick his wrists and lay on all the showmanship tricks he can muster, but if it's a facade, people know. They can feel it. The best showmen learn to cross that hurdle so that even on a bad day they are believable.

Six years had passed since Brian Boitano won the gold medal in Calgary. I was shocked when I saw him at the US Nationals. He looked like an old man, though not because of his appearance. It wasn't just that his hairline had receded or his body had changed shape, becoming a little chunky in the process. It was his attitude on the ice, a subtle something emanating from him that said, "I'm tired and wondering why I'm doing this, but I'm here now and better keep going." He didn't have the fire and raw energy and punch. He looked like a comfortably retired professional. He hadn't kept up the quantity of appearances, being very selective about what he did. He trained hard, but the flash of amateur competition seemed to come as a surprise, something he seemed to remember but he couldn't quite put his finger on the right button to get going. A competitor who can't find the magic doesn't know where to look, doesn't know where it lives.

Both Boitano and Petrenko had gained immeasurably from their professional experience, honing the very best talents they had, but they did not have the edge for competitive skating. They still had all the technical skills to get the job done, but competitive skating involves such fine motor skill and athletic prowess beyond just endurance that when you're having to do jumps in hundredths or even thousandths of a second, the body had better be pretty well tuned. The sport had passed them by.

There's a naiveté to youth that many skaters call on. Not knowing anything else, they have a sense of "I have the right to be here. I deserve to be here and it's wonderful." For the professionals, it was hard to muster that awestruck "at last my fantasy has come true" attitude. For Boitano and Petrenko, skating seemed to be a job.

Brian's second-place finish to defending title-holder Scott Davis in the US championships didn't surprise everyone. What did come as a shock from Detroit was news of the end of innocence in the genteel skating world, as an assailant wielding a metal club smashed Nancy Kerrigan on the knee of her landing leg the day before the women's technical program. Rod Black and I were sitting in the CTV newsroom in Toronto when the news of the attack came in. We looked at each other, smiled and both said, "Tonya." Then we both felt a little embarrassed about our overly quick judgement. After all, the poor girl hadn't been implicated in any way.

The news of the whack on the knee was just the beginning of a story that would colour the upcoming Olympics and, for both good and ill, would reverberate around the skating world throughout the rest of the season and beyond.

In the biz, we call it "the O word." The Olympics is quite unlike anything else in its magic, proportion and symbolism. For figure skaters, the Olympics are in some ways no different than the world championships. The competition usually consists of exactly the same people. Yet because of that one little word, the event takes on a different face. It is more significant simply because it means more to the rest of the world. People who are not even sports fans watch the Olympics.

The feeling is different for the athletes too. At most skating events, only the skating world is represented. The Olympics is where figure skaters see bobsledders, short trackers, skiers and every other kind of athlete. The interaction, camaraderie, friendship and sharing that goes on amongst all athletes from all countries and all sports is a unique and wonderful experience. No Olympian can ever quite look at his or her own country in the same way again, nor look at people in quite the same way. The best thing about sport is its tremendous potential to bring people together. The competitive aspect just measures one person's talent against another's to see who is better on a given day. At an Olympics, there is a great union between athletes that is beyond description, a commonality, a sharing of purpose that is almost palpable. In any given event, there is only one winner, but in some respects all competitors have a share in that gold medal, no matter how far down the roster they appear. They all push each other, react to one another and depend on one another to a great degree.

There is an intermingling and a sharing of ideas and attitudes. Many competitors, maybe most, show enormous progress during an Olympic event. When training at a little rink, always with the same coach and other people around and with no influences from the outside world, a skater focuses narrowly on particular techniques or elements. Exposed to other athletes and other ideas, the best athletes try those new ideas on to see if they fit. "Is this good for me? Can I use that? How can that make me better?" There is growth emotionally, physically and athletically. Some people may never skate so well again. Some may never skate so poorly.

Calgary set the stage for the way the modern Olympic Games have unfolded. The Albertville Games in 1992 were a step backward, seemingly set up for everyone but the athletes. There was nowhere to warm up with weights, cycling, stretching, no space to do lifts off ice to get the muscles going. In organization and layout, the Lillehammer Games were far superior, bringing the good feeling back by paying attention to all the little details that make athletes' lives so much easier.

The capacity of the Hamar Olympic Amphitheatre, Northern Lights Hall, was quite small—6,000, which is unusual because figure skating events traditionally draw 20,000 people—but the Norwegians had elected to construct buildings according to what their needs would be after the Games. Despite the legacy of Sonja Henie, Norway is not a figure skating country, so the building would be used for concerts, figure skating or short track if ever the need arose. The Norwegians put their efforts into making it a friendly building for the athletes, with pleasant colours and lots of wood that gave it a piney feeling of golden warmth. There was lots of walk-around space, beautiful weight rooms and exercise rooms. Every area was well-equipped with juice, fruit, coffee, tea and, since Coca-Cola was a major sponsor, gallons of Coke were available everywhere. The dressing rooms were nicely equipped, with no extras, but were generally first class. There was also space for privacy, which becomes very important. The media always hound athletes because that is their job, but athletes can get the screaming meemies if the media can get to them all the time. Access was strictly reduced. CBS and CTV could get down, but we were the only two, and we were careful about respecting the athletes who were also there to do a job.

Some skaters—figure, short trackers and long trackers—were concerned that they were in Hamar, nearly 60 kms south of the main venue, living in their own village while the other athletes were in Lillehammer. They were concerned that it would be like Albertville, off the beaten track and that they would miss the wonderful exchange that happens when all the athletes are in one place. I felt the same way, with the International Broadcast Centre in Lillehammer. But when the Games got underway, both the athletes and the press in Hamar were grateful to be where we were. Lillehammer was a zoo. Even the simplest things became difficult, with long, long line-ups to buy a T-shirt or get a hamburger. Hamar was just right.

One difficulty with living in an Olympic village is that only athletes, team leaders and others directly named to the team have access to it. When you are used to a support group close by, such as parents whose presence you have come to depend on for moral support, living conditions that are dramatically different can play on your psyche. Feeling homesick or pining for someone special can interfere with the concentration needed for good practices and competitive performances. In stressful situations, even the most minute things can loom large. Windows that don't open may keep you from sleeping at night. The team managers are clued in to who is having trouble. The team becomes a close-knit family trying to deal with each other's problems.

The Canadian skating team is schooled like no other in how to cope, going through dry runs so they know exactly what to expect. They are told to bring certain things to make the village seem more like home, they go on a time change program as soon as the Canadian championships are over so that by the time they got to Lillehammer, they were not losing another week to the effects of jet lag. The CFSA is on top of everything. They are superbly organized and understand the effects of competition and changed lifestyle. They school the kids on things such as how to dress and how to handle the media, without forcing them to toe the line as to what they can and cannot say. Coaches also have their own techniques. Louis had a day at the Granite Club for his skaters where people were invited and skaters were judged, duplicating as many detailed conditions as possible to simulate the pressure of the situation and so diffuse it. When his skaters finally got to Lillehammer, they felt they had been there already, which is a nice bonus for competitors to have when they're faced with the real thing and need as much reassurance as they can get.

An Olympics is also the world's biggest and most complex television extravaganza, and the media village was a state-of-the-art high-tech playground, a friendly home away where print and electronic journalists from everywhere struggled to communicate and happily swapped hats and jackets at all hours of the day.

The CTV skating crew has an opportunity to work together throughout the year at other events. Crews for many of the other sports at the Olympics don't have that opportunity. The Games may have been the first time they had ever worked as a unit. It takes a fair amount of time to work the bugs out over who does what and to develop the kind of bonding that makes a unit intimate enough that you begin to feel comfortable with the situation and the people you're working with and begin to anticipate each other's needs. The figure skating unit worked together all year long and, with the exception of our new analyst, Brian Orser, we have all worked together for years, which makes everything run much more smoothly.

One other change was that because CTV was the Host Broadcaster for figure skating, hockey and short track, our regular producer became the producer for "host," while for domestic coverage—Canada only—our producer was Laura Mellanby. She had been a big part of the production team in lead-up events, but we had worked with her as a producer only on events that were taped, edited and aired at a later date, not as a producer on a live event, which is a very different ball game. For her, it was a baptism by fire.

Besides Brian and Lynn Nightingale, who was working on slow motion replays of program elements, two other skaters were with the crew. Doug Ladret was the associate producer for figure skating for "domestic" at the Games. He had worked on boxing at the Barcelona Games, where he came to understand TV schedules, routines and priorities. TV never has the luxury of time and Doug was instrumental in making things happen, finding the right people, taking short cuts, knowing exactly who to go to and how to get what we needed. If we wanted an interview with Gordeeva and Grinkov, Doug would get them. Having been around for so many years, he also has a sense of protocol and is beginning to know in broadcasting the kinds of things he already knows in skating. He is a wonderfully calm and clever guy who sees through all the crap and has become experienced enough that he could produce small package items on his own.

Another pairs skater, Scott Grover, did not compete at as high a level as Doug, but still gained 99 per cent of all the valuable experience competitors enjoy. In Hamar, he worked with the associate director to define the content of every program, skater by skater, a painstaking, tiresome job, recording practices on VHS and re-playing them over and over again. Scott would identify any tricky information and the time of each element once the music started so the director could choreograph his cutting of cameras down to every detail. He would identify, say, a spin combination with three changes of feet and five changes of position that should be on super slow motion.

Being skaters, both Scott and Doug could put a perspective on the competition that helped it make sense so the director could shoot it in a way that showed the highlights. Every second of every program was studied and blocked out. By the time of the competition, the crew knew the programs almost as well as the skater. A skater, of course, has only one program on any given day. The TV people have 30 programs to memorize. It's a huge task, but it pays off. Things do get screwed up sometimes because the skater falls, gets lost in the program or has to leave some element out. A director flies by the seat of his pants if the skater changes the choreography, but mostly it works and when the skaters end their programs, there they are smiling sweetly in closeup.

Along with the athletes, everyone on the TV crew had to work around the herd of American reporters and photographers stampeding around the practices trying to get good shots or the latest juicy information about Tonya Harding and Nancy Kerrigan. The athletes were generally upset about the "Nancy and Sluggo" affair, as it was called by many in the press. When the attack happened in Detroit, all athletes felt vulnerable and frightened, thinking that it might just be some wacko going around beating up on people. Oddly enough, knowing that the attack came from within the skating community let everyone relax a bit. But security was tight in Hamar, right down to dog units in the rink. It was not pleasant. The skaters just wanted to get on with their work and forget about it.

In the village, there was no one more upset over the flap than Katarina Witt. As the press concentrated on the next episode of the story—what happened today and did you see them talk to each other in the Olympic village and did they pass in the hall and what happened on the ice—Katarina seemed almost in shock, disappointed she couldn't hold court and carry the women's event on her name and style alone. She wandered around saying, "Vhat about me? I am two-time Olympic gold medalist. But nobody talks to me. Vhat about me?"

There was obvious tension on the American team. Nancy Kerrigan—one writer dubbed her the K-Mart Katarina—is not the little princess many think she is, although as long as her coaches were able to keep that lady-like, aristocratic aura they had created, in other words, as long as they were able to keep her mouth shut, it was a good sell. She conducted herself beautifully until the last moments of the Games, but before the competition even her coaches were heard to say, "Oh, Nancy. She won't practice, she doesn't do anything, she expects us to pull it out."

Some tension also developed on the Canadian team. The team press book was a very nicely done publication with pictures and biographical information on all the competitors and features on the world champions. Kurt and Lloyd and Isabelle each had a special page. On the front cover was a stylized picture of Kitty and Peter Carruthers, former American champions and Olympic silver medalists in 1984. The Carruthers weren't named and their faces couldn't be seen, but it is a famous photograph. Everyone looked at it and asked, "What are the Carruthers doing on the front of the Canadian team handbook?" Many wondered whether it was a deliberate slight to Lloyd and Isabelle, the CFSA's way of getting across some message.

"That was probably a mistake," David Dore says. "I didn't catch onto it until I was in Lillehammer. I think they were looking for something generic to put on a cover so that nobody would be offended and it happened to be that picture. Tom Collins used an image of Nancy Kerrigan on his poster this year. Is everyone else offended? People try to read things into everything."

The night before the opening of the Games, a welcoming reception was held for all the Canadian team members and officials. Mark Tewksbury and Sylvie Frechett spoke about their Olympic experiences and a video about the team, produced by the CFSA, was shown as a motivational tool to get the athletes pumped up before the first day of competition.

As the program ended, one of the athletes sitting beside Elvis Stojko said, "I guess we weren't good enough to get in the video." Elvis looked at her and started laughing. But when he went outside for the reception afterwards, he wasn't so sure it was funny.

Doug Leigh joined him in the lightly falling snow. "In my opinion, I thought you deserved to be in that video."

"I thought so too, but I wasn't. I guess I won't cry over it. It's no big deal. It's only a video."

"It still wasn't right. But don't let it bother you because we still have a job to do and we're going to go and do it. That's what counts."

"Yeah, I know what you mean."

Elvis says, "I guess in my head, it might sound kind of funny, but it kind of felt like a slap in the face. All those years of always being second in nationals and then finally winning and so many people being positive for me and supporting me and maybe I don't have a shot at a medal because so many people are coming back, but I'm the Canadian champion. I'm going in as national champion, the best in my country. It was like a perk. It wasn't just something that goes by. It's the Olympic Games and the Olympic video in front of the whole Olympic team. It's special and I wasn't part of it. I was an Olympian in '92 as well, so it's not like they didn't know me."

"I know on the bus going home that night he was furious," Louis says. "I kept thinking, what's wrong with him? I thought it was because Kurt was the flag bearer. I guess he just thought, 'Enough of this shit'."

Elvis had been skating brilliantly in practice up to then. The next morning, I said to Doug Leigh, "What's wrong with him? He can't do anything."

Doug said, "Oh, something's troubling him and he's just trying to deal with it."

"Come on, Doug. What's he dealing with?"

"Well, you know, the reception. He was the only one who wasn't there. He feels slighted."

"Yeah, it was bothering me for a little bit," Elvis says. "I put it behind me, but subconsciously it takes a toll on you when you're skating. It was bothering me during that practice. But I talked to Uchi and Doug. They laid it down and said, 'This is an opportunity to fire up the guns. That's what it's for.' So it bugs you for a while, then you add a little bit of fuel and say, 'Okay, let's go.' I came to compete and enjoy the Olympic Games, not to get frustrated over a stupid video."

Rightly or wrongly, many people had felt for years that the CFSA bandwagon only rolled for Kurt, leaving Elvis out there alone, without any help or emotional support. But David says, "What the Olympic Committee asked me to do nine months before Lillehammer, when Kurt was the four-time world champion, was an evening representative of 13 sports. One of the big concerns of mine was that this didn't come out to be a figure skating evening. I had to make a choice of leaving some people in and some people out. I had to do it in every sport. I was trying to pick leaders in each, so I picked Kurt and Lloyd and Isabelle. I thought that the Kurt-Elvis thing was overkill. We did leave Elvis to the side, as we left Nathalie Lambert. She was furious too. But I had to make it look like everyone was a member of this Olympic team, whether they were going to come first or forty-first, so I chose. I guess in hindsight it would have been easy to throw all those kids in and everyone would have said I was a great guy and so forth, but I don't think I would have done the job right."

But Elvis, along with every other competitor, focused intently on the job at hand as soon as the opening ceremonies were over with. While some people are energized by the Olympic experience, others are terribly undone by it. There are two motivating factors in any kind of competition. One is the search for success, which is positive, and the other, which is negative, is fear of failure or fear of success too. People react very differently. Younger skaters can be traumatized by the O word but know they may have another shot. For older skaters, the Games are often the last event, the culmination of their careers. The desire to go out a winner can be overwhelming, as can the disappointment when winning is beyond the skater's grasp.

In 1976, as the first Canadian man to have a chance to reach the podium since Don Jackson won bronze in 1960, Toller tried to make "cheap deals" with God to ensure success. "A frozen moment in my life is standing on the podium at the Olympics after coming third. I didn't deserve any more than third. Well, maybe second, probably, but I didn't really care. I was standing on the podium with John Curry to my right. The cheap deal with God was, if I can just do it, then I'm finished, it's over, I don't have to do this anymore. It would be the end of everything. As I was standing on the podium, I knew as clear as day—it was a shard of a thought that went through my brain—I'm back in kindergarten and I've got to go through thirty years of proving myself again. The guy to my right had finished. He had graduated from university."

No disappointment was greater than Brian Orser's in Calgary. He had already won silver in Sarajevo and, when many of his friends moved on to the professional world, he decided to stay an amateur. "They were really surprised that I was going to stick it out for four more years, which was always something I'd considered doing. I could have easily turned pro in '84 and made a pretty good living, but I wasn't ready. The Olympics were in Canada, I hadn't won a world title and I knew the door was wide open. Scott Hamilton was retiring and it was sort of to be my turn, which I guess was a way of keeping me going. I was young and the way that it worked actually set up the Olympics beautifully because there were three different world champions, Alexandr Fadeev, Boitano and myself, so it was really exciting."

A lot was riding on Calgary, and not only for Brian. After his disastrous long program at the Canadians in Victoria, David Dore suggested he get away, go to Florida for five days, walk on the beach and get some sun. Brian said, "David, I can't. This is my last year. I've never done it before in my life, so why now? I'm glad I skated like shit. In '84, I had a shitty Canadians too, but I had a great Olympics, so I'm looking forward to a good Olympics again." He didn't go.

The loss to Brian Boitano by one-tenth of a point was devastating for David. "I went to pieces after that because I really felt that he was the child of my system. I sat there and said he was the one to whom it should have gone and I couldn't accept that he never got it. I went AWOL in Calgary for three days after that. I went nuts. I just could not accept it. I truly believed in my heart that he had to win it for himself. I really believed it was his and somebody stole it from him. I knew the decision was close and that we had to accept the decision, but I kept thinking, all those years and someone snatched it away."

Brian had to cope not only with the loss after a brilliant skate, but with the way the press covered it. "All these terrible headlines. The one that sticks out in my head the most was the article by Jim Proudfoot. The headline was 'Orser Magnificent But Still A Loser.' I'll never forgive him for writing that article. I know he didn't write the headline, but the article dictated it and I'll never forgive him for that, ever. That was something that I had to deal with and still go on to the world championships."

The wounds took time to heal. Going to Albertville as part of the media helped. "I was working for Macleans magazine and I was hanging out in this press room where all these people who criticized me in '88 were saying, 'Gosh, Brian, it was pretty good skating four years ago. You guys skated great and it was only one-tenth and what a great night of skating and we didn't see it this time around.' Everybody felt differently."

It helped, too, to see some of the people from Calgary come to the Lillehammer Games. "It actually made me feel kind of good. Here was the guy that beat me by one-tenth and everybody was scared to death of his talent. Our team set a standard. Brian and

Katarina sort of represented all of us from the class of '88. I was very proud of them."

The return of the pros promised to make the Games the greatest figure skating competition in history, but only two stars from Calgary could recreate the magic. Ekaterina Gordeeva and Sergei Grinkov came to Norway still young and exciting. At practices, other skaters stood by the boards and watched in admiration. They retained a freshness that did not look contrived or overworked. They still had the sparkle of vitality. And how refreshingly beautiful to see Ekaterina, who has such a beautiful body, so lean and graceful, come out in a plain, flimsy chiffon that looked like it had been designed by Chanel, a simple, classic, uncluttered costume that let the skating shine through. They did not skate all that well, but still won their second Olympic gold medal.

As a G & G fan, it pains me to say it, but it was Natalia Mishkutenok and Artur Dmitriev's night, although only one judge had them in first place. Gold medalists in Albertville, they are often more like two single skaters sharing the ice than a great pair, but their long program was inspired and truly exceptional, earning them the silver.

Herb and Isabelle performed their program as well as they had at the Canadians. Izzie was again radiant as they skated to the bronze. It was just so unfortunate that their lustre had been tarnished by Herbie's constant complaining about the re-instatement of the pros and how they were taking places away from younger skaters, this from a man skating in his fourth Olympic Games. They had proven themselves. They were defending world champions and should have come to the competition with grace and serenity, letting coaches, parents or somebody else make their views known for them. Their competitors, despite their Olympic history, were not even ranked. Right to the end, he made so many disparaging comments that people started turning him and Isabelle off. Judges are practiced in staying removed from extraneous matters, but the relentless comments alienated many people, including Canadians. The emotional commitment of an audience is not tangible, but it is a powerful force. He created one more hurdle he and Izzie had to overcome, and it was a shame.

The hype for the men's competition focused on the battle of "the top guns." Brian, Viktor and Kurt, world champions all, were supposed to have a lock on the three places on the podium. As pros, Brian and Viktor could still do the tricks, but when it came to put their money where their mouths were at the Games, they just looked like old people skating around. In men's competition, the quality of amateur skating—the ideas, the crispness of the skills and the cleanliness of the moves—had advanced so much even in the two years since Viktor took the gold in Albertville. Both the jumping and the artistic end of skating had catapulted itself into the future.

Brian skated first in the short program and couldn't land his triple Axel-double toe combination. The program went from bad to worse. He looked as if he wished he wasn't there. It was as if somebody had taken a black paintbrush and just painted in his eyes. After the short, he was in eighth place. Viktor had so many problems in his short program that he ended up in ninth.

It was the perfect opportunity for Kurt to come through and put the memories of his sixth-place finish in Albertville behind him. The Albertville performance was not devastating. He was battling hurt and had been off the ice for a long time that winter, nursing his back injury. No one expected him to come out and skate like Kurt Browning. An athlete cannot enter an Olympic event without having had competition beforehand. It was amazing that he skated as well as he did. In Hamar, he could prove that staying in the sport two extra years wasn't a mistake, as many people believed.

He started well, landing the triple Axel that had often caused him so much grief. Then he went into a triple flip that looked clean in the air and on the landing, but he couldn't hold it. After that, he packed it in, turning a double Axel into a single. He did not receive even one technical merit mark over 4.8. He was in twelfth place.

Forty-five minutes after the program, Doug Ladret brought Kurt over to Rod Black. Rod said, "Are you all right with this?"

Kurt said, "Yes."

Rod was sure it would be a good interview. Kurt looked mad, staring out at the spot where the triple flip went down. As he started to speak, Kurt saw his parents approaching, and his eyes filled up. He had nothing to apologize for, but he did anyway, as the tears flowed. A great champion through and through, no one could have handled the moment better. "I don't know what to say. It's gone. It's really gone this time. My Olympic dream is gone. I know a lot of people are sad in Canada. Sorry."

Oddly enough, many people were outraged. Even Sheldon called Louis to give him hell. "You've got to protect your skater. Rod Black doesn't give a damn about your guy. He cares about how he's selling himself and selling the time on the air. It doesn't mean he doesn't have compassion for him, but you can't let your guy be exposed to that."

Kurt's agent, Kevin Albrecht, disagrees. "It was the best thing that happened for Kurt," he says. "He had to get the emotion out of him right away. It helped him get ready for the long program, that cleansing, even though he had a tough night that night. And what else was Rod to do? He would've got killed in the media if he hadn't done his job."

The death of Kurt's dream was devastating for the entire Canadian team and skating community. David Dore had once more seen what he thought was the best hope for a gold medal dashed. "David tends not to be very warm to people," Louis says, "but certainly the night of the short program, if anyone was ever going to come out as a best friend, he did. He was fabulous, so supportive. He tried so hard to help that he cried in frustration at not being able to. A reporter asked me a question, but I told him if I said a word, I would lose it. But those kinds of stressful moments, when you look back at them from another perspective, are so neat. My son, who's a great big six-foot-three 250-pound guy, phoned that night and said, 'Are you all right, daddy?' I've been 'dad' since he was eight, yet he could sense the vulnerability and went back to his childhood to talk to me. That probably affected me more than anything that night."

With all the top guns crashing in flames, the young guns took over. Alexei Urmanov, the last men's champion of the Soviet Union and the first men's champion of Russia, led after the technical program, with Elvis and Philippe Candeloro close behind.

There isn't anyone who looks less like a skater than Candeloro. Like Elvis, he is not pretty, though he drives the young girls wild. He is stooped, bent over, sort of sloppy and has terrible positions in the air. His technical skills are questionable, but he makes people look at him through the force of his personality. He has the basics as far as the jumps are concerned, but artistically he's gone in a brassy direction with a Rocky look. It is not recognized as classically good skating, but he developed a style and dared to be different. It looks wonderful because it's not cookie-cutter skating. It's dashing, with a gutsy feel. He's committed. His competitive performances to music from *The Godfather* were brilliant, beautifully thought out and integrated, smooth and polished with a touch that saw his personality shine through.

Urmanov has a more classic appeal, with a balletic style the skating world has come to expect from Russian skaters. He almost crashed into the boards in his operatic long program and I thought he wandered around the ice, but the judges gave him high marks for artistic impression.

Elvis clearly outskated both of them, but only won silver. There were many theories about why he lost the gold, from the slightly bent position of his body on a landing to the line of his leg in a spin. There was much emphasis put on his quad, but when his first triple Axel didn't work, he had to instantly change choreography. In terms of his repertoire, a triple Axel was infinitely more important because it was a measure of comparison between him and the other top skaters. The quad was the gravy of the program, but the only way he could do it was if he completed everything else successfully. He made a wise decision, displaying great presence of mind to leave the quad and do the Axel, but it set up the "disappointment factor." Judges all say that they judge what is skated at the moment, but it does not make them immune to human feelings. They knew he could do a quad. They had seen it all week in practices and were waiting for it. When it didn't appear, the program became diminished in their eyes.

When looking at the most minute discrepancies in skill, technical perfection or artistry, the top three skaters in any category might be a hair's breadth different. Then it comes down to personal choice. Elvis was considered fairly new wave. Even though he was second in the world in 1993, the program was still a bit shocking for some judges. It was not that it had anything too terribly different, but it wasn't the tried and true look of men's skating. The disappointment factor, plus the unusual presentation and the atypical skating look Elvis presented was something that took time for the judges to accept. But Elvis has never had an easy route. He has faced those kinds of judgements all his life.

In the ice dance event, Victor Kraatz and Shae Lynn Bourne got everyone tingling with their look. They were doing terrific warm ups with their hydroblading, a very low movement where they almost sit on their skates as they stroke around the ice, almost like Cossack dancers, only backwards. By rights, they should look like waddling ducks, but the way they do it, it looks beautiful. What is shocking is that they make it look so easy. They do it as if not one hair is going to move, it's so controlled. The move helped them win the practices and they incorporated it in one or two moves in the free dance. They made a name for themselves and came in tenth, a great place in their first Olympic Games.

For the top three spots, the results were even more controversial than in the men's event. To my mind, no one on the ice came close to Torville and Dean. After they had won the Europeans and saw all the boopy stuff the other dancers were doing, Jane and Chris thought they had to change their free dance program. Eighty per cent of it was re-worked in the weeks between the two events because they felt that the judges wanted tricks instead of dancing. As it turned out, they didn't. They only won the bronze because, in the judges' eyes, there was very little new. It was all old stuff rehashed and warmed over, something from Mack and Mabel, something from Bolero, something from Barnum, all of which have become, in skating terms, clichéd moves. Torville and Dean invented the moves and, for the most part, are still the only ones who do them because they are so hard to do. They were penalized for staleness.

I don't care how many times they do Mack and Mabel or Bolero. They still smack me silly and knock me off my feet. The other two dance teams were strictly amateur. Evgeni Platov and Oksana Gritschuk won the gold in a program that I thought was messy, sloppy, inexact and generally all over the place. They could be awarded an A++ for personality and energy, but skaters have skates on their feet. Ice dancers are not supposed to pose. Standing and tip-toeing around while you shake your butt can be done on the floor. Ice dancing is supposed to give floor dancing an extra dimension. With Platov and Gritschuk, there was no extra dimension.

The defending world champions, the husband and wife team of Maia Usova and Aleksandr Zhulin, came second. Aleksandr had had an affair with Oksana Gritschuk, which worked in Gritschuk's favour. How can a woman appear to love a man on the ice when she really wants to kick him in the shins with her skate blade? Their material has always been exquisite, displaying an elegance and other-worldliness about them which, unfortunately, life infringed upon and ruined. Maia Usova, the primmest prima ballerina ever seen on ice, was reduced to trying to be Gritschuk, coming out with a bebop ponytail doing a fifties jive.

Jane and Chris were graceful about the result. They did feel humiliated and put down, but rose above it, essentially saying "Well, we'll always be the greatest ice dancers. Thanks, but we'll move on."

Of all the events at the Games, the women's competition is always the glamour event, the most watched figure skating competition in the world. The American media did their best in Hamar to carry the Nancy-Tonya rivalry right up to the podium, but Tonya never really had a hope. The contenders were always Nancy, Oksana Baiul, Surya Bonaly and Lu Chen, with an outside chance for Katarina and Josée.

As a returning pro, Katarina skated early in the draw. There are written rules about apparel, but the unwritten and unspoken rule is that women should wear dresses. The fashion trend for several years has been the more expensive the dress and the more sequins, jewels and other dripping stuff, the better. Trust Katarina not to play by the same rules. She came onto the ice to do her Robin Hood number dressed, symbolically at least, as a man. From sex kitten to earth mother, from bustier to tights. She skated with great confidence, but without the more difficult triple jumps, her marks weren't high. She wasn't disappointed, saying, "What the hell, I just wanted to have a great program and I did."

When Josée's turn came in the short, she looked into Louis' eyes and he thought he had her focused and ready. A few seconds later, she walked past the broadcast booth. Her eyes were glazed. She looked as if her skin had fallen off. She fell on her opening triple Lutz and wound up out of medal contention.

For the favourites, the results after the short program saw Nancy in first place, followed by Oksana, Surya and Lu Chen, setting up a dramatic finale between the American Ice Queen and the two polar opposites of women's skating, Oksana and Surya.

Oksana can skate to typical ballet music and the audience feels as if they have stepped out of the rink and into the seats at the Bolshoi. This isn't just skating that looks like ballet. This *is* ballet. You're enchanted and swept away. There is not one step that is unnecessary, not one note that isn't examined and used musically. Surya may be a great jumper, but she's no artist. She thinks she's being artistic by waving her arms around, but that attitude is strictly YMCA. Her program is not a work with a beginning, a middle and an end. She doesn't weave a spell. Certain parts can be appreciated. She has wonderful positions and some great moves within the context of the program, but it doesn't work as a unit. Her programs are a series of things put together, with a nice section, then nothing, another nice piece, then nothing. Her set-ups are so blatant everyone knows twenty seconds ahead of time that a jump is on the way, which removes the audience from the program.

"We need a separate category for those people," Sheldon says. "This isn't figure skating. Glide is involved with skating. You could do that in golf shoes."

With Surya there's no consistency, no flow from one thing to another. She does not stay in character throughout. Oksana never loses it. Oksana might be standing in the centre of the rink doing absolutely nothing, but that nothing is awesome in its meaning and feeling. When Surya stands there doing nothing, it's nothing.

When it came to the long program, Surya had trouble landing her jumps, and with nothing much else in her choreography she slipped off the podium, yielding the bronze to Lu Chen, the first skater from China to ever win an Olympic medal. Who took the gold and silver involved a decision as controversial as every other at these Games. Nancy's program was balanced, with very beautiful choreography and beautiful music, and she skated very well. Oksana did the same, skating to a Broadway medley and landing a double Axel-double toe loop combination at the very last moment to just squeak out a win. Each had four first placings. The ninth judge had them even, but gave Oksana the edge in artistic impression. It was one of the closest results ever. Many people thought Nancy was robbed.

By the luck of the draw, Katarina skated last. Her long program was performed to an instrumental version of *Where Have All the Flowers Gone*, a tribute to the besieged city of Sarajevo, where she had won her first Olympic title in 1984. She performed to have the world remember that once upon a time, Sarajevo had been such a peaceful city that it represented the Olympic movement. She wanted to draw attention to that again, at a time when the arena where she had won was being ripped apart to build coffins and provide winter fuel.

She wrapped up her competitive career with a beautiful piece of ribbon. It was brilliantly managed and beautifully skated, not with a lot of pizzazz, but quietly. Such understatement was another departure for the Katarina skating fans have come to expect. The rule with her always seemed to be if a little is good, then a lot must be terrific, but she stepped back and showed that she was capable of subtlety. The program was not cleanly skated, but despite the mistakes, she never lost sight of its purpose of talking about peace through movement. It takes great strength for an athlete to carry that off knowing that the technical skills are not being performed well. The ten seconds she spent in the air were not her best, but she hung on to the other three minutes and 50 seconds with grace and finesse. It was a perfect end to the final competitive skating moments at the Games and perfectly appropriate for her own final moments as an international competitor. It was a quiet statement about what skating meant to her and it was lovely.

She didn't feel too badly. She never wallows in disappointment or lets poor marks consume her in any way. She told Brian Orser, "I tried really hard. I was pleased though with what I did." He gave her a hug and off she went with a smile on her face that wasn't the least contrived. It was another meet, another event.

As the Games ended, all that was left was the post-mortems. For younger skaters who succumbed to the pressure of their first Olympics, there is always a look ahead. Susan Humphreys had battled so hard at the Canadians that she had really blown her wad, so badly did she want to make the team. Yet there she was in Hamar going full-out, looking exhausted as she worked out on the bicycle, just training, training and training some more. There comes a time when a skater has to back off a bit from training. At a competition, especially the Olympics, the time for training is over and a more gentle maintenance is called for. Physically exhausted, she was mentally and emotionally bombarded. The O word just did it to her. The surprise for her and her coach, Christie Ness, was that by placing so far down she didn't even qualify to skate her long program, an outcome they had never even considered. She can at least look forward to the 1996 Games in Japan.

For Josée, there will be no other Olympics. In two and a half weeks of practising in Oslo, she fell on her triple Lutz twice. It wasn't always perfect, but she stood up. When it came to competition, her nerves did her in, but not in the usual way. The night before the short program, she was so nervous she cried in her bed, thinking she would never make it through to tomorrow.

"I've lost sleep during my career," she says, "but I've never been like that. I couldn't control it at all. The next morning, I had to get to the rink half an hour earlier because when you're nervous you can't move. I said I'm not going to be able to warm up. I went to put on my skates, step on the ice and there was no way somebody could be in my way because I had no reflexes. I would have just hit them. I told Louis and he was laughing and saying, 'Don't worry, it's only tonight, it's not this morning.' I said, 'Yeah I know, but I'm so nervous.' I did my physio, I went back to sleep and I was getting less and less nervous. I was controlling it, but when I woke up, I was not nervous anymore. I kind of controlled it a little bit too much. I was nothing when I woke up. Usually mascara is so hard to put on, I can't find my eyes. But I was not nervous. I was ready before the time and usually I have to run. I got to the rink, I thought it's going to come. It's not possible that I'm not nervous anymore. I got to the rink and still not nervous. I had nothing. It was almost like a normal day. I had nothing left."

In pressure situations, Josée tends to get very tense and starts to skate with her shoulders. As soon as that happens, she appears to lose confidence with what her skate is doing and lose contact with the ice. Everything tends to get a bit rushed, her timing becomes self-conscious and things that she could normally take for granted aren't easy anymore.

"My short was so easy for me this year and was just perfect for myself. At the Olympics, even on the ice, I looked at Louis and I couldn't believe it. It was like I was in a dream. When I started, I felt so good. I fell and it was like part of my body stayed down. The rest of the body was following music, but I was dead inside."

Many people think that the blame for Josée's poor skate in the long program could be laid at Tonya Harding's door. Tonya is renowned for equipment failures—a broken dress strap, a loose blade—that allow her to skate last. At the Olympics, she almost missed her two-minute call to start her program, came out and tried a jump, then made a teary appeal to be excused so she could fix her skate lace. There was a strange energy in the building when it happened, a tingling with little sparkles everywhere.

Louis knew her reputation. "We had discussed all kinds of things. Either the audience would love her and when they announced her they'd throw flowers and it would take 15 minutes to clean the ice off or they would boo her and she would come off the ice crying. We knew that there would be some type of interference. I certainly don't say that Josée didn't skate well because she was affected by the commotion that was going on. I truly don't believe that was true. It would have made a good story, but I think if you're properly prepared, you can handle those kinds of things."

Josée says, "Oh, I blamed God. I blamed everything. People say why don't you blame Tonya? It was a factor in a way. When she came off the ice, they said I was going to be delayed. I never thought I was going to be pushed onto the ice, so in my head I just set back all my preparation and started all over again my visualization and my programs and breathing. Then twenty seconds later they said just go whenever you're ready. I started running. Louis yelled, 'Walk.'

Okay. So I walked. But I think that with the experience I had, I should have done it. In the long, I was still the dead body going on. I still wanted to skate well because I had Worlds after, but I didn't have the aggressiveness like I would have had if I would have still been in the game. In the long, I was not nervous. I just didn't recover from my short. "

It was a different story for Kurt. He recovered from his disastrous short program beautifully. The plane for Casablanca took off for the last time as he came out and skated almost flawlessly to move from twelfth place into fifth, calling on the reserves that had deserted him two nights earlier. He salvaged a moment of self-respect to cap a year that had been tremendously tough for him, the last nail in the coffin being the intensely personal struggle to cope with being beaten by the person he had beaten for so many years. Kurt and Elvis like to pretend that they're good friends as far as the public is concerned. They certainly have fun with each other and get along very well, but the bottom line is there was never one moment where it left the other's mind that "this is the guy who can beat me." As the final standings were announced in Hamar, Elvis grabbed Kurt by the shoulders. No one could hear what he said, but by the body language, it looked like he said, "Sorry." When Elvis had gone, Kurt said rather wistfully, "I don't mind losing. But why did I have to be beaten by him? Anybody but him."

The Olympic championship had always been part of Kurt's dream, but to win at the Olympics an athlete must have a maniacal commitment to doing it. The goal must be all-consuming. If it isn't, there's a crack in the shield. Between Albertville and Lillehammer, Kurt started to have a life. He found someone he deeply cared about and became incredibly successful, famous and wealthy. So what was the point?

"He never wanted to be there. Right from Prague last year," Louis says. "It was over. Competing was over. He proved then that he was still the world champion. He needed to prove that and he proved it. After that, he just said let me out. It's too bad because the *St. Louis Blues* was perhaps his very best piece ever and the world never saw it as it could have been."

Sandra Bezic had noticed the same thing while working with Kurt on his TV special the summer before. "Prague was his Olympics, then he lost the hunger. He tried to convince himself—we all tried to convince ourselves—that there was one more year. But he'd moved on, folks."

Even Kurt, the master of motivation and master of getting himself into a hole and being able to dig himself out, couldn't come up with the magic formula for the O word. It did not matter to him the same way. It did not have the same edge, the lustre and enchantment that it had in the past. He didn't have the intensity needed for the moment. When your name is called and the eyes of the world are upon you, if you can't count on yourself, if you don't know that you are there just for you, you may do all right, but to win takes a connection to your soul and to your self that you've never felt anywhere else. Without that connection, you might pull it off. You might get lucky. But luck doesn't have a lot to do with skating or any other sport.

It almost makes no sense to have a world championship event during an Olympic year, but every March following a Games, most of the competitors travel on to the Worlds to follow up on their Olympic performances. In 1994, the Worlds were in Chiba, Japan. Many stars who either shone or were eclipsed in Lillehammer didn't make the trek from Europe to Asia. Kurt turned professional and passed on the competition, but went to Japan to do analysis for NBC. Nancy Kerrigan turned pro even before the closing Olympic ceremonies. Tonya Harding had a few other things on her plate to deal with. Oksana Baiul had to nurse her injuries received in a collision with German skater Tanja Szewczenko before the Olympic long program. Lu Chen had to withdraw with a stress fracture in her foot. Gordeeva and Grinkov, Mishkutenok and Dmitriev, Usova and Zhulin and Torvill and Dean were all no-shows at the Worlds.

But the Worlds still had great moments, especially for Canadians. Shae-Lynn and Victor were only aiming for a top ten finish in the dance competition, won by Gritschuk and Platov, but they did much better than that. Their rhumba knocked the socks off everybody and they ended up in sixth place, an excellent position in only their second Worlds.

Despite their best year of skating, Herb and Isabelle couldn't defend their title, losing it to the fourth-place finishers at the Olympics, Evgenia Shishkova and Vadim Naumov, but that they skated at all is a tribute to their guts and stamina. Izzie cracked a rib during a practice at the Olympics, landing on Herbie's shoulder coming down from a triple twist, and it only got worse in Japan. Even breathing was painful, especially after she aggravated the injury during a practice. They weren't even sure they were going to compete, but decided to do the technical program and then re-consider. They placed second in the short and decided to go ahead with the long. After each of the first few elements, Lloyd kept asking if Isabelle wanted to stop. She refused. She wouldn't even replace a throw triple toe loop with a double, despite the agony it caused her. She winced every once in a while and doubled over in pain at the end, but her courage brought tears to their teammates' eyes. They only won silver, but went out as true champions.

Josée had a good shot at reaching the podium with Oksana, Nancy and Lu Chen gone. She won a qualifying round and was right in the race with the eventual gold and silver medalists, Yuka Sato and Surya. Every skater has a blowout every once in a while. All you can do is hope that it doesn't happen at a major event. Having two devastating performances at major events where you're cleaning up the ice is almost unimaginable. For Josée, the unimaginable became real. She was in third place after the short, but fell three times in her long program and ended up fifth.

"At Worlds, I was out of it," she says. "I was so nervous in the short, you wouldn't believe it. It's stupid. I guess I just put more pressure on myself with no reason, like I've got to do it now or else. It shouldn't have been that way. I was always competing against the performance that I did a competition before. But the ideas and people changed around me. There were things that were more important. Before, I didn't have to prove anything, I was only trying to prove it to myself. Now it was different. I think it's my fault because I put pressure on myself. It's harder to stay at the top than trying to reach it."

When it was over, she was cradled in Kurt's arms, not wanting to talk to anyone. They had become very close friends while training together and he understood as perhaps no one else could how devastating her performance was.

The Worlds were a triumph for Elvis. Although he is not a pretty boy or considered a classically beautiful skater, he is nonetheless beautiful in the perfection of his sport and it only took about a month from the time the Olympic Games ended for that to be understood and appreciated. In the short, he won all nine judges and in the long he blew everyone away with a quad toe loop with a triple toe tacked on the end. Even Doug Leigh was surprised. He was sharp, focused and his sincerity showed through. He was brilliant, easily beating Philippe Candeloro, who had probably the best skate of his life, to be named best in the world.

What was very refreshing in the men's event was that the judges did not protect the Olympic champion. Traditionally, in both the men's and the women's division, the placement protocol stays exactly the same in the Worlds as it was in the Games. In Japan, Alexei Urmanov came fourth. That was a big step that was good for the sport because skaters always know who should win and when the best doesn't win, every skater wonders, "What in the world am I doing here?"

When the Worlds are over, especially at the end of an Olympiad, many skaters ask related, similar questions: What am I doing now? Where am I going? Is this all there is? The end of a competitive season is a time of transition. There comes a point where the motivation of a medal is not enough to stay in the sport, particularly if the dream is winning Olympic gold. Four years is a long time to wait for a chance to make the dream come true. Are next year's results going to be significantly better to make staying for even a national medal worthwhile? Or is it time to leave the amateur scene and try to make some dollars to offset the enormous investment that skating demands?

For skaters at the top, those questions, and far more complicated ones, can wait. The champions always set out on tour after the Worlds. If the event is in Europe, ISU tours wind there way around the continent. In the days when I was skating, the tour played three or four cities and that was about it. Now they go on for months.

In North America, the biggest show is Tom Collins' tour of champions. In the skating world, if you're on Tommy Collins' tour, you've made it. It's the big time. Tommy was a skater himself in Kirkland Lake, won a few titles in Ontario, joined Sonja Henie's Ice Review in 1949, then did a feature turn in the Holiday on Ice show in the fifties, doing double-duty selling candy floss during intermissions. He's an old-time, barnstorming showbiz promoter who eventually managed Holiday on Ice before moving into merchandising T-shirts and posters for sixties rock 'n rollers like Alice Cooper and Crosby, Stills and Nash. He still makes piles of money on Neil Diamond merchandise. He started the Tour of Champions with his brother-in-law in the mid-seventies and took over the show in 1979. It was a fairly small affair until after the Calgary Olympics, when big bucks first came to skating. After the Albertville Games, his tour sold out in 40 cities and grossed $20 million. Over a million of that went to the United States Figure Skating Association, making up almost 20 per cent of the USFSA's revenues for the year.

Tommy is honest, fair and treats his skaters very well. He's first class all the way.

Different world champions are invited to perform depending on where the show plays. Some take a few shows off to rest or fulfill other commitments. His tour has always been successful from many angles. He goes to great cities, plays in great buildings, draws big audiences and gives Americans a chance to see skating at its best. For the skaters, the tour is a terrific education. It's where they learn whether they like showbusiness and are prepared to go the distance to learn to be good performers. With a few polished pros also taking part in the tour, an amateur with an open mind can learn a lot and become a much better competitor. Skaters have a chance to test out material, learn the tricks of showbiz in front of huge audiences and be treated like stars. Many skaters, particularly those coming out of former Soviet countries, have nothing. They barely have a coach. On the tour, they have a chance to make very good money with all expenses paid while they hone their performance skills. It is very hard work, combined with heavy travel, so all the performers are pretty wiped by the time they're done, but it is a passage. The tour changes lives.

On any tour, there are all kinds of things to learn. On a purely practical level, you have to discover how to skate in spotlights that make you totally blind. It is very easy to get lost on the ice when you can't see any of the visual cues that have been worked into your choreography. Not only can you not see any hockey lines, but you can't see anything in the audience either. A red light at one end of the arena and a green at the other end are critical. They are basic port and starbord indicators that can still be seen in the spotlights' glare. Skaters coming out of a fast spin at the end of their programs can check the lights and say, "Ah, there's the audience."

It is particularly hard to do multi-rotational jumps while skating in spotlights because you lose your horizon line, which is as important in skating as it is in flying a plane. Without it, you don't know whether you're on your head, on your feet or sideways. In shows, the border of the rink is often outlined in tiny Christmas tree lights, especially when the ice surface extends directly to the audience. The lights are not something you look at directly, but when you're in the air in a double or a triple jump, the horizon line the lights provide saves your life. The line simply creeps into your subconscious to tell you whether you're going to land on your feet or on your ear.

The most important thing to learn is how to make an audience respond. Everyone's double Axel is the same as the next guy's, more or less. So what are you going to do to make the audience like your double Axel best? That requires learning to skate with your soul or with your heart hanging out and learning to play the audience like an instrument. Amateur competitors rarely know how to do it, although Brian Orser developed those skills in the last years of his competitive career. He says, "The showmanship in my amateur days came because I stuck it out for the extra four years until the '88 Olympics. That was really the time that I brought some entertainment qualities into my skating. You learn what the audience likes. They're not crazy about the triple Axels. They love the back flip and speed. An audience can tell when you're sincere and they can tell when you're having a genuinely good time out there and then they can have a good time too. There are some skaters who are doing it only for the paycheque. They'd rather be elsewhere but have to be there because of their contract. But that comes across. I love being out there giving the audience the tricks they love to see. I like to have fun with them. I like the rapport and the chemistry between the audience and performer."

The best skaters learn that they have to develop that rapport no matter what. They mature and come to realize that every member of the audience has paid $35 or $50 and expects to see a good skate. The audience doesn't care if you're having a bad day. You can't have a bad day. You've got to skate. Performing is all about consistency and learning to get the job done even when you can't. You're tired? So what. Got stomach flu? Tough. Got your period? Too bad. Do it on blades that are dull, on ice that's crumby, with lighting that doesn't work and music that plays too fast. If you need a sharp edge on your skate to do it, figure out how to get one. The show must go on. There are no excuses. You've got to entertain them and give them more than their ticket's worth.

Perfect facilities can become such a crutch. Amateurs won't skate unless everything is just right. As a pro, nobody cares even if conditions are truly horrible. A few years after I retired, I did a feature turn with a group at Expo '67 called The Howard Cable Troubadors. Three stages travelled through the grounds entertaining the huge line-ups waiting to get into the pavillions. The main stage was an 11 by 18 rink with real ice on top of a refrigeration unit. Three people could skate on it at the same time. We took great pride in trying to show the public good skating, so we were doing at least double jumps.

We performed from the time the fair opened in the spring right through to the fall. In the summer, it was so hot and humid it took every bit of power the little ice machine had to keep the ice frozen. With so much water on the surface, our boots would be soaked by the end of the day and without ample time to dry them out before the next day's performances, they soon began to rot. No one had ever performed in a situation like this before. In the middle of one performance, I kicked my leg up and my blade flew off, hitting someone in the face. We began to understand the toll the conditions were taking on our equipment.

The next summer, Howard moved the tank to the Canadian National Exhibition in Toronto. One of our skaters, Ross Garner, once did a double Axel, flew right off the tank and fell four feet or so onto the ground. I'll never forget the look on his face as he landed skate blades first in the hot asphalt and got stuck. We pried him loose, he walked across the pavement, hopped back up on the tank and kept skating.

That first of several stints at the CNE was very important for me because Howard hired his nephew, John Darroch, to help run the show. Now a television producer, he has been my husband for the past 22 years. In the summer of 1970, John and I produced the show for the run at the 'Ex' with our merry band of skaters. We hired a friend of his to drive the jeep that pulled the tank through the grounds, a big, lovable aspiring actor, John Candy, who kept us all laughing so much we had to insist he shut up. Over the next few years, on the tank and on an artificial surface called "slick" we played shopping malls, industrial shows and anywhere else people wanted to see us. It wasn't the big time, but it paid my way through university.

Performing in a really big show like Ice Capades or Ice Follies was something I sort of wanted to do. Ice Capades was a motivator to me, athough I never thought seriously about going on the road. I was too much a suckie stay-at-homer. As long as I had my support group I was fine, but I didn't even like travelling for competition. Living out of a suitcase in fleabag hotels was not my idea of a good time. I did try out for a starring role in Ice Follies as a singles skater, auditioning to the tune of Second Hand Rose. I thought they'd be wild to get me and was sure they'd offer me millions. It was quite a jolt when they said, "No thanks." Considering that I had never skated as a single in my entire life, I shouldn't have been too surprised. But the experience of touring with those shows gave many skaters an opportunity to see the world and get some return on their investment in skating.

When they were at the height of their popularity in the fifties and sixties, the shows in some respects gave the term professional a bad name. Professional in skating had always meant simply making money at it. To the general public, if anyone said he or she was in the chorus of Ice Capades, that was as good as being an Olympic champion. The skating community knew those skaters were a dime a dozen at your local rink. The only requirements for the show, according to an Ice Capades audition call in 1964, were: "should be able to perform '2nd Test' figures and simple 'Free Style'and be 16 to 21 years of age, with attractive appearance and personality." Show skaters could do enough fancy stuff to get an audience to applaud, but they couldn't really skate. The headliners were good, but there was a vast difference between quality amateur skating and show performance. Amateurs were athletes doing great technical work, but in those days any artistry or emotional involvement was unusual. Competing was as simple as a runner getting from points A to B in the shortest time. Skaters had to do a couple of good double jumps and by the sixties it was awesome if they threw in a triple here and there. The emphasis on choreographic artistry or innovative moves came much later. Until very recently, skating was about the only sport where moving from amateur to professional was a step down.

The big shows started to fall apart about the same time as variety shows disappeared from TV. The public's love affair dropped off dramatically in the sixties and seventies. Through the seventies, Ice Capades only made money in three cities in North America, Toronto being one of them, and that money carried them through the rest of the year. There were no more box office killings. Everything changed. There was so much for the public to choose from, transportation and the other costs of doing business became prohibitive and producers had a tough time coming up with new ideas. As the competitive stream and the show stream came closer together, the shows could no longer afford the calibre of talent needed.

Sandra Bezic was another skater inspired by the ice shows when they were magical. She says, "When I was a kid, I sat in the front row and fantasized that they would push the spotlight over to me and ask me to skate. That was my life. Going back to what Sonja Henie started, they were magnificent works. Then they started to deteriorate and became more vaudevillian and tacky, cheaper and weaker in ideas. The marketing of it got confused. Who was this for? Was it for children? Was it for adults? Disney is very clear. It's for children and will always be successful. It's not about skating. But Ice Capades and Ice Follies got confused as the market started to change. Were they spectacles or were they the Smurfs? They tried to be something for everybody and couldn't be anything for anybody."

Ice Follies disappeared in 1981, transforming itself into Walt Disney's World On Ice. Bob Paul has been the resident director and choreographer since the Follies' last days. Ringling Brothers and Barnum and Bailey Circus runs the operation now, with six units touring Asia, Europe, South America and North America. The productions are all based on Disney movies like *Beauty and the Beast*, the big hit these days being *Aladdin*. Cynthia Coull, one of Kerry's pairs champions from the eighties, has made a splash playing Princess Jasmine.

Ice Capades  still exists only because Dorothy Hamill rescued it from protracted bankruptcy proceedings and turned its main company into a Cinderella-themed show that is breathtakingly beautiful and doing very well. When she bought it, there was a promise of "more quality skating," but it is a show geared strictly to kids. One parent gets assigned and off the gang goes. For the children, it's like going to a theme park. Dorothy and her group identified a market and designed a product to suit it, so all the more power to her. In the spring of 1994, International Family Entertainment, which operates The Family Channel cable operation in the States and also has a live entertainment division, bought the assets of both Dorothy Hamill's Ice Capades and Dorothy Hamill International. Dorothy became CEO and her husband became president of a new IFE subsidiary that will produce specials for TV and home video markets while her Ice Capades will still tour productions built around Cinderella and Hansel and Gretel.

Those kinds of family-oriented attractions are still the backbone of the live entertainment touring industry. But the face of skating entertainment has changed. People want to see the big names like Kurt Browning, but they don't want to see him in a stifled environment where some producer tells him what to do. Today's great names do what they choose to do. The last to fit in with the content of a major show was probably Liz Manley, a perfect show skater because of her "Miss Energy" personality, her bubbling enthusiasm on the ice and her ability to pull off some amazing tricks. Ice Capades was made for people like her.

"It's a shame the shows are gone," Ozzie, the Ice Follies veteran, says. "The touring shows don't suffice for them totally. The skaters repeat themselves. They take a bow. They sing and just mouth the words. It's not a show. It's a bunch of skating, although they'll have the pairs change partners. I believe music could unite the world and to have Russian music with a Russian skater skating with a Canadian skater and doing the lifts, you feel Canada and Russia are one for a moment. That type of thing I like. There is still room for an ice show, but I think the format has to be of a different type, like the Ice Theatre."

Skaters themselves have been driving the development of the new breed of ice shows, built around their own talents, with star turns by hand-picked co-stars. Toller starred in his own simply named Ice Show in 1977. John Curry put together a show that was too high-brow to be a commercial success. Torvill and Dean organized their first world tour in 1985 and a few months after the Lillehammer Games began their Lets Face the Music Tour in Britain, before going on the road for a year and a half, touring Australia, Canada and the States. Their show has lots of production numbers, although not in the old Ice Capades style. According to Chris, the production is playing a part in the evolution of skating away from sport and towards theatre, with more creativity and artistry than today's tours can usually muster. He says, "The show that we produce now is not a skating show, not an athletic performance. It's an evening of entertainment."

American champion Scott Hamilton, along with his agent, International Management Group, started Stars on Ice in the early eighties. Now directed by Sandra Bezic, Stars on Ice, with different headliners appearing in the American and Canadian companies, has become enormously successful. "The audience was ready for it," she says. "They were becoming more educated, they wanted to see something more than just nice costumes and big sets. They wanted to see the stars and the technical content. When Scott started it, it was very much a 'we've got the barn, so hey kids, let's put on a show right here' sort of thing. It got to a point where it needed to expand. In the meantime, Brian Boitano and Katarina wanted their own vehicle. The common denominator was a certain standard of skating, which was terrific for me. I used to do work for Ice Capades for the principals, but although I liked the people I was working with, artistically it was unsatisfying. Stars on Ice became a good place for me to develop my directorial and staging skills, but on a purer, more modern level. Each year we talk about pulling back and keeping it simple and not getting overproduced, not going back to Ice Capades just because we're bored. There are temptations, but then the restricting factor is budget, anyway. We still have to make it economically feasible. We have this great big surface with minimal props and no BS. We just have our bodies and our feet and good quality skating."

The timing was right and the public responded, but now tours are popping up all over the place and everyone is worrying about a glut. How many dollars are out there to see skating and how can the quality be maintained so that the whole business doesn't self-destruct? There are only so many really good skaters out there.

Fortunately, the skating audience is growing, especially after so many people discovered the sport while following the saga of Nancy and Tonya. The audience is also becoming much broader. Sandra says, "It started out being more of an older audience, but it's getting younger and funkier because of people like Kurt and Elvis. Skating is now a place that you can take a date. It's starting to be a cool thing to do. The audience in the States is different from in Canada because the stars are different. Our audience up here is funkier, younger, wilder, louder, although we're getting quite a funky audience in New York and LA and those places. In Minneapolis we get the blue hairs. It's sort of all over the place, so I have to do a show that makes everybody happy and be very careful that by doing that I don't just make a very bland show. On the other hand, I'm working with these stars who can't possibly be bland."

For the stars at the top of the heap, performing in shows extends their skating careers beyond the norm. But even at that level, careers tend to be short. Once skaters hit the age of 30 or 35, they're lucky if people will still pay to watch them perform. There are exceptions. Toller is well past those years and still hasn't stopped. For him, skating has been a passport to seeing the world. He's performed everywhere from Rio to Beijing and Vladivastock, from South Africa and Australia to every major city in Europe. He never will stop. He says, "The only time that I can actually ever feel in harmony with the self is through the act of skating or the act of painting. Certainly not, 'Gee if I could just win the world championships, I would be happy.' I can only experience tranquility and peace of mind through the act of doing. That is my curse. Or maybe it's my joy. Maybe it's my luck, maybe it's my gift, but that is my only channel to heaven."

Some competitors who never make it into the top flight have long careers ahead of them in smaller tank shows and Las Vegas productions, quite lovely and glamorous in their way, where age is not such a criterion. Others have to get a life and make their way in the real world. Once a talent is identified in a skater's mid-teens, the skater spends maybe ten years working in the cloistered world of competition. They are important years in the cycle of life, what with all the socialization and adult adjustments going on. Skaters have some unreal expectations about the rest of life because of what they experience during those formative years. They expect a lot of success and a lot of patting on the back. Just as in other sports, the adjustment to real life is a jolt.

When my career was over, I found myself very confused and quite bitter. I felt slighted by the skating community. I used to think I was terribly interesting because people would hang around and talk to me. When I retired, I was saying the same things, but no one was interested in hearing them any more. It's a fickle world and when you have become accustomed to special privileges and applause, it's hard when the applause dies down. You feel like a nobody and feel angry at a sport that has used you for it's own purposes. It took a couple of hard years to adjust. Some sports and other disciplines like dance, where careers are short, have mechanisms to handle the decompression needed to emerge into normal life. In skating, it's pretty much "thanks, you were good and good-by."

High level national and international team members, from Canada at least, usually stay in the sport somewhere. It's hard to break out of it. Some become involved in judging, where they must remain amateurs. Some linger in other areas. So many skaters get so caught up in training and competing that they don't finish school, then stay involved in skating, not by choice, but because they have nowhere else to go. They often lead narrow lives and often without a lot of happiness. If the pinnacle of your success has come at age 22, what's the encore? It seems to happen so often that old champions walk around as if they still have their medals around their necks. It's nice to be revered, even idolized for what you accomplished, but you've got to move on and apply what you learned.

"Skating is its own little world," Marg says. "You are quite protected as you move in this very safe space. Then when you get out in the real world, it's a rude awakening. It is tough, it is rotten, it is a jungle and you have to be ready for it. Unless you have the training to go from this safe space that you've been in for years and years and have a profession or a definite goal or place to go to, it is rough. I don't envy anyone out on the edge wondering, 'now where am I going to go?' They're going to get slapped around out there because people don't care. They don't care one bit who you are, what you've done or anything."

Marg and I both know how tragic the results can be when success at an early age seems to define a life forever. Guy didn't have much of an education and when he joined Ice Capades after we retired, he became a gypsy. He loved the road life, living in a different city every week. He was very good at what he did, but shows always wanted skaters out to make way for new faces coming in. Guy didn't understand that. He thought he was going to be around forever, a Richard Dwyer type the shows would always want. He was certainly very talented, but the shows didn't see it his way. They changed headliners rapidly to keep the production fresh and new and give the audience a reason to come back.

Guy just moved on to a lesser show. Ice Capades and Holiday on Ice owned productions all over the place. Guy went from Capades to Holiday on Ice's main company in Europe, then to the B company, then down to the C company, worked in some of the "Boobs-on-Cubes Revues" so beloved in Las Vegas, until finally he was skating in tank shows in the Far East where the girls all dressed in G-strings. It was the kind of experience that does awful things to a person's self-esteem and their sense of who they are. There is nothing sadder than an old showman at 35 trying frantically to re-capture the best moments of a long career.

He left showbusiness and tried to settle back into the real world, teaching skating at Unionville, unhappy and disillusioned. He couldn't understand why his skaters wouldn't follow his words as if they were straight from the Bible. He took the geographic cure and moved to Vancouver. There were many unhappy things going on in his life. He was struggling with his sexuality, struggling with alcohol and drugs. Every time I saw him, which was not often, he would be engaged to some young college girl. For someone who was so honest with himself about some things, he could deceive himself in many ways. I always thought that his falling in love with sweet young things was a facade, but was never sure whether it was a "make believe" for his own piece of mind or a result of his burning desire to look good in the public eye, to fit into the mainstream and be like everybody else. I'd tell him, "Guy, there are women who would be very happy living in the kind of arrangement you need, where you are simply good friends who share your lives with each other. These trophy girls aren't the ones. They think you are who you're pretending to be."

I had long had the sense that Guy was withdrawing from life. He was having serious emotional problems, trying to figure out who he was, where he was and what he wanted to be when he grew up, even though he was nearing forty. He was a perfect example of the athlete who has had a long and good career but never gained any experience in a normal world where not everyone is a champion. He could not accept an average life. In his own mind, he was a failure. If he couldn't produce Canadian champions right away from his students, somehow he wasn't measuring up.

We talked on the phone quite a lot. When my first child, Chris, was born in 1977, he came and stayed with John and me, then went back out on the road with a new partner on the "seedy side of life" tour. When he came back, things were somehow never the same. My second child, Jilly, was born in 1980, the same summer my mother died. I phoned him in Vancouver to tell him the news and it was like he didn't even know who I was. He had started to retreat from the world. This was not the Guy who was like a brother to me, who I had spent so much time with and liked so much. He didn't seem sympathetic or offer condolences on my mother's death or say much at all about my new daughter.

We exchanged Christmas cards that year. The world championships were in Connecticut a few months later. The people Guy had grown up with, the skaters who had been part of his social family, were on TV from Hartford, Louis with his competitors, Otto and me with Johnny Esaw's broadcast team, and there was Guy teaching skating to kids in Vancouver. I've often wondered whether that wasn't some sort of crowning blow to his self-esteem. It was only about a week later that we got a call to tell us he had killed himself. I was shocked, but not surprised. Louis and I flew to Vancouver for the funeral. The coffin was decorated with his Olympic medal. I was told that he would be buried with it. That offended me so much I wanted to march up to the casket and shake him and say, "Get on with it, Guy. The Olympics was a long time ago. Life forgets fast. That medal wasn't your ticket in this life and it won't be your ticket in the next." Too late.

All the qualities and skills elite athletes develop will make them successful at anything else they choose to do. It doesn't work at all if they think they're going to be successful simply because they have been at the top. But if they're prepared to set goals again in other areas and pursue them the same way they pursued their skating goals, they'll be successful. Everything our mothers told us is true. Work hard and be good at what you do. Be the best you can be and it will always pay off.

Participation in sport supplies a certain kind of insight into the workings of the competitive mind and the knowledge and experience gained can be parlayed into income in all sorts of ways. There are plenty of options. Michael Slipchuck, the men's national champion in 1992, went to Lillehammer as part of the Olympic team, almost like an executive assistant, and became an important support service for the athletes. He knew them all well, knew the ropes, had been on Olympic teams before and provided a good sounding board for the loneliness that exists at high levels where skaters are often inhibited about talking to a judge or the Association.

Doug Ladret has been straddling two worlds for several years, working in television while still skating with Tuffy Hough. They have a longer career ahead of them than most because they are not in Stars on Ice for their title-winning history. They are there because they are two of the best show skaters the world has ever produced and will be sought after for as long as they want to continue. They have a look, showmanship appeal and can do anything. Tuffy is the real showman on the ice. Doug is not incredibly animated, but is intense in a way that shows her off beautifully. They have a great set-up that works very well. But Doug is not a kid and he sees that those days will come to a close. The big money-making days are not unlimited, so he is looking to create another industry for himself. He is planning for the future. Freelancers are becoming more commonplace in the broadcasting industry, and as long as he has something unique to sell, he will continue to find work. In his TV activities, as on the ice, he has intensity, a no-nonsense feel to his work and tremendous dedication.

Too many skaters don't explore all the options and too many drift into coaching for want of something else to do. Spending every night of your life teaching children how to skate is not glamorous. The hours are terrible, the return is poor. There are some vital people who have contributed enormously to the sport and get a good payback in return, although not necessarily in monetary terms, but they are few and far between. For most coaches, skating is not the money making machine it used to be in the sixties when skating had no profile and coaching was a nice little cottage industry for a handful of people. The great majority of coaches today work in out of the way places, putting in long, cold, tedious hours from seven to nine in the mornings and from four until ten at night. It's hard to be fully booked. Teaching five hours a day makes for a pretty full schedule. Twenty-five hours a week isn't exactly big time when the higher end of the fee scale in many places might reach $40 an hour.

For most coaches, the largest percentage of their income comes from everyday skaters who may be competitive, but not at the highest levels. Even the highest profile coaches don't make a lot of money from competitive skaters. They have to spend much time travelling to competitions and doing more work than they are actually paid for, losing regular teaching time in the bargain. How are you compensated for spending two weeks at the Olympics?

Team teaching was partly developed to eliminate the insecurities of traditional coaching schedules. What made Kerry's Preston Skating Club so attractive was that the membership fees for the school per week also included their lesson fees, whether the skater had one lesson or ten. It worked well because Kerry was good about making sure everyone got at least their fair share and often more than they paid for. It was wonderful from the coaches' standpoint because they knew they would be making so much money a week, didn't have to do their own bookkeeping or juggle their own schedules. They'd get their assignments and that was it. It was a much more secure situation than having to do everything piecemeal.

At most other schools, everything is modular so that you pay a certain fee to cover ice time, possibly including stretch classes, dance lessons or lectures one or two days a week on motivation or nutrition by experts paid by the school. Some other schools bill for every individual element: freestyle ice, patch ice, lectures and lessons.

Team teaching bridged nicely into the age of the freelancer, specialists called in by head coaches to work on particular elements of technique or performance, which has created many new opportunities for competitive skaters, even some still on the circuit. Like Sandra, they are carving out new kinds of careers in the sport they love. Brian Orser can work with Sebastien Britten to develop his triple Axel. Paul Martini became part of Louis' team, with Kurt as his first pupil. Toller has worked with many skaters on their choreography and style and was even called in to tame American bad boy

Chris Bowman, who never followed the rules or trained properly. That kind of job took experience, perspective and knowledge, all of which Toller has in greater measure than almost anyone else in skating. In his longevity, he has achieved the ultimate goal for skaters who pass through the bizarre world of elite competition and wonder at the end, is this all there is?

"The number one thing about this great machine that rolls and rolls and is the history of figure skating is that it is kind of like a huge merry-go-round. It whirls around and some people are able to cling to it for awhile and some people are thrown off, never to be heard from or seen again. There are moments in your life when you feel, 'My God, this is the best, it can't get better than this.' Being the star of Holiday on Ice in Paris where you live in the Latin Quarter for three months, your picture is on every subway wall and you're the skater of the century. Couldn't I come back next year? But that never happens again. But then, a show on Broadway? Yes! You do that and you think, 'I'm in Judy Garland's dressing room, oh wow and gee.' But it doesn't happen again. Then it's a show in Radio City Music Hall or a tour to Brazil. There's always something else around the corner. I have learned that all those great things that happen have to be taken for what they are. You savour them and enjoy them and when it's over, it's over. You can never repeat the good things. The opportunity of having a career that has spanned decades was my gold medal. The career has been fraught with frustrations, disappointments and bullshit, but all things considered, maybe my shake of the dice really wasn't so bad. I've been able to pass through this world—the skating world—and at the end of it, I'm going to come out tranquil."

The 1994 Tommy Collins Tour of World and Olympic Champions hit the road in April, with Elvis, Alexei Urmanov, Philippe Candeloro, Herb and Isabelle, Gordeeva and Grinkov, Oksana, Nancy Kerrigan and a host of other skaters. Thirty thousand people saw the show at the Thunderdome in Clearwater-St. Petersburgh, Florida, the largest audience in the history of skating. Extra chairs were being brought in up to an hour before the performance, but thousands of people still had to be turned away. Scheduling another show was impossible.

For three months—right into the middle of July—the tour wound its way up and down the United States, hitting almost every state before finishing up in San Francisco. The tour used to involve maybe thirty shows. In 1994, there were 70, grossing an estimated $100 million plus. A good many of those millions were handed back to the skaters. Some were pros and some still amateurs, but that distinction doesn't matter any more. The split between amateur and professional is disappearing. The words have become meaningless as far as skating is concerned.

In my skating days, if we went on tour we went to maybe half a dozen cities, had our expenses paid and were sometimes slipped $50 under the table to go along with the honour of being asked to be on the tour in the first place. We were allowed to accept $25 Eaton's gift certificates. I used to give them to my mother and make her give me the cash. Sandra and Val Bezic used to gather all their certificates at the end of a season and, just for fun, buy the ugliest thing they could find in the store. One year, they bought a hideous sculpture. Val went back the next week and said "I received this as a gift, but I've already got one." The refund was $175. We would have been considered professionals if we took a job selling skis in a sporting goods store. Guy couldn't even teach swimming.

Everybody wants to make money doing something they love and that's what more than a handful of skaters are finally doing. Skaters' choices have been multiplying for over a decade as some old and new powers in the sport have created opportunites.

Dick Button is a good businessman, very well educated and a real trend setter who did triple loops long before triple anythings were very common. In the early fifties, his name was synonymous with figure skating in the U.S. and pretty much in Canada too. He parlayed his interest into big business, becoming a producer and a promoter. He was the first TV commentator to work full time on the sport and his company, Candid Productions, along with ABC Sports, held the rights to broadcast the world championships from 1962 through to 1980. He also began developing professional events. In their earliest days, they were never regarded with much credibility in the skating community. The competitions were between all the old pros who couldn't hack it anymore. If you didn't go into a show, well, you went and did Dick's thing.

His competitions were full of big names and Olympic champions, but the level of skating was not as high as in amateur competition. Within the skating world, professional was still considered a dirty word without the appeal or the whiff of excellence attached to it that amateur competition had. But his events were important because, for the first time, skating performances were marked out of 10.0 and the winners were decided by cumulative marks. Placement ordinals by individual judges had no bearing. The final result was strictly a matter of adding up the points to see who had the highest score.

In some early pro competitions, each judge was responsible for a particular element. There was a jump judge, a spin judge, a choreography judge, a footwork judge, music and costume judges and a group of ten people from the audience who were allowed to ride gunshot on the process and come up with a mark themselves. What the system taught professional skating was that there is a lot more to judging than just sitting there and watching. It is hard to evaluate a performance and put a mark down. Famous people would come from the skating world or the arts to judge. They had big names but may have never judged anything in their lives.

When Robin Cousins, Toller, Peggy Fleming and others performed a sensational show on the stage of Radio City Music Hall, they kicked off the modern age of pro-ams and agents. That was when everyone started getting delusions of grandeur. Many people in the sport still have delusions of grandeur. There were a couple of years when awesome amounts of money were bandied about, even though there were very few agents around.

At the time, I was part of a company formed with Mel Matthews and Gord Crossland called Performers Management. Mel and Gord were the founders. They had both coached for several years and saw that skaters coming out of Canada were not prepared for professional careers. They didn't know what kind of programs to use, how to dress, how to train, how to perform. The idea was to take on these people as clients in exclusive contracts for what we considered a finishing school. We had good skaters like Lynn Nightingale, Ronny Shaver, Heather Kemkaren, Brian Pockar. Mel and Gord also started to organize a Canadian pro championship. We took the idea to television and it was, "Get the sponsor, we'll give you the TV." The sponsor said, "Get the TV and we'll give you the sponsorship." It went around and around. We were too honest in those days. As soon as people think you have a sure thing, they'll pay you to get in on it, but we didn't know that then.

At the same time, Concert Productions International, run by Michael Cohl and Bill Ballard, and an American promoter were starting to put together the first serious professional competition, Pro Skate. When Michael Cohl called Canadian skaters to compete, they all said, "You'll have to talk to my agent. That was the beginning of a fascinating roller coaster ride. We'd come in all full of bluster and pretend we knew what we were doing. Mel and Gord would stay quiet and make me talk. I'd pull 'girl' and stomp up and down, absolutely refusing whatever they were demanding. I used to think they were standing in the shower in the morning laughing their heads off at us, but we had a good time, learned a lot and made a few bucks. In the end, our skaters were the only ones who got paid."

They treated the event like a rock concert. There was respectable prize money, but it got out of hand. It seemed that the winner was whoever had the highest guarantee. That didn't last long because the public wouldn't accept it. Then the skaters started to demand such high fees they priced themselves right out of the market. The competitions didn't make much financial sense. The whole effort was premature. It took a rest for a couple of years and then started coming back again under different names when the few agents started developing new business.

Mel, Gord and I were working with Brian Pockar after he won his bronze world medal in 1982. Brian was an extremely ambitious young man with enormous talent, personality and people skills. He could work a room, was comfortable with anyone from royalty to skid row, had a great sense of humour and was a great skater with dynamic sex appeal on the ice. We found work for him, but felt we didn't have the wherewithal or the know-how to push him in the American market. The fact of the matter was that there was not enough money to be made in Canada. Any big money had to be made in the North American market and to do that, a skater needed people who knew the U.S. market like the back of their hand and could pick up the phone and call Roon Arledge at ABC and get through. We couldn't, so we recommended he consider going to a U.S. agent while we would happily stay involved with all his Canadian gigs.

Michael Rosenberg was just starting out in California. He had managed Dorothy Hamill in the early years and I thought he had done a good job with her. Michael was very very good for Brian. Got him a lot of work. Michael had a good balance in his head. He wouldn't tell you he could make a million dollars for you if he really couldn't make a million dollars. He was honest and straightforward about who he thought you were and the kind of money he could make for you.

Brian was exceptional in that he was very smart. His family was behind him, his dad was a very successful businessman. Common sense and good brains is a dynamite combination and Brian used both to the very best of his ability. He wasn't caught up in only doing top of the line shows. He realized that he wasn't going to be able to make the money gold medalists did and was satisfied with being second choice. But no one worked harder and gave better value for money. If you told him that doing cartwheels down Santa Monica Boulevard was going to make him a better skater or get him a particular job, he would do it without question. He followed direction impeccably and Michael gave him that direction.

There is always talk about every agent being a snake in a Gucci suit, but I always found Michael reasonable to deal with and without any inflated idea about who or what he is. He does his business well. His agency, half owned by Tommy Collins, represents most of the Russian or former Soviet skaters such as Oksana and Viktor Petrenko, and has done great work with Liz Manley. He's the sort of person, before IMG, who if he couldn't sell his skater to something that already existed, would make something for that skater that he could sell. That takes courage.

But Michael is pretty much a one man show, without the resources of International Management Group. IMG was started in 1959 by Mark McCormack, a lawyer in Cleveland who played golf with Arnold Palmer and suggested to Palmer that he could get some people to pay some money to play golf with him. It was the beginning of the sports marketing industry. *Sports Illustrated* has called McCormack the most powerful man in sport. Britain's Sunday Times listed him as one of the thousand most influential people of the century. IMG has an amazingly long client list of athletes in every sport, musicians, orchestras, and organizations from the Nobel Prize Committee to the Mayo Clinic. IMG now has 62 offices in 28 countries, with divisions for hockey, tennis, golf, baseball and winter sports, including figure skating. Subcommittees of the winter sports committee cover athlete representation, pro events, touring and so on. It sounds big, but it isn't. In winter sports, there are about five people who get together and call the shots. Trans World International, its television arm, is the largest independent source of sports programs in the world.

When the New York office decided to get into figure skating, its first client was Toller. By 1984, the office was also representing Scott Hamilton, the Carruthers and a few others and approached Brian Orser. "They had a real subtlety with their approach. They understood completely what my responsibility was, and that was to go to the Olympics and win. They were not going to stand in the way of that or try and tap into making money on the road to the Olympics. There was a huge market, but I didn't want to deal with it. I didn't want to have on my shoulders the weight of a company I was representing. Come the beginning of July, at the very latest, in the Olympic year is when I said no to everything, even interviews. Through the rest of the season, it was practically nothing as far as any other distractions. Now I see these guys are touring and doing TV specials."

Just about everything in skating changed after Calgary. Brian Boitano left the 1988 Games with his gold medal and single-handedly changed the face of professional skating, gaining it credibility and prestige. He continued to train at the same level as he had as an amateur and was still able to do the triple Axels and combinations. The caliber of skating in professional competition advanced to the point where the amateur and professional streams started to mingle, finally merging in the 1993–94 season when the pros came back to scare the daylights out of the amateurs. Great skaters who never really made it as amateurs because they couldn't handle the pressure, or whatever other reason, can do well in pro competitions, the best example being Paul Wylie, who was never a national champion, world champion or Olympic champion, but found his niche in professional skating where the pressures aren't the same. He's a great entertainer and crowds love him.

Now that the calibre of skating has given pro competition more legitimacy, everyone within the skating world has to take a fresh look at amateur events and re-evaluate everything about them—schedules, how many people are allowed in, practice times and especially judging because the 10.0 format has been easier to understand. But the calibre of judges in pro events is still a problem. Brian says, "The judges in amateur competitions have to go through the tests and meet certain criteria to get to that level. To be a pro judge, you just have to have a pulse. I'm the first to admit that I wasn't a great professional competitor. I was crowd pleasing and all those things, but they could always justify placing me somewhere because of not being technical enough or not entertaining enough or whatever it may be. They could always justify it because there were absolutely no criteria to the judging system. None. It made me nuts."

Tours became big business after Calgary. IMG's Stars on Ice went from a small tour of small towns to a major attraction in major cities. Even on tour, skaters' competitive natures come out. "It's who can get the most applause," Brian says. "If I get a standing ovation, I'm the first one to say it when I come into the dressing room. That's the payoff in professional skating, if you can get a standing ovation. I love the entertainment world and everything that goes with it. Brian Boitano doesn't love it. He loves to compete. He thrives on training and someone holding up the mark. That's his payoff. He always kept it in the back of his mind that he was going to compete again at the amateur level. That's why he kept his skating up and was so brilliant at the pro competitions."

IMG has become the most powerful entity in skating with the increase in the number of pro competitions, tours, special events and TV programs owned, operated or promoted by the company. The number of skaters looking for and finding work is also increasing, most of them represented by IMG. The competition is getting tougher and skaters have to adjust their attitudes. "I cannot throw my weight around," Toller says. "I cannot say at the age of 45, 'What? I'm not getting that? How dare you?' I'm lucky to be part of the A-group still. What I try to do is be credible. I don't think what I used to think, which was, 'I am the star.' I think rather, 'I am part of this group.' As long as someone says, 'Oh, Toller Cranston was really good,' I can keep afloat. I am not hungup about skating. As a matter of fact, it's pouring out of me. I feel that I've done everything that I possibly can."

For Brian, "When I was an amateur and jumped into the pro circuit, I felt a little relieved that I didn't have to deal with the politics anymore. Then I realized it's just the same. When you're hot, everybody wants you. As an amateur, everybody wanted to be around, everybody wanted to have a piece of the pie, everybody wanted to be involved. Turning pro, everybody wants to represent you, everybody wants you to work for them, they're all waving big dollar signs around. But then somebody hotter comes around and it's out with the old, in with the new. I'm going through a transition right now, a passage. I can't be performing all my life. I don't want to be begging for jobs all my life. I don't want to be saying to my agent, 'How come I'm not doing that show?' I want them to be calling and asking me. That's why I want to pursue television and commentary and production, and if people want me to skate, I'm available. I can't get too uptight. It happens in every business. For IMG, it's more of a conflict of interest when they own the competitions. The Dick Button event is an IMG event, so when they are negotiating my fee, whatever they get for me on one end, they get back on the other. But for the tour, they make a bad offer, then say, 'But this group wants you to do their show and we're going to go after this amount which would be double.' And I'm thinking, why am I worth double when somebody else is coming to the door? You're the guys I'm loyal to. They have to wear many hats."

Kevin Albrecht, who operates out of IMG's Toronto office, says, "When we negotiate for a client to go on Stars on Ice, which is owned 100 per cent by IMG, we negotiate with the man in charge of the tour. You have to be up-front and let the skaters know that IMG owns and controls that tour, but we've never run into a problem. People from outside find it hard to believe, but we negotiate hard internally. We're all in our different divisions and we all have our bottom lines to look after and if it ever gets to a conflict where we really can't resolve it, then it moves up the ladder, which is pretty rare. The couple of times I've seen that happen, the people at the top, the

Mark McCormacks and Bob Cains, will always go on the athlete's side because the athlete is still the core of IMG's business. The events don't happen without the athletes, the television doesn't happen without the events, the merchandising doesn't happen without the television, et cetera. The focus of the universe for us is still the athlete."

Kevin began his career with Mike Barnett in CorpSport. It was a small agency in Edmonton that really only had one client, but the client was Wayne Gretzky. They had no plans to move into figure skating, but they had seen Kurt at the Calgary Olympics and thought he was a pretty good athlete. "We were still leery of getting involved in figure skating. Anytime we get into a new sport, the learning curve is so steep we really have to be careful. It was a very political sport, then all the connotations with male figure skaters and how do you market them. All that kind of thing."

But Kurt's natural athletic ability was too hard to ignore. They checked out his vertical jump and other stats. "His chart was outstanding. Then watching him play tennis and baseball and everything else, how acrobatic he was off the ice. We knew he was a good athlete. On top of that, there was obviously his personality, his talent in front of the camera, how the camera likes him, his look and his manner and how creative he is. He had what we call 'the entire package' from day one."

They met with Kurt's father, Dewey, at the ranch in Carolina, then met with Michael Jiranek and Kurt at the Royal Glenora Club in Edmonton. The next day, Kurt rode his bike to the office and sauntered in wearing his biking shorts. As he came in, Wayne Gretzsky was walking out and said, "Hi, how you doing." Kurt was impressed. Kevin and Mike explained what they could do for him and what would happen when he became world champion.

Kurt walked out of the office thinking, "Yeah, right."

Kevin felt much the same way about figure skating and the CFSA. "When I first came into it, I thought it was totally screwed up. From a marketing standpoint, it was in the Dark Ages. Where it's come in six years is absolutely incredible. It was like a B-level national sports governing body on the verge of becoming a name, going through what track and field, alpine skiing and swimming had gone through. They had high profile athletes for the first time and were dealing with agents and outside people. They had a lot of questions about how to market the athletes and the team and the events and how to do it right so that everybody was satisfied. They were at a fork in the road of their career too in '88."

It took a couple of years to develop a relationship of trust. "Figure skating from a personal relations standpoint is very sophisticated. There's a very strong and tight community. It took us about two years to break into that inner community and be trusted by people. At first, with David Dore there was just so much tension from his side because he just didn't understand our business and what we did. It's now come to the point where he calls all the time when he needs someone to speak with parents or to the executive."

In Kurt's first year as a client, the message was to keep training, the family would be helped out with finances and the marketing plan would kick in when he became champion of the world in Paris. When he did, they were ready, starting him off slowly with one corporation and one charity—Toshiba and Muscular Dystrophy—and telling him, "You should just have one this year, because this is going to be a very difficult year for you. You're going to have to learn how to be a world champion and that's not something you can teach somebody. You have to learn by experience."

The first year as champion was tough. He was drowning in fan mail, requests for his time and the attentions of the media. The CFSA also organized a fall tour that year, never a popular idea with skaters who feel they should be using that time to train and focus on the year ahead. Tour contracts were tough to turn down in those days when fees weren't very high and any money was welcome to offset parents' huge invesment in skating. The plan was for over 30 stops. Kevin worked Kurt's appearances down to about ten, but the tour affected him badly.

"He went to Skate America and NKH, he came third, he just barely got by Canadians that year through sheer natural talent. He took two weeks before Halifax and pulled his socks up and pulled it off. But he learned a lesson. He said, 'I'm in charge and if I don't want to do fall tours or don't want to do this, I have to say no.' That was the year that Kurt learned how to say no." Kevin had him repeat the word over and over and over again while they were in a taxi stuck in a traffic jam in Paris.

Some hockey agents may not talk to their players for the two or three years between contracts, but IMG handles all the media and PR for athletes to keep control over their image. "Our job with the athletes and the figure skaters is to bring them and their families all the options. When they say they want to get into a certain area of the business, we research it for them and bring them all the options, then they make the decision. Sometimes they ask our advice, sometimes they don't. When someone wants to go on tour, we'll go to Tommy Collins, we'll go to Rosenberg, we'll go to Stars on Ice, we'll go to Ice Capades, we'll go to Disney and get all the options, lay them out, then talk to them about what direction they should go."

Kurt turned into a marketer's dream who understands business, contracts and marketing, knows how much energy he has to spend for various commitments and sets pretty clear priorities. Kurt Browning Enterprises is involved in nine areas from television and video projects to licensing and merchandising. He was also something of a trailblazer, breaking through several barriers keeping skaters from control of their lives. He spent $25,000 in legal fees so that skaters can have their trust funds outside of the CFSA and can direct their own investments. He spent more money lobbying Revenue Canada and Parliament so amateur athletes can keep their trust funds and draw money for eight years after they retire. In the past, ten years of income had to be taken out in the first year. The tax bite was crippling.

He was also the first male figure skater who could overcome the reputation of male figure skaters and land a big-time endorsement contract with the likes of Coca-Cola. In his autobiography, Kurt felt constrained to write, "Let's just say I like girls," which may be one of the understatements of the century, but he obviously felt the comment was a necessary nod to the still wide-spread perception about skating that homosexuality goes with the territory. That never has been the case. As in any artistic field, there has often been a higher percentage of gays than might be found in the general population. But there are also quite a few male skaters, top notch ones at that, who are terribly homophobic. In public, they display friendship and real cameraderie with gay guys, but behind the scenes they make crass, insensitive and totally unnecessary comments.

The story has floated around for years that the CFSA has encouraged gay competitors to stay quiet because the Association wants the "boy next door" look to the sport, middle of the road and straight. Some skaters who are gay are concerned that their corporate sponsorship or the way the CFSA thinks about them could be affected. The only time the question is acknowledged is when benefits are held to raise money for AIDS research. Tracy Wilson and Brian Orser have been instrumental in organizing Skate the Dream in memory of Rob McCall. AIDS has devastated the skating community. Many friends are already gone. But they find it harder and harder to get people to commit their time to the benefits. They know they can always count on Herb and Isabelle and Gordeeva and Grinkov to just say, "When do you want us?" But the interest is not always there.

"In any artistic sport it is perceived that you might have to be a little light on your hooves to be able to go out and do it," Brian says. "But the perception of gays in figure skating isn't as strong as it used to be because we've had so many successful male skaters and a lot of pretty good role models that suit the image of what society wants to see. Society itself is a little bit easier and obviously there are a lot more men who figure skate now at all levels. Every year it becomes less and less of an issue. It was a big issue when John Curry announced that he was gay, then it became a big issue through the AIDS thing. People thought you could get AIDS from figure skating. That was tough. There was a bad spell in figure skating and it's going to happen again. But I don't really think there are that many gays in figure skating, male or female."

The apparent taboo on the subject can reach silly lengths. Toller performed in a benefit for AIDS research in England and was announced as one of the greatest skaters in history. Not far away, his competitor from the podium at the 1976 Olympics, John Curry, was dying of AIDS. His name wasn't mentioned.

Skaters generally are a very graceful bunch. They are well behaved, say and do the right things in public and are fantastic representatives of the sport and of their country. No gay skater has ever been out for himself, pursuing a political agenda. After 40 years in the sport, I cannot think of one high level gay skater who has not represented his country in the most upright and positive fashion, handling the media's difficult questions well and being an outstanding example of the sportsmanship, intelligence, dedication and perseverance that figure skating demands. A skater's sexual orientation has nothing to do with anything.

"People still care from a marketing standpoint, especially in Canada," Kevin says, "because the corporations and the advertising agencies here are still much more conservative about that than they are in the States or Europe. It affects corporate involvement to a small degree, but I think Kurt broke it down. Corporations are seeing the sport now for what it brings them from a sales standpoint. The bottom line on all sponsorships is that you had better sell some product or they're not going to be around. When Proctor and Gamble runs a Kurt promotion for two months against Pringles Potato Chips and they sell 34 per cent more potato chips, that's all there is to it. If that didn't happen, we wouldn't be involved with Proctor and

Gamble. If Diet Coke didn't sell more Coke with Kurt on it, we wouldn't be with them. Skating brings an image and it brings the demographics of very loyal consumers, much more loyal than any other sport. What's unique about him and the sport from a marketing standpoint is the female demographics. Gretz is with Coke Classic and Kurt's with Diet Coke because their demographics are so different. For figure skating, the demographics used to be 80 per cent female, now it's about 65 per cent female, high level of education, high level of income and extremely loyal consumers. Once they're hooked into a product, they stay there."

Kurt is unique in many ways. It seems strange to say about a four-time world champion, but there is a widespread view in skating that Kurt never reached his potential, given that he is the most talented, gifted skater this country has ever seen. "The tough thing about a Kurt Browning," Kerry says, "is that it's like breaking a colt. Once you break it, are you still going to have the very thing that makes him great, that magnetism he has with the audience and the ability to go out and turn an audience wild with his raw talent. If you made it so that he trained as most top athletes train and he conditioned as they did and did all the other things most top athletes do, would you destroy the beast in trying to control the beast?"

In the 1993–94 season, he was beaten in Canadians, in the Olympics and in his first professional competition, the Miko Masters, in Paris. None of it matters. He will be beaten many times again, but it will not affect his reputation. The staff in the Toronto IMG office were busier than ever when Kurt didn't win first place at the Olympics, and the office has had a few gold medalists. "It's bigger just because of the way he handled himself," Kevin says. "The impact has been zero."

He said to Kurt, "What would be different right now if you were the Olympic gold medalist? You do all the competitions that you can, you're on the tour and have signed a four-year deal, you're still doing your variety special, you still have your companies. You can't take anything else on anyway and do it well."

Skating seems to be going off the gold standard and moving to cold, hard cash as a measure of worth. It used to be said that in the States Olympic gold could mean up to $10 million. Kristi Yamaguchi and her handlers thought she was going to strike it rich after Albertville. It didn't happen. To think that her race might disqualify her from embodying the Ice Queen icon would be very sad, but the fact is she's had few sponsorships. She has done okay, but she's been no Dorothy Hamill or Peggy Fleming. Nancy Kerrigan did much better just winning silver. The gold medal has lost its lustre. The only current measure of its worth was revealed when, after John Curry's death in April, 1994, Sotheby's auctioned off his gold Olympic, World and European medals. They brought $32,000 U.S.

There's much better money than that around. Toller says, "I believe that Kurt, in the Last Stars on Ice, made so much money that it would make our heads spin. It's a good thing we didn't know how much because it would've been too difficult to skate. I think $50,000 a night is the lower end of it. But in the found market in Canada with his renown in Canada, it truly was Kurt who was selling out those buildings. It wasn't anybody else. If you have the ability to sell out the Gardens two nights in a row where you—not Katarina Witt, not whoever else—are The Star, you deserve the money."

Figure skating now depends on the revelation of personality for success, so it's not surprising that personalities have now come to predominate. Personality and temperament decide whether a skater becomes great. A multi-facetted, fascinating personality has staying power. That's part of Kurt's magic.

Louis says, "He makes contact with every single person. There is a common touch about that boy. People can relate to him. They know they can touch him. He's a star, but he's them, so they can share it. Crying on television, saying 'I'm sorry.' He always does the right thing and I think that's what makes them love him. He's kind of an extension of themselves."

Many people have witnessed Kurt speak words to a crowd that could be chiseled in stone as to how to give the perfect speech. In the spring of 1994, he was awarded the gold cross and inducted into lifetime membership at the Granite Club in Toronto, which hadn't happened to anyone since Barbara Ann. The Granite has a very rich history in all kinds of sports. The night of the award, Canada won a gold medal in hockey, 50 years to the day since the Toronto Granites won Canada's last hockey gold.

"He thought he was there to get a green jacket like I got last year," Louis says, "the president's jacket with the crest. Every time I wear it, people ask me where the bathroom is. The other guy that they awarded was Frank Bogart, who has been the orchestra leader at the Granite Club since 1940. I think Kurt realized the enormity of the honour while he was speaking. All this history was before him. He said, "Every time I go to the gym and walk across that hall of fame, I feel like I should be on my knees. These are such giants, and not only in skating.' Then he said, 'Mr. Bogart, I have never met you, but I think we should get together soon, maybe sometime next winter. You come and play and I'll skate and we'll invite a few of our friends.' The place went wild. What an idea, Bogart and Browning. I said to Marijane, 'How did he think of that on his feet?' He had no conception of what was happening before he got there. He didn't know who Frank Bogart was. But did he ever piece it together. Of such super stuff is stardom made."

"Kurt Browning is a mega-star, the biggest star in Canada," Toller says, "and deservedly so. Charisma in many ways can be a manufactured thing. Some people know how to turn it on and become charismatic. With some skaters, it's performance-innate. His is a mixture. But he does have star quality and that is a star's body."

Few people have seen so many stars, real and manufactured, as Toller. He still skates with some of the best of them and had a fascinating time watching performances of the Tom Collins Tour in New Orleans and New York. Nancy Kerrigan, after coming through beautifully under the incredible pressure of millions watching every twitch at the Olympics, seemed to be suffering the nasty whiplash of success. But he saw her do a triple Lutz 20 feet high under the spotlights. "She was polished. She was absolutely to perfection, but did not have the star-quality that the other girl had. She is vacuous, but that's no crime. She's just not deeply passionate. Baiul's a Drama Queen. The antics that happen before the performance are much better than the show out there. Oksana Baiul is a major, gigantic star. I have not really run into one of those for quite a while."

It was the audience reactions to the men's performances that were the most interesting. From the beginning of tour, word had been spreading that Elvis was tearing up the joint every night. "The Urmanov boy, the audience doesn't know who he is. He's the Olympic champion and they don't have a clue. They don't know and they don't care. The first time Elvis did Stars on Ice, he was very gauche and wet behind the ears, but Elvis Stojko, for who he is and what he is, knows how to work that crowd. He is not an 'oh my God star-star' like Kurt. Kurt really has something rather mystical and Elvis is not a mystical creature on the ice. But he has been able to parlay whatever he has going for him, and what it comes down to is a complete and total lack of inhibition. In New Orleans, Elvis was a major star, way bigger than [American champion] Scott Davis. Big. In New York, in Madison Square Garden, they knew him. When America knows you, you're in."

Elvis' effect on the audience was almost matched by Philippe Candeloro, another major player on the tour, skating around half-naked and driving people wild. It's a new look for men's skating, very different from 20 years ago when Toller took Rudolph Nureyev as his model for the character he developed on the ice. "There was a very rich, creative cultural period of skating in the seventies, a very thoroughbred, Arabian stallion approach. John Curry would have aspired to that same level. It was all deliberate in retrospect, a facade that was affected and cultivated, but there was something rather imperious about us. 'Don't even look at us the wrong way, we're intelligent, we're untouchable, we're gods, we're artists.' Janet Lynn, a great skater, the kind that comes along once in a century, but completely forgotten now, certainly in America, had exquisite programs. Her coach told me she wanted Janet's opening positions to reflect the attitudes she discovered on ancient Greek vases in the Metropolitan Museum. If you were to tell a skater today, 'Now, for your opening, take this motif from a Greek vase...' they'd think you were out of your fucking mind. They're not into it. It doesn't exist. They don't want to be artistic, interesting, bizarre or be whoever the top ballet stars are. They want to be Bruce Springstein. They want to be jeans and a T-shirt and milk the 14-year-olds to the max. I never thought about 14-year-olds. They never entered my head. It's a whole different approach to skating and a whole different market."

"The teenage group, 13 to 18, are starting to become a key segment of the figure skating market," Kevin says. "They're becoming larger and larger and that's important because of the merchandising side. They're the people that buy the T-shirts, buy the posters, buy the videos or ask mom to do it. They're a very important demographic that wasn't that big in the past, but have become more so because of the male image. There were always girls who saw the Karen Magnussens and the Dorothy Hamills as the little Barbie Doll princesses on ice. Now the teenie-bopper magazines are reaching younger ages with all the male heart-throbs with their shirts off. That wasn't part of figure skating. Now it is. That's a brand-new market segment that's moved in. But overall, it's varied. Unlike hockey, you can't pigeon-hole the female viewers of figure skating. They're from five years old to 70 years old, with the key groups being the 24 to 45 and the teens."

What has changed significantly in the demographics of the figure skating market is that more men are becoming fans. For attending an event, the audience still breaks down as almost 70 per cent women and about 30 per cent men. But more men will watch skating on television, even if they don't admit to it, than will see a live show. Television viewership is about 60/40. Kurt gets a lot of fan mail from males.

Kevin has noticed a change in attitude toward the sport from men of very different ages and backgrounds. "Guys I went to university with, drank beer with and played pickup hockey with are now talking to me about how someone got ripped off by the judges. Six years ago, I would've been in a figure skating clique. Now they stop and say, 'Oh, Kurt's on.' They all have good athletic eyes. They know these guys are amazing. CEOs and those types of people want front-row seats at Stars on Ice, they want to be at the reception afterwards, they want to know about Katarina. Their level of knowledge is very high. Try to get someone to a skating show six years ago? Forget it."

What is most wonderful about the expanding market for skating is the variety it supports. Torvill and Dean, Paul and Isabelle Duchesnay and many others obsessed with skating can sell the art of skating and draw crowds. Elvis and his friends can sell the raw power of youth and athleticism. And there is still room for the embodiment of a great era of figure skating that has almost passed now, an era that saw love and romance between a man and woman on the ice, put there by the couple who did it better than anyone. From the moment I first saw them at the 1960 Worlds in Vancouver, Liudmila and Oleg Protopopov became the only idols I ever had. To stand next to them on a podium in Innsbruck was an honour. They define for me a moment in time, a moment of elegance that I remember now like the first strains of a graceful waltz.

Toller saw them in more recent days. "On the same program, Calla Ubanski and Joe Mero were skating their Americana deluxe McDonalds hamburger shtick. Then the Protopopovs came out and they're 60 and grotesque in a certain way—he wears this horrible toupée and eye makeup out to here—but if you can get past the grotesqueness and the absurdity of the time-warp, what they actually do is skate straight down the middle of the road of refinement, a kind of refinement that is beyond reproach, even if it is almost without any virtuosity. It's still a sliver of sophistication and refinement that is almost non-existent today."

The skating world has been turned upside down and inside out and no one knows what is going on anymore. There's a brand new world in the making, but the shape and contours are not yet defined. All the parameters are changing, from ice level up to the highest reaches of international skating politics and business. Everyone is trying frantically to exert some control, but no one can. Everything is far too fluid and fast flowing for that.

For the skater, control means knowing that when you step on the ice you're going to be in control of your feet well enough that you can stay standing and do what's required. For the associations, it means being in control of the skaters and being able to predict with a fair degree of consistency that they are going to produce what is needed, thereby giving that association more influence within the ISU. The ISU is just trying to maintain control of this rather jubilant express careening to such heights and at such a speed that it threatens to go off the rails. But there are far more players in the game today, all so dependent upon one another that it makes for a very interesting family. Figure skating has become something that no one anticipated. From a rather stodgy, precious little sport that many people thought didn't even belong in the Olympics, it has become the glamour sport of the Games and a multi-million dollar global entertainment business.

Will the sport even still be called figure skating by the end of the century? Figures as we know them have been on the decline since 1990 and may soon disappear altogether, to the delight of some and to the great regret of others. I came to love figures. Marg and Bruce could always relate each section of skating to another, and Marg appealed to the intellectual process of doing it, telling me that a figure was something you built, that you drew from the very beginning. She used to talk about the feel of the circle and the feel of the edge. When I was trying to learn to jump, she said "It's just figures. Think about how you would do that as a figure."

"Figures in the field," Bruce says. "There's not that much to skating. It's just repeating itself in different shapes. Jumps are the same. You learn a double loop and you can do all your jumps up until a double Axel without a problem. They all make it so different and difficult now. [Coach and former national junior champion] Bob Emerson passed his third, fourth, fifth, sixth and seventh tests from April till September. Now they make doing one test a whole year's job."

In Florida, they now work with a teaching system devised by the recreational skating organization, the Ice Skating Institute of America. Marg says, "They have to do certain jumps and certain spins and footwork set just like a dance step footwork. But if they haven't done figures, they can't do it. This is just a little flicker of what's ahead with children who only have to have their third test. We now have new testing coming in, all set footwork like old dances, except that you have to go back and teach them how to do the turns, which is right back to where the figures are. Figures are still the basis. A girl was trying to do a double Lutz and I said, 'What was the last position of a back outside eight?' She stopped and thought about it, then she did it and said, 'Oh, that's the position I should be in for my take off.' Yeah."

Louis chairs the CFSA's technical committee that reviews all of the technical components required to develop technique from a child's first steps on the ice through the testing system and on to becoming a competitor. "People have paradigm paralysis when it comes to figures," he says, "and the worst are the coaches because that's how they've been training all these years. They say the reason they do them is because figures develop balance, line and flow. Figures as we know them are manipulating your skate with any type of body distortion to stay one line on another line. If this is developing balance, line and flow, it's a problem."

In the early part of the century, people just used to design little things on the ice. Figuring, as it was called, wasn't even done in a formal way. When giant 25-foot school figures became part of the formal system, medals were still awarded for original designs. But tracing became the most admired skill when the world changed after the 1936 Olympics at Lake Placid.

"When the Olympics were over," Louis says, "there was this huge arena in Lake Placid, New York, which is still in the middle of nowhere but, in 1936, it was really in the middle of nowhere. They decided since they had the ability to refrigerate ice, they would do the unthinkable and have a summer school. They sent out brochures around the world and to their amazement, people sent them back with money attached and said 'We're coming.' The arena manager wondered what he was going to do with them and he was parking his car when the idea occurred to him. Each car has a place, so when they came to practice their figuring he'd give them each a place on the ice. The number of people he had was 24, so he drew a line down the middle and cut the rink into sections that looked like patches of ice and decided they would charge a fee to rent each piece. How much money has been made on patch ever since? He, who knew nothing about figure skating, dictated the size of school figures which stands today. Can you imagine if he had had 50 people? This is our glorious past in school figures."

As the new dimensions of the figures were established, there were also changes in the way skating skills were evaluated. Figures used to be marked out of six, with two marks awarded for style and flow. "In their wisdom," Louis says, "the skating mafia decided that style and flow are really hard to judge. You have to know what you're looking at and a lot of people didn't, so it was much easier to look at the prints on the ice and decide if they were round and traced and the turns were clean. In the meantime, somebody had been commissioned to write a book called *The Evaluation of Errors in School Figures*. That was the beginning of negative evaluation. Judges looked for errors and deducted them from a total mark."

"The guy who wrote that was a civil engineer," Sheldon says. "When you take the errors he described you can end up with negative points. I competed when he was around. He used to wear golf cleats when he judged. They made him stop because we had to skate figures on that ice. The next year, he wore skates. They made him stop that too. He was going to be secure on the rink."

The focus on clean turns, round circles and retracing were the doom of school figures. "What we're trying to do," Louis says, "is turn the clock back to why we did them in the first place. Stand up tall over your skate, get your head up and perform these wonderful edges which are joyous. Retracing doesn't come into it."

His committee has designed a series of skills, linked together musically, so that skaters begin at at a very low level, then constantly adds turns and edges. The basic skills will take the place of figures eventually, at least in the competitive field, for the pre-novice, junior and senior levels. It may not become a third element of competition to go along with short and long programs, although many people believe that if you want something to develop, you have to compete at it.

The system is already in place and has been demonstrated to coaches and officials. Learning the system and learning how to teach it will add a few more courses to what is already a heavy load of courses coaches now have to take. Sometimes it seems everybody has to stop teaching so they can study hard to pass all the exams in physiology, biomechanics and a broad range of other subjects. Most coaches are former skaters and most skaters are not terribly well educated—they don't have the time—so they can feel quite intimidated. For one of the coaching courses I did, I was grateful that I had a university education. I certainly couldn't have absorbed the information through the seminars. I knew some of the answers because of my psychology background, not because of skating, and I didn't even do that well on the exam. It is amazing that most coaches can cope.

In the spring of 1994, a professor who is a skater and did her masters in skating biomechanics, Moira McPhereson from Lakehead University, spoke to coaches at their annual conference. Louis says, "She could come down into our language. People were intimidated by her intellectualism. She knew that, so she would constantly retreat into our language and try to draw people up into the biomechanical language. She'd say, 'When you do a flying camel spin, you bend your body over and you throw your leg around. We all say that. We all do that. What we're doing biomechanically is creating an off-centre force.' So she was perfect."

All the courses aim to train young people to take on loads that their bodies have to be conditioned into accepting. Sheldon says, "Divers have an easier time. They don't have to take the load of the entry, but our people do. There are very few sports that emulate standing on a totem pole. But almost every sport has the interchange of muscular action and reaction and the timing necessary for its function. And its function is dependent upon what is the task. When you start to prescribe that a geometric figure is the basis by which you get this control, sure, you get control, but is it the control that you want? Start with gymnastics, not the gymnastics we know here, but the acrobats that probably started it. Kids could do a layover cartwheel. Now ask them to stand still in there somewhere and you see how you are diametrically opposed to the physique, the physical reactions within muscle systems and the motor systems of the human being. There are certain school figures that were very beneficial, especially for the unison of motion, timing, control and the reduction of the arc for a faster rotation. Now we talk about decreasing the inertia, which is a nice term the people in the theory department like to talk about. I'd rather just say make it spin faster and let the boys and girls adapt, because they are the ones who are going to make it happen and they have to understand the terminology that gives them something to go on. We've got to get some of the biomechanic boys straightened out if they are going to make a contribution. They better get on ice and find out how reaction is taking place and what is pre-loading under ice skating conditions."

Ozzie says, "The three sessions of free skating are killing to the legs at an age when they're too young. The figures naturally divided that somewhat. There was also a warmdown when you were doing your patch and now there's no such thing. You just sit there then go back to free skating. Injury is very prominent in skaters because of the extensive jumping and the triples at a young age. The legs haven't developed enough. That's why we're running into a lot of skaters with shin splints and tendonitis."

The challenge is to find out what exercises bring the right muscle systems into play but don't inhibit their development. Skaters no longer need the big buttocks and the big quads to perform all the jumps. It's the fine-tuning of the small muscles and motor systems that have become important in skill training. There has to be a balance. If the muscle develops at a faster rate than the bone and ligament connections, skaters are leaving themselves open to long-term injury. "Look at those lower legs of Midori Ito," Sheldon says, "and you'll see they've destroyed some of the development and growth. Maybe it's necessary."

People are always surprised when they see skaters in the flesh for the first time. They tend to be tiny, especially the singles skaters, because without a perfectly proportioned body or at least one where the centre of gravity is very close to the ice, no skater can do the jumps with any degree of consistency.

The quality of men's skating is the best of all events now. They do more and take risks that other competitors don't, not necessarily physical risks, but artistic ones. They are more open to trying new things because they are comfortable with all the jumps expected today. Pairs skating is going in the direction of the incorporation of outstanding skills with great difficulty—pairs skaters will do assisted quads with great regularity—yet still has a story to tell.

Women's skating is in the worst shape. In the free program, women have been trying triple jumps for years, but with little consistency. Even when they have done them in practice, under the pressure of competition they were falling all over the place. The ISU clamped down on the triple jump hysteria that affected women's performance by ruling that triples were not allowed in the short program in the hope of increasing basic skating quality. Women have to develop some comfort with triple jumps and start to see them as accomplishments rather than hurdles. Triples should be something they know they have, not something they're going to try. Having to climb the same step each time they go out is not good for performance. As the search for triples has continued, the programs reached an artistic plateau. Now that a few leaders , Oksana the most notable, have mastered most of the triple jumps, we'll begin to see some artistic progress.

There should be some consideration for triple jumps, but they shouldn't be the focus. They have become a cheap way to differentiate skaters, but they also have the effect of excluding many talented women from competitive skating.

"I think the triple jumps are a tragedy because they're mandatory," Barbara Ann says. "A lot of people can't do them who would otherwise be very lovely skaters. And look how they do those wretched cutbacks and always a triple Lutz down in that corner. It's too bad that it's so structured, that you must do this triple and that combination. It isn't a gymnastics event, it's a figure skating event which should be beautiful and lovely as well as technical. If you do a double jump, you prove you can rotate in the air without being terrified to do it or terrified that you might fall and spoil your routine. Peggy Fleming was lovely and she didn't do triples. She did the doubles but they were just there, part of the whole thing without any big to-do about it. Now the one exception was Liz Manly in '88. She did them all and she did them with fire, but she probably would never do it again. That was a magnificient performance. But you can't do that day in and day out. Figure skating is not triple jumping."

The ability of the human being to rotate in the air is finite. The physical limits can only be pushed so far and since 1988, the

ISU's emphasis has turned from the technical side to the artistic. If Brian Orser had skated in 1989 instead of 1988, he would have been the Olympic champion. Brian Boitano's margin of one-tenth of a point was in the technical mark which then determined the result. Since the 1989 ISU Congress, it has been the artistic mark that breaks a tie in the free program. Now people are wondering where skating should go in the next ten years.

"We are too short on theory associated with free skating and theatre," Sheldon says,"And theatre is expression in an acceptable form where you can demonstrate fulfillment of anticipation. That's the greatest reward you can get as an athlete or as an artist. Take Pavarotti. When he starts to sing, you already know how good he is. When he fulfills those notes, that's achievement and that's what you give to the audience. This is where it's got to go. What do we want to give? Now we can make a triple rotation. Fine, providing we give all of this other to it. And the only other is that which has been known for centuries, which is showbusiness or the presentation of quality skills in a controlled environment on a controlled timing. That is to say, I paid for my ticket, I am here tonight, please show it to me now."

What skaters want to give to an audience changes with age, experience, the moment, the circumstance, the people in the seats and a host of other things. Fans who are content to see skating only on TV miss out on experiencing the dynamic interaction of live performance.

I remember the first time an audience ever applauded for me. Even at seven years old, I felt a weight of responsibility. It's thrilling and inspiring when people tell you they like what you are doing. At each stage of a career, the expectations rise. The most experienced performers can assess an audience in the twinkle of an eye. They breathe the building and take a taste of the crowd. Some know how to do it instinctively, others learn.

On the Tommy Collins Tour, Elvis did his Van Halen and Elvis Presley numbers back to back, not the easiest programs to do almost fifty times within a space of a few months. He found keeping it fresh to be the hardest part. "Uschi came on tour for a bit here and there and we tried out new things to discover something new to play with. The first one was to learn how to be out there and not have to worry so much that when you're on the ice you're doing something all the time. Just be comfortable with the fact that you're there. People come to watch you skate, but just you being there is the first thing they really enjoy. If you stand there and not do anything and let the music play, it's funny the reaction. A lot of times I took up the idea of playing a bit more with the audience and spending more time with them instead of rushing to them and then rushing back on the music. Let the music play. Just bring them into it and shock a few people. Each time we would try something new because every audience is different and every person is different. Sometimes I felt kind of drained. At times I was tired of skating for them and wanted to skate for myself. And it was good. It got all that skating for them out of my system so I could come home ready to train."

As skaters mature, the relationship they develop with their audiences deepens. The longer the career, the more personal and intimate it becomes. There is a great interchange of energy. The audience can become a source of strength and comfort, as Brian Orser found when he retired from amateur competition, battle-scarred and wounded, and skated to Neil Diamond's *The Story of My Life*. "That particular piece was just perfect for me to make the transition from amateur to professional. Basically, it was my way of thanking the audience for all that they'd been for me. The audience was a support group when I was making the transition from amateur and when I was dealing with coming in second at the Olympics. Their message was that it was okay and that's really all that mattered. They didn't care what the contract said or some of the headlines. They were the ones who made it okay. I needed someone else to say it was okay and they did."

Every skater also has moments when the audience never even enters their consciousness. In a disastrous performance or a wonderful one, many skaters report having almost out of body experiences. At its best, the skater and the skate become one. Toller has had moments of "spiritual cleansing," most recently in Moncton, going out before thousands of people without a twinge of nervousness. He went into his number and found himself somewhere else entirely. Even such intensely personal moments don't go unacknowledged. His agent received a letter from a school teacher whose class had never seen anything like his performance before and took up a school collection to buy one of his paintings.

Toller has performed on every continent. He has already been inducted into figure skating Halls of Fame in the U.S., Sweden and Germany, although not in Canada. In the fall of 1994, he was invited to the Nations Cup in Germany where the venerable and still-powerful German skating federation honoured him as the Skater of the Century. Some skaters take from an audience. I've only ever seen Toller give.

"I was dragged up with a pistol to my head to skate in Corner Brook, Newfoundland," he says. "Most people don't even know where it is. So I go to this freezing rink, a hockey rink, and it's absolute torture. I practice, but I am not into it. What am I doing here? The long and the short of it was, the show they were having for the 2,000 or 2,500 people there was really only me and a precision team. The precision team skated on the clean ice and when they were done, instead of getting off the ice, they all stood around by the boards. They introduced me and the moment of recognition was, 'You are a species they have never seen here before. They don't know about this. So what you have to do is give them a moment that they will absolutely never forget.' I performed in a way that eclipsed the way I would have performed at Radio City, madly theatrical with eye contact to all those people. The kick was the expression on their faces. There was a glint of euphoria. Maybe skating in Corner Brook was the highlight of my life."

For people watching skating on television, the experience depends on the event and the context. Many people are drawn to the sport of it, the athletic contest with all the thrill of victory and the agony of defeat. That has always scored big ratings in Canada, especially since the coverage helps viewers get to know the skaters personally. It's better than *The Young and the Restless*. It's real live drama.

David says, "The highlight of the information age was Karen Preston, last to skate for a place at the Olympic Games in Lillehammer. Only two girls were going. Obviously Josée Chouinard has won it. Susan Humphries has had the skate of her life and is now in second place and Karen Preston skates really well but kind of loses the last minute. This is tough. In .004 seconds, she's gone. As sad as it is, that's life. O.J. Simpson in his Bronco, that's what people watch today. Think of the ratings. I hate to say it at the expense of Karen Preston, but that's how the sport has changed. Think of what you got watching this girl's life crumble in front of the TV camera. I'm not saying it with joy. I'm just saying it's a description of the sport and how it happens. The upside of that was an hour and a half later, seeing the audience's reaction to her when she came out to do her exhibition, because they skated it with her. We've created this involvement."

There are always ways to make the production and presentation of amateur events better. Doug Beeforth says, "The sport has to seed its skaters better. This makes for a far better presentation on live television. The last group of five skaters should skate backwards so the leader after the technical program skates last. You need that particularly in a Canadian championship where you've only got two contenders. The Sebastien Brittens aren't going to win, but you want to see them skate. When Kurt and Elvis skate first, someone's pricked their balloon. We want to keep the viewers watching until ten minutes to eleven. Other sports have moved in that direction. They do give some significance to an athlete's prior performance and standing."

TV and the sport also still have to work together to take the mystery out of what happens and how events are judged. It's an information age. The big news is so and so won. All the other information is down the pyramid. Figure skating does it the other way around. In Calgary, 20,000 people sat in the Saddledome and didn't know for 20 minutes that Liz Manley won the silver medal.

A leader board showing every competitors' ordinals after every skate, rather than reading out individual marks, would speed things up, help the skater and help the audience. It would also solve a problem the CFSA has when commercially sponsored water bottles, jackets and clothing appear out of nowhere. "I lost a contract last year because Coca-Cola wanted these little cups brought in to people and it got into such a mess, I finally gave the money back," David says. "They're turning all kinds of these little tricks now. The kiss and cry has become a nightmare. It's very difficult to police. If we pulled off those marks we wouldn't have that situation. I'd like to say to the competitors, 'Just step off the ice and stand at the boards and we'll let you know how you did.' All I want to know is, how are they doing? Oh, she's second now. Thank you. Got it."

The bigger problem that figure skating has is the glut of figure skating out there. How does a network know what to put on? Will anybody still be watching amateur competitions in five years' time now that professional events created for television are proliferating at a great rate and prizes are getting up into the hundreds of thousands of dollars?

The explosion of events is an echo from the whack on the knee in Detroit. The potential of that incident to drive dollar figures to ridiculous heights was proven within a matter of weeks. Nancy's agents, Jerry Solomon and Lon Monk from ProServ, held court at a Hollywood hotel, hoping to land a good deal on a TV movie of the week. The proposals came so thick and fast, each one bigger than the next, that their stay in town became known in the business as "Jerry and Lon's Excellent Adventure." Eventually, producer Steve Tisch brought in the deal clincher in the person of Disney chairman Michael Eisner, one of the most powerful men in Hollywood. The package, worth millions, eventually included the movie, a TV special, a book, commercials, Disney World appearances and an exercise video. After he landed the deal, Tisch said, "You couldn't write a script this good. It's noirish, it's Disney, it's America." Nancy was a millionaire before she even set foot in Norway, let alone landed a jump.

For CBS, the Olympic coverage ratings were up 45 per cent from the Albertville Games. The week of the women's final was the network's highest rated week ever. When Tonya and Nancy squared off in the short program, CBS' share of the American TV audience doubled the number watching ABC, NBC and Fox combined. In the end, the two women's events in Norway were the two highest rated television programs of the year in the States, the fourth and eighth most watched programs of all time. That might have been enough to make the network throw some resources figure skating's way, but CBS was also dealing with the loss of NFL Sunday afternoon football, after 30 years, to Fox. CBS' top executives floated a few trial balloons on alternative programming at a meeting in January, none of which the affiliates liked. Instead, the affiliates pushed the executives to go after women viewers with figure skating events. In the fall of 1994, CBS planned to air Ice Wars: The U.S. vs. The World, with Kurt, Katarina and Viktor Petrenko representing the world and Kristi Yamaguchi, Brian Boitano and Paul Wylie representing the States. The winners would pocket $100,000.

ABC Sports signed a five-year television and marketing partnership deal with the USFSA for an undisclosed, but likely enormous, sum. Under the terms, ABC bought exclusive rights to all USFSA events and will televise the American Nationals, two pro-am events, Skate America and the Tommy Collins Tour. The network also becomes the Association's official promotional arm, with the two outfits working together on packaging skating events, TV production, media sales, sponsorships, marketing and licensing.

NBC decided to get into the game by contracting with IMG to broadcast the Gold Championship in Edmonton, pitting Katarina, Oksana and Kristi against each other for the women's title and Brian Boitano, Viktor Petrenko and Scott Hamilton battling it out for the men's. The winners would pick up over a quarter of a million dollars.

There isn't one champion anymore. There's a whole bunch of them and people are getting as confused about figure skating as they are about boxing or wrestling. Is it still sport when the agony of defeat means you only pick up $50,000 for the night instead of $100,000?

The concept of championships will have to change now that there are far too many of them. They are particularly worrying to the CFSA. David thinks, "They'll go into the marketplace like ice shows did in the fifties and spew all over the place because there isn't enough talent out there to sustain viewer interest. There's not enough variety. The tour promoters better be careful. Everyone's trying to make a quick buck. Somebody's got to be killed off here."

"Figure skating has always been the purest," Kerry says. "It really has been a true amateur sport. But it's going the way all sport is going and all sport is going to money, TV, the highly visible athlete. It was inevitable. There's no room in the world of sport for amateurs. It'll go the way tennis has gone and I'm not sure we'll have a good system to funnel kids up. I see the Canadian championship ending up being a professional event. The Canadian Open they're going to do professionally is what the Canadian championship is going to be ten years from now. What scares me is the people in charge of the direction of it, the promotion companies and the agents—and when I say that I'm not against IMG—but it's a scary situation when a group controls the skaters and that same group controls the competition."

"I think it'll be tennis," Louis says. "A circuit. And soon. It'll be world cup oriented. Who has the most points at the end of the year will be perceived as the best person for that year. Being champion of the Games will have less significance. Try to recall who won the gold medal in tennis at the Olympics in Barcelona. Do we care? The pro-am competition structure has already been struck. Professionals and amateurs can enter into the same competition. It's very soon down the road where there is no difference. When the words eligible and ineligible go away, then the judging problem will be solved. When it's Brian Boitano against Kurt Browning against Elvis Stojko, the word professional looms and it won't take long for the audience to say, 'What are those amateur people doing judging those professional people? Shouldn't you have qualified professional people judging those professional people and if they don't do a good job, get them out of there and get some other ones who will?'"

A world cup may improve skating. Basing a whole year's worth of training and an entire career on six and a half minute make-or-break performances makes competition very exciting, but doesn't always deliver up the best skater. The danger of skating becoming like tennis is that tennis is in terrible shape. Pro tennis players, especially the younger ones, in their attitudes and in the way they approach sport, are often held up not so much as heroes but as horrible examples.

In this industry called skating, the CFSA is a business, the sponsors are running a business, the ISU is running a business, the competitions are a business, for coaches it's a business and for agents it's a business. And for the skaters it's supposed to be sport? It needs to be a business for them as well, except that doing it for love and not for money is part of what makes skating wonderful. But skaters may get smart and start organizing themselves as the tennis players did. The agents say they are looking after the skaters' interests, but agents look out for themselves.

Even coaches in the U.S. are starting to wonder what their cut is. To get to the world championship level, there's much more than the payment of lessons involved and some coaches are discussing handling their students' professional careers as agents so they can get something out of this all this development too.

Not every skater thinks the scramble for money and control should be won by business. In Brian's view, "It's going to be a long time before there's one entity and I don't think it should be in the hands of the professional world of skating. I think the CFSA and the ISU should still be in control by the pros being able to go back and work under that umbrella and work with them like at the Olympics. I can't imagine any of these professional entities running that. They have no standards or track record and the only vision they have is dollar signs."

But the ISU is in no shape to take a stand. Canada does take a leadership role in the organization. No other member country has a resource base or a membership base like the CFSA's, but that just translates into one equal vote in the world of international politics. "There are now 50 members of the ISU," David says, "and I think if you ask anyone who the most important members are, they'll always say Russia, Canada and the United States. You've got 300 million people there and 250 million people there and 29 million people here. There's lots of money in the States. They're always going to produce good skaters. Russia is also always going to produce good skaters. Don't try to be number one. Just try to be seen as a leader. As long as they keep talking about us as among the top three, be happy. In the last ISU Congress, we had an influence on the proceedings. That's all I want."

The ISU is like most international sports governing bodies: a European-based, male-dominated old boys' network. Many members still operate according to the "old school" rules, manipulating other associations to their own advantage and pulling rank in any dispute, even though many countries at the international level operate without any real system and only produce two or three skaters that come and go.

"The ISU really needs to provide some help for these countries administratively," David says, "because it's difficult to have any respect for them. In dealing with Skate Canada, it's very difficult. These countries have no respect for the fact that we have television contracts and newspapers. It's a business and if I advertise Tanja Szewczenko from Germany, then I need Tanja Szewczenko. I can't have somebody telling me five days before, 'We've changed our mind, She's not coming now.' It doesn't work that way. With the Russians, you send the invitation, they answer a month late, send their fifth place skaters and say, 'We'll fly Aerflot and give us the cash when we get off the plane.' Object and they say, 'We don't have to answer you, we're Russia.' I wrote back and said, 'Well, yes you do. Those days are over.' I'm playing hardball. We canned the whole team. We told them we would let them know in September if we had some room for them and if they fly, they'll fly on a Canadian airline."

But, as always, Canada is caught between Europe and America and the ISU is powerless to do anything about the volatile situation in the United States. Everything is up for grabs in the American market. There aren't any rules and the game keeps changing all the time. USFA president Claire Ferguson wants her association to control the professional movement. The USFSA jumped right into developing a pro-am competition to compete with Dick Button's World Professional Championship and his Challenge of Champions and to compete with the U.S. Open run by the Professional Skaters Guild of America.

The CFSA has taken the time to come to terms with new realities of the skating marketplace, keeping some distance as IMG organized the Canadian Professional Championships.

According to Kevin, "We'll keep that as just a pro event in the first year, because my long-term goal is to be involved with the

CFSA. They need an open competition. It would just become part of the development triangle of each sports governing body. Open competitions in the United States, with just Americans, pro and amateurs, have been a good testing ground for developing the rules and setting standards for judging. It'll come down to four or five key ones around the world and then you'll see the Skate Canadas and the NHKs becoming a little bit more developmental than they are now. Still important, but probably like what Triple A or Double A ball is to major league baseball. The grass-roots is very important and that's where the CFSA is very good, the best in the world. That's what David has concentrated on and he's smart because the top end of the development pyramid is showbiz. Major league baseball is showbusiness. What happens at Maple Leaf Gardens every Saturday night is showbusiness. The Canadian Championships is show business. Everything below that is development and that's where the sports governing body should be putting their emphasis on their priorities. The USFSA has lost focus on that. They're trying to be in the show business game. They are volunteers who know figure skating. Why would they get involved in showbusiness? Concentrate on the grass-roots and what's happening at the bottom. The top takes care of itself."

The consequences are apparent in the lack of depth in the American team after the Olympic Games. Canada has far more depth in its skating system and intends to keep it that way.

David says, "The Canadian Figure Skating Association, despite all that's going on in the world, cannot lose its focus and its mission and its purpose. If we should become enamoured by what's going on in the upper echelon of the sport and lose our focus of children and clubs and programming and teaching people to skate, we are going to lose it. That's our reason for existence. We have to be constantly revitalizing our development and organizational programs to reflect economic impact, social impact, family values, divorce, single families, working mothers. We've got to keep adjusting our sport and our systems. We've got to adapt children's programs, how people teach, the evaluation system, group teaching. The upper echelon is going to go into chaos in the next two years. There's too much on television and there are too many people trying to make a quick buck. My attitude is, let 'em go at it hammer and tong and show passive interest, but don't really get involved yet because I think it will be a bloodbath between the television networks, the agents, some of the families that may get into all this, the promoters, the entrepeneurs. The ISU will not understand all this and the end of the line will be that out of this bloodbath emerges somebody who will have the power to dictate to the ISU how their system will be run. I don't think the ISU will take control because they don't know how to take control."

A good candidate emerged in the past two years after the Swiss marketing firm, Gloria Transparente, went bankrupt. Since 1972, Gloria had been managing and selling the space on the rink boards at all ISU competitions. The ISU, spending great sums on programs against the expected marketing revenues, was left holding the bag when the revenue stream stopped flowing. The ISU needed to find someone to bail them out financially in the short term and someone with ideas about how to expand globally and cope with so much change. Several companies gave presentations on where they thought the sport was, where it should be going and what the companies thought they could do for skating. Who had the cash, the global network and the vision was IMG.

"People equate that relationship with the ISU to somehow taking over," Kevin says, "but when you do a marketing contract with an international sports body, you do the mandate that they set up for you. The mandate that they've set up for us is to market the ISU and its properties, figure skating, speed skating and short track. There's a high priority on the last two, especially since most of the people on the Council come from those two sports and now the president is a short track person."

In the first year of the relationship, the ISU committee within IMG concentrated on the ISU's figure skating properties, the World Championships, the Europeans and and the Juniors, selling rink boards, arena signs and tickets. The committe looked at the properties the ISU has and reported to the Council on what is valuable and what isn't and what other options the ISU might pursue.

"They'd never done any licensing or merchandising programs," Kevin says, "so it started off basic, getting them up to speed on where most of the top level international sports governing bodies are from a marketing standpoint. That was the first year. The second year is getting a little more sophisticated as we start to tie in the television contracts, going out country by country and selling the television rights. Before television is up, there's nothing much you can do about sponsorship. Now that the television has come up, we can start packaging a little more, which is our expertise."

Looking at skating as a big time sport, IMG recommended ways of maintaining and improving skating's position in the market and pointed out areas where the ISU was weak in consumer education, right down to things like judging. "Everybody within the sport was pretty happy with the judging, but the average person who is not a huge skating fan will watch the Olympics and the world championships and say, 'God, it was such a mess.' That's an education gap, so they have to get out there with the videos, the newsmagazines, et cetera, et cetera, educating people on why everyone in the skating community thought the judging was fine or above-average and why everyone else thought it stunk."

Part of the plan IMG devloped to deal with the issue is a television newsmagazine program much like the ones the company has produced for golf and tennis for many years. The profile of figure skating is now high enough, its demographics broad enough and the reach wide enough that the sport now merits its own show. The program will be distributed to 60 countries. "The ISU has its core markets and they've got to take care of them, better care of them than they do now, but they also have to expand. That's where we can help the most, especially from the television side."

The IMG union with the ISU makes good business sense, but it scares the living daylights out of a lot of people in the sport. How much power can one organization exercise responsibly? IMG represents the skaters, creates the pro events, runs the biggest tour, produces the television shows, employs all the talent and now shapes the response of the ISU to the massive change spinning the sport dizzy. Even though Kevin says that IMG isn't taking over entirely, one does have to wonder.

The 1993–94 season was a watershed year that saw the amateur and pro streams meld into one and witnessed the greatest field of skaters meet at the Olymic Games in Hamar. The season was a critical juncture in figure skating, effectively ending an era of development dating from the end of the Second World War.

At the end of the season, Kevin spoke to the CFSA technical committee, still developing skills programs and working out ways to tell coaches what the future of the sport will be and how rule changes for open competitions and the pros coming back will affect the way skaters develop. Kevin says, "They needed someone to come in and say, 'Hey, this is your time-line. This is when it's going to happen and this is what you guys have to prepare for, because the pros aren't going to do amateur competitions and they're not going to do all these special requirements and they've got back-flips and they've got vocals and you've got to incorporate them somehow.'"

It might take until the next century before the figure skating world arrives at its new destination and discovers for sure what works, what is good and what is appropriate for skaters and all the other members of the skating family. The journey will be one hell of a ride.

"We're at the point where control is the name of the game," Sheldon says, "Or relinquishing it. The public is still going to be in charge through media and if the display is not pleasing, or the conditions of the display, it won't survive. But it will. We should bless all development. Whether we can give it first place or not, let's give it credit. Because that's where inspiration and stimulation come from."

June used to be the month almost everybody took off to wind down and get refreshed for the upcoming season. But skating is a year-round business these days and the best anyone can do is just slow down. Even if the training schedule isn't as demanding, skaters and coaches search for new music and ideas and ask the perennial questions: How am I going to look? What am I going to say? What's the message I want to get across? Who do I want to be this year?

Almost everyone involved with the sport gets together in some fashion to review the past year's events. In June, 1994, Barb Strain and 150 of her skating friends met at the Toronto Cricket Club to sort out the winners of their "podium picks" pool and start handicapping the competitors for the next season. During the reunion, they received word that Karen Preston had retired from amateur competition and would be skating the role of Snow White with Walt Disney's World on Ice. Their consensus was, "Good girl."

The CFSA held its annual general meeting to review the year and look ahead. The meetings used to be small affairs, with maybe 30 people attending. Around 700 gathered in Montreal for the 1994 edition, an event laid on with the David Dore touch, with videos, banquets and dry ice wafting through the room as the stars were introduced with fanfares and light shows.

Kurt, Lloyd and Isabelle said goodbye to the CFSA. For some people, it was like being at a funeral in that it marked the end of something they had come to care so much about and love so deeply. David knew he'd never be able to keep his emotions in check, so he left the task of saying the official good-bys to outgoing CFSA president, Doug Steele. Kurt was a mess and Lloyd was a mess, both weeping as the ceremonies went on. The only one who stayed together was Isabelle.

All the members of the world and Olympic team were there, except one. Elvis, the Canadian and world champion, stayed home. His absence generated all kinds of speculation. "Big, big mistake," said one coach. "A major tactical error," said another. People wondered whether it was his way of paying the CFSA back for years of non-support during the Kurt era. David took it as a message of who was boss. "It was Kurt's retirement and Isabelle and Lloyd's retirement, but with all the videos, all the visuals," he says, "it was to be Elvis' evening too because he's world champion and he didn't come. I may be a lot of things but I'm not stupid."

Elvis says there was no message. "I'd been flying all over the States, I'd been doing the tour, I'd been doing stuff for people. That was the only time I had where I was leaving the tour to get away from everything. That was the one thing in my life that was really for me and that was out of skating. I'd already told them that I wouldn't go and everything was fine. I don't mind if ahead of time they say, 'We really don't think that's right, you should come.' Then we can discuss it. End of deal. No problem. But I don't like the fact that I say that I'm not going and everything is cool, then I get letters saying, 'We missed you da-da-da.' Not after the fact. That's wrong. But I always try not to look at someone else as choosing something right or wrong. It's their perception of how they see things and you have to adapt to that because you're not going to change the perception."

The tension between him and the Association has always been evident and the dramatic flare up of that tension at the Olympic Games has yet to die down. Elvis says that after the first day of the Olympics, he never said anything more about his glaring omission from the team video and asked others not to say anything either. But others apparently took up the cause on his behalf.

David says, "This since Lillehammer has been hugely upsetting to me. This has been blown so totally out of proportion. I've explained it so many times I want to say, 'Read my lips and if you can't accept the explanation, you have a huge problem with your image.' They've magnified it into other incidents and other examples. I don't understand that after 42 years people treat me like this and have said the things they've said. I'm having a real problem with that. My first favourites were Paul and Barbara, then Brian was a favourite, but my absolute favourite is Kurt and I think this is the problem in the Elvis situation. I've never hidden it. I just enjoyed the naturalness of Kurt. I enjoyed the fact that he is what he is and nothing else. He has such a wonderful sense of humour and such a wonderful brain. He has such an awareness of people and a marvelous, marvelous sensitivity that most people don't know about. He speaks his mind. He's spoken his mind to me many times and dead on. There's the difference. He would have come to me and complained directly. I wouldn't have gotten out of the room. He would have come to me and said, 'Why did you do this?' And I would have explained it to him and he would have said, 'I don't have to like it, but let me think about what you're saying' and he would have come back a day later and it would have been dealt with. I get very hurt when people perceive that I'm doing something to deliberately hurt someone else. I don't do that. There's this innuendo going on that just keeps getting worse in the other camp and this is the first time I've felt helpless. There are so many things going wrong and I can't help them because they won't listen to me. They've decided that I don't have anything to say."

With Elvis as Canada's very best example of what skating is and perhaps the country's first bona fide truly global skating superstar, someone has to take responsibility to set things right. This should be a happy marriage, but resolving the relationship won't be easy.

"I consider myself a bit of a loner," Elvis says. "On my own a bit. With the CFSA or with the team, I'm part of the team but I'm very much an individual on that team and if I feel like something is infringing on me, I stop it. That was the hardest thing this year because no one used to bother me too much before. I wasn't the champion so it didn't matter. Now as soon as someone starts doing this and that and I say,' Whoa, time out,' they think, 'What's wrong with him. He's changed.' I haven't changed. I'm no different than I was before Canadians or Olympics or Worlds. I'm the same person. It's just I've learned a lot more, I'm understanding more, I'm more confident in just being me. The CFSA do their thing to bring in funds with sponsors and they're doing an incredible job. They are the best at it in the world. We have a huge junior team now and a senior team that's growing. That's so positive and it's the skaters and the personalities we've had that's making it work. There are times where we do things at competitions for sponsors and for the CFSA and doing that is a lot in itself. For the rest of it, I just like to be associated as Elvis, not as Elvis the skater. I'm Elvis the kid who likes to do a lot of different things and I'm not attached to anything. I don't like to be attached to anything."

After the CFSA annual meeting, the coaches held their annual conference in Laval. Louis took the opportunity to have lunch with Josée. They talked about the Olympics. He said, "You know, in all the years I've done this, you're the first person that's had me completely fooled. Because I said to myself, yes, she's going to do it. Right from the moment you left me and I looked in your eyes and you were very focused and I thought, yes."

Josée said,"You were right. It was yes. When I was with you, I was going to do it. It was when I turned my back and you weren't there anymore, that's when I lost it. From that moment to when I took my spot. I know I have to work on that 30 seconds now."

"It was nice to watch her self-confidence grow," Louis says. "And it's neat that she's got it down that fine. We'll have to work very hard to give her stuff to think of in the bridge between there because no matter if she skates first or last, there's always that last moment she has to leave and go and do it."

But Josée's amateur career is over, although she's left the door open to reinstate. In the summer, she made the decision to turn pro. "It was harder than I thought," she says, "because if everything would have been how I was expecting and wanted them to be, it would have been easy and I wouldn't take that long to decide. But I took my time because I didn't want to decide either on a bad feeling or for the moment. I wanted to get over it a little bit and then make the best decision. I've been so disappointed for three years in a row. I have good moments, but always followed by a disappointing moment. So I'm just looking for something that will make me happy."

The women's and pairs titles are up for grabs in the 1994–95 season, but Bourne and Kraatz seem likely to retain the ice dance title and, barring injury or major, major upset, Elvis will have a lock on the men's title for many years to come. The 1994–95 season will be a very important year for him because everyone in the skating world—judges in particular—will want to know, "Did we make the right decision last year? Is he a one-shot wonder?"

We have not yet discovered artistically how many people Elvis can be. We have seen his Bruce Lee and his rocking tough guy type—perhaps they are the same—but now we need to see whether he can be something else or if he will be stuck in some form or other of martial arts. Champions have been known to be one-dimensional.

Viktor Petrenko has one side that he is comfortable with, but it is his only side. It is the only thing he can do. He does it brilliantly, but the true artist is one who can be anybody.

Elvis is very aware of the process and seems to be having as much fun uncovering the layers of his personality as many people are watching him try to do it. "Last year, with the short and the long, they wanted something that was me and something that had a theme, something they could put a finger on and say, 'I know what that is.' So I took the two things that come most naturally to me, martial arts and techno dancing, and put that on the ice. Everyone thought it was great and I enjoyed it and I loved doing it and I was still trying to show that you can be yourself and not be docked for being yourself. Skating should be really flexible. I wanted to open doors so that other kids can do what they wish. Now that that door is more open, I picked something that is based on what I did this whole year. Each program I do every year is based on what I've done. You live skating, right?"

The long program for the 1994–95 season, skated to music from the movie *1492: Conquest of Paradise*, is built around the idea of "the discovery of what is true, what is right, what you strive for. The idea is you're always learning and always discovering things. A gold medal hasn't been spurring me on. It's been the consistency to keep growing and keep getting better and to push the limits as far as I can. I've been pushing more and more and getting more excited and more focused and more into it because I'm discovering new things. Discovering myself as a person is one thing, but I never realized so many different things, so many ways I can skate. That's the most fun. If you keep doing the same thing over and over and over again, it's boring."

The short program is skated to music from *Total Recall*. "I've tried different ideas with it. I've put on the music and played serious, I've played mysterious, I've played ridiculous, many different sides. I wanted to see what I could get out of the music. I've picked serious and mysterious together. I think it's fun because the biggest thing about last year was, 'Okay, he's a martial artist. So what's he going to do next year?' People are waiting to pounce. You got to do what you got to do. There's no way I'm not going to be competitive."

Elvis' success will have an impact on skating school registrations for years to come, only adding to the effect that the Olympics always has during the autumn after a Games. Even that effect was heightened by the Nancy and Tonya soap opera. "The coverage it got the Olympics wasn't bad," Kerry says. "Registration in our recreational programs is 200 per cent higher than it's ever been. I keep thinking I should send a thank you card to Tonya."

With so many more children drawn into the sport, it's a safe bet that many more will one day say to their parents, "Come and watch me skate. I'm going to be a champion." That can only be good for skating. But with the great upsurge in interest, alarm bells seem to be going off everywhere. For the elders of the sport, there seems to be a spirit of something at work that makes the blood run cold. David sums up the concern by saying, "The issue of professional sport and this ability to make money now has changed, very despondently to me, the issue of why someone skates. Are they skating for money or because of the passion for it and the love of it? Clearly Brian Orser skated for the passion of it. Now I'm finding a lot of the younger ones are really after the money."

All parents set certain goals for their children, assess their aptitudes and do their best to get them into music or dancing or skating or gymnastics. Children don't understand that achievement requires work, discipline and routine, so the parent imposes those things on them, hoping that eventually they love the activity so much that they impose those things on themselves. But there are many cases, not just in skating, but in other passionate disciplines such as dance and music, where talented young children are forced into the life of high-level competition when they don't really want to be there. Their families want it for them.

This sport can make people crazy. That was true long before the stakes became so high. Parents could alway focus intently on stardom and sacrifice almost everything for fame and glory. Some families in skating do everything to ensure their child's opportunity and promote their success, selling or re-mortgaging their homes and even short-shifting other children who may be denied opportunity in their own chosen fields. The sport is very expensive. To have a high-level competitor requires a full-time job from one parent to pay for fees, equipment, lessons, memberships. But how many kids make it? Hardly any get to the top of the national scene, let alone move on internationally. We have a 12 to 14 member world team drawn from 180,000 skaters registered in Canada. Those are pretty bad odds.

The high costs of skating can extend far beyond financial ones. Parents have to try to see the experience through a child's eyes so they can recognize the stresses their children experience right from the beginning. The way tests are done today are much different from when I skated, but the pressure situation hasn't changed. At the very earliest test levels, there they are, out there on their spindly little legs, all alone on a rink where they've never been all alone before, being viewed by scary adults mucking around the ice in great big galoshes. Their legs are shaking, they have butterflies in their stomach, they have to pee, they're feeling sick, they can't think and they're supposed to do well. They know they're trying to do something special and if they've been well-trained they'll know they can do it. But many tests are attempted when a skater isn't really confident. The parents push and the coach pushes. It's a horrible experience when the children are not sure they can do it.

The stress gets worse in the transition from childhood to the teen-age years. Until puberty, a skater is like a racehorse. Somebody opens the gate and off you go. You know what you have to do and you do it. It's a thrill. With puberty, self-consciousness begins to take over, although not in the sense of feeling shy or moody on the ice. Many things taken for granted somehow just don't feel the same anymore. You're gangly and awkward and begin to feel self-doubt. Some kids make it through that transition, some do not. Sometimes tests can give them a smack in the face and help them get a grip on reality, preparing them for the rigours of competition. Other times, the pressure can push them off the ice and out the arena door forever.

Dealing with stress and nerves in a test situation is something children can do, if given guidelines and good support and if they are assured by parents and coaches that it is not a do-or-die situation. But the load can seem overwhelming if parents see passing a test as a sign of getting value for their money or if coaches are trying to live their lives through their skaters. Certainly skaters put a lot of pressure on themselves. We're quite a group of perfectionists.

There is a reason we grow up in families. That little cluster of people, even when dysfunctional, is important. The sense of being loved no matter how well you skate is elementary. The solitude and loneliness a competitor feels out on the ice can be an exhilarating experience, as long as the skater is aware of and in touch with support from a family.

In a high performance discipline that requires such commitment, life becomes skewed. Everything, not only for the athletes, but for everyone around them, becomes so focused at such an early age that life is not normal. As in many sports, there is a sacrifice to be made in the form of normal socialization. You don't have lifelines to an average existence. Your friends are only skaters because the rink is where you spend most of your time. You probably don't spend a great deal of time in school or participate in school activities. Yet all those things teach you how to make friends, how to have friends, how to be a friend, how to relate to members of the opposite sex and how to live happily in a normal, everyday world.

In the skating world—and there is both good and bad about this—you still learn how to have friends, how to be friends and make friends, but because the major focus is achievement, all those other things either fall by the wayside or become less important. You don't learn from your mistakes. You learn from the technical mistakes you make on the ice, but don't gain the valuable experience of learning how to live. When I got through skating, I was very good at talking to adults, but I couldn't talk to someone my own age. I didn't know how to be seventeen years old. I didn't know how to be thirteen years old either because when I was thirteen, I had to pretend to be nineteen so I could keep my motivation up to compete against real nineteen year olds. When I was fourteen, I went where my friends and fellow skaters went, which means I was in strip bars in Germany watching Lady Chinchilla take her clothes off in a cage.

A skater attains a certain maturity early on, but a maturity that cannot be retained. When I was thirteen and fourteen, I had a view of life that I lost when I stopped competing. I had tried to skip some stages between eleven and fifteen that didn't seem important at the time. At that age, all you want to do is be grown up. The life and the setting require skaters to be older than their years. They are judged on composure, on how they handle nerves, on their ability to deal with success and disappointment. Skate well and everyone will pat you on the back and say you are wonderful. You're everyone's hero. That experience can distort anyone's view of the world. I was lucky in that my climb happened quickly and was over fast. I have scars. There are things I'm still not able to deal with effectively, but that's probably not because of skating, that's probably just me. I was also lucky because even the "skating mother" in my family—my father—insisted on my having two months off each year where I could, as he said, "just be a kid." Ambitious as he was for me, he sensed I needed something away from skating and the skating milieu.

I was never allowed to quit school, though Lord knows I tried. At the magical age of sixteen, many of my friends, most of them skaters, dropped out. Skating and school are both full-time jobs, leaving little time for anything else in life. But at sixteen, there should be lots of other things in life—dating, partying and just hanging around. I could never do any of that because I had to be on the ice at six in the morning, be off to school for a couple of hours, back to the rink and then off to tutors who could make up the deficiencies caused by missing school. Every day was the same: skate, school, skate, school. At sixteen, I approached my mother with a plan. I said, "I want to quit school. It's getting to be too much. I'll have more time to train, I'll be a much better skater, you won't have to pay for tutors," blah blah blah.

She said, "I've got news for you. Not only will you not quit school, but if your marks drop even one per cent, you'll quit skating. What happens if you break your leg and never skate again? You don't know you're going to be an Olympic champion. You don't know what the sport has in store for you. You better have some choices." I don't think I talked to her for a month. I am so glad she stuck to her guns and had the foresight to consider what the world would be like now.

Coaches have a responsibility to make their students as good as they can be as fast as they can be. The CFSA has a responsibility to produce as many champions as it can, while also trying to examine young skaters and suggest what might be in their best interests. Young skaters often feel like pawns, trapped in the middle and trying to please everyone. Parents should enter into this mix on the side not of "the skater," but of their child. If the pressures to achieve become too great, parents should intervene to say, "Not with my child you don't."

With big dollar signs now luring both parents and children into the sport, the pressure to achieve can become relentless and dangerous. But the potential for disaster such pressure holds was revealed long before money was an issue in skating. When Tracey Wainmann was prematurely moved into senior competition, I thought, "Oh my God, this kid is a sacrificial lamb. They're moving her to senior because they know she can get into the top ten at Worlds so Canada will be able to send two women next year instead of just one. That's what this appears to be about."

This talented, smart child, hooked on fame and success, had no positive self-esteem, no backbone built into the system so that when trouble inevitably came along, there was nothing to build her up, nothing to hold her or help her stand up straight. At thirteen, she was Canadian champion and one of the top ten in the world. She found herself on the top of the heap, not knowing how she got there and not knowing if she could do it again. At puberty, never having had to deal with a nerve in her life, nerves were suddenly sticking out of her body everywhere. There was such enormous expectation put on her from such an early age and she was never shown how to get through that time.

Tracey is still lost and running. For any individual there can come a moment of incredible success or incredible failure where time stands still, a moment the individual cannot get past without therapy that can lead them to the kind of self-understanding that allows them to move on into a future where they can accept more responsibility or begin to discipline themselves in a productive way.

She married Joseph Sabovcik, the Czech champion who was one of the finest technical skaters the world has ever produced, but just as wild as Tracey in those days. They married in Germany and tried to join a couple of shows, but couldn't follow any rules. There are parameters within which skaters must behave and no one has much patience for very long with those who show up late, drunk or stoned.

I had an opportunity to work with Tracey and Joseph a couple of years ago on an American TV special where they were part of an outstanding chorus of national and international skaters. They had come to some understanding that they were messing themselves up and were trying to start out fresh and clean. They were delightful to work with. They honoured their commitments, worked very hard and were given a fair amount of individual star skating. They were wonderful, but had both lost the spark that had made them the best. Their eyes seemed to say that they had lived too much, seen too much, been to too many places. There was a sadness about them that hadn't even advanced to cynicism. It was a sadness that made me as a parent want to run over and hug them. It was as if they had been eaten up by skating life and had no strength or reserves to call on. As skaters, they knew what to do. They went through the motions and performed beautifully. But the people inside had withered from being so badly hurt, maybe by their own actions. Even with all their experience, their show faces couldn't hide it. They were not the first and will not be the last to come away from skating with so much potential richness gone sour.

We discard our heroes quickly. As soon as they reveal that they have chinks in their armour, that they are human and have weaknesses, we don't want to hear from them anymore. In the skating world, things change so dramatically that few people have the time or take the time to get to know the skaters. The skaters don't even always take the time to get to know each other. In the end, a skater is out there all alone. So many of them are withdrawn because of it, especially girls.

Boys have it pretty good in the sport because, relatively speaking, there are so few of them. They are sought after as pairs partners and dance partners. If they show even a hint of talent, they can just about call the shots. Young women, on the other hand, are often treated with little respect, with few opportunities for self-validation and no real support or concern. Young teenagers are treated like adults when they're not. They are still children, many of them moving away from home for the first time, without the support of their family. It takes something very nurturing to put these kids through the system and have them come out the other side a winner.

Coaches from the old school of negative motivation, who believed in breaking someone down into small parts and building up again and that any behaviour was justified to get the end result, are becoming fewer as coaching becomes more scientific. All coaches in Canada must do certification courses within the Coaching Association of Canada and the negative ones are being weeded out. Generally, coaches are a very caring bunch who take their sport very seriously, but as in any field there are good ones and not so good ones and parents have to be careful.

A lot of what makes people good is having success. Men in Canada under this system are good for a variety of reasons. There have been great role models over the last thirty years. We had many, many world champions or men right at the top of the ladder. Because there have been so few competitors in comparison to women, success is statistically easier to achieve. For women, competition is so severe, there are so many good skaters to compete against, it's desperately hard to get anywhere. It's a crush 'em kind of system for women, not through anyone's design. It's just the nature of the beast.

The system is built on criticism: You're doing this wrong, your program stinks, the hair's not right, the music's wrong. Sometimes people get hurt and sometimes skaters respond to criticism by attacking their perceived deficiencies with all the strength of the obsessive-compulsiveness that helps make them successful athletes in the first place. So many girls are told that if they want to be successful skaters or gymnasts or synchronized swimmers they have to lose weight.

Dorothy Hallis has operated The Skating Boutique in Toronto for over twenty years, selling all the equipment and paraphernalia a skater needs or wants. She's seen several of her regular customers grow out of their beginners' skates and make their way to a place on the Olympic podium. She has also seen a lovely skater she had known since she was six years old die of starvation at age fifteen. This is figure skating, for heaven's sakes, and fifteen-year-old girls are dying?

Howard Winston is a physician specializing in primary care sports medicine at Scarborough General Hospital in Metro Toronto. He's seen the effects of an overemphasis on success. He says, "The athlete may not feel they can achieve a certain level of ability because they weigh too much. They become focused on that and depressed about that, then don't compete well because they have to be mentally focused. It spirals from there. They become preoccupied with achieving a certain level of weight as the solution. They lose objectivity about what the problem is. They no longer can see themselves for what they are but for what they perceive themselves as being. The common denominator is the end point. The route to getting there varies greatly. Anorexia in medical terms means depressed appetite, but people who are anorexic tend not to have a depressed appetite. They force themselves not to eat because they are so driven to lose weight, the main way being to eat like a mouse and exercise to exhaustion. Restrict calories, expend many. An intense fear of being fat when there is no obvious reason to fear being fat is one tip off. Another, by definition, is someone who has lost 25 per cent or more of their ideal body weight, calculating ideal weight by body mass and a ton of other ways.

"A person who is bulimic will eat and eat, but their weight doesn't fluctuate very much. What sometimes sets the binging off is some kind of upset. They sit down for two hours and have a box of pasta, two boxes of raisins. What stops them eating is abdominal pain, diarrhea or distraction of some sort. Then they realize they've got to lose the food. They tend to abuse laxatives to induce diarrhea, use diuretics and induce vomiting. Anorexics also abuse those things, but it's more typical of a bulimic.

"Before there's a full-blown eating disorder, there are early warning signs that we sometimes miss. Quite commonly, a lot of these kids have an underlying depression and are never taken seriously or allowed to open up and talk about why they're depressed. When they develop an eating disorder, if you look at their knuckles, you'll see a lot of cuts and scabs from trying to induce vomiting. A lot of our secretions come from the parotid glands, so they work overtime because of all the eating and the glands swell as if the person had mumps. With induced vomiting, stomach acid tends to erode the enamel of the teeth over a period of even a couple of months. They all need some form of behaviour modification, individual counselling, family counselling, sometimes emergency help for the anorexic who is emaciated and may need intravenous re-hydration and nutrition. Young women are the most susceptible. The high risk group is girls from the age of twelve to eighteen or nineteen. The mortality rate is very high. Five to ten per cent don't make it."

Eating disorders can cause tremendous turmoil in families, tearing them apart or bringing them closer together. Denial, a big component of the victim's psychiatric state, affects the parents too, who'll say, "Oh, she's all right. She's just a little thin." It can take two years of treatment before a person with a full-fledged eating disorder can get to the point where they are back functioning and not at risk of relapsing. They may have to fight it the rest of their lives. An American gymnast, Christy Heinrich, fought anorexia and bulimia for five years. She was dead at twenty-two. She weighed sixty pounds at the time.

The role parents have in the game is so important. They have to be the buffer between their child and the coach or their child and the CFSA if the child has moved into the big time. Some parents give up that role, tempted by the chance at success and achievement. They give up their rights and surrender their duty to protect their child against too much success too soon. Being exceptional at anything at an early age can eat anyone up.

Protection does require discipline, which some parents don't seem willing to exercise. Dorothy says, "The cynicism sets in around age twelve. When I see children come into the store and be really nasty to their parents and the parents take the abuse and don't chastise them, they don't change. Years later, they come back and the children are telling the parents what to do."

There's a worrisome nastiness in the skating world, maybe only because there is so much of it in the real world. It has driven some good people out of the sport altogether. I've worked with Mel Matthews, my old skating friend from Unionville, in his many capacities, from coach to agent to ice show manager. He finally couldn't take it anymore and moved to another field. "I thought skating was changing a lot and changing in ways that I didn't like and it just wasn't for me anymore. The dominance of the amateur mentality. The manipulation of the children in the sport, the good people getting driven out before they get a chance to get there. Not funded, not chosen. They don't win when they should and they leave. What was happening to the parents of the children as a result of their participation in the sport. Greedy, vicious. Two women fist fighting in the gallery while their children were skating. Those kinds of things don't appeal to me."

In the late fifties, in the old, dilapidated Weston arena, fifteen-year-old Louis Stong skated up to centre ice at great speed and took the strange, Scottish-style hat Marg always used to wear right off her head. Marg marched him into the arena office and said to a sweet woman named Mrs. Macdonald, "Phone his mother." Louis sat there quivering. "My mother never came to the rink. I mean, never. She was a very busy lady, but she drove in and they were deciding whether I could stay in the school. My mother said, 'Do you understand the implication? You're outta here. Think about this.' I kept saying, 'All I did was pull her hat off.' But the thing was, it was so disrespectful."

Toller put in his usual training time at the Toronto Cricket, Skating and Curling Club in the summer of 1994. A pubescent girl going into her program crashed into him. "She told me to fuck off and get out of her way. I could have hit her, but I did not lay a finger on her. I just stopped her, then went over and reported it to the teacher. The girl came over and apologized. The next day, the parents were in the office saying they were going to sue me for attacking their daughter on the ice. Thank God there were many witnesses."

There is more to life than skating. There are wonderful things to be gained from it, but parents have to keep some perspective. To be a champion does take burning ambition. It does take obsession. But somewhere along the line, the smartest people realize that the obsession has to play out within a framework. When the obsession completely rules a life, what is at the other end?

In this big new world of figure skating, many people are naive, none more so than parents. To its great credit, the CFSA is one of the very few sports organizations that involves parents in its summer National Training Camp for skaters, coaches and officials so that the parents are exposed to the realities of skating life. At the 1994 camp, David spoke to the skaters about a variety of issues, especially an emerging drinking problem. He wanted to give them a wake up call. To the people flocking to the sport with dollar signs in their eyes, he said, "There is no money in skating. The money in skating is five people and the rest of them have to live a life. There's not a lot of money in being a coach and that's a hell of a life. With no figures, which has changed the whole look of the sport and how a skater trains, there is a lot of time for skaters to prepare themselves for something else, to do a computer course or a communications course or something. I'm very concerned that that's not being done."

Kevin Albrecht spoke to 85 parents, 82 of them mothers, to clear up some misconceptions about what agents do, the biggest one being that agents choose the coach and choreographer, tell the skaters what outfits to where, choose the image they should portray on the ice and control their training. "Now it's different once you become a pro," he says, "but this misconception about control was hilarious. If I ever gave a music suggestion to Kurt, he'd laugh me out of the room. I like Jimmy Buffet."

It was one of the most spirited seminars at the camp. They peppered him with questions. He put up a series of his own questions—Do your off-ice activities now take more than eight hours a week? Are you answering more than four hours a week of fan mail? Have you been approached by corporations? Have you been asked to go on a national figure skating tour?—and told them that if they could answer "yes" to all of them, then they just might possibly need an agent. The only mother in the room who could was Irene Stojko.

He said, "Let your kids have fun. Skate hard, train hard and if you're having a coaching problem, call the CFSA."

The parents asked, "Well, how will we know when we need an agent?"

He said, "Because one will call you."

The camp is a good place to see the young talent rising through the ranks in this country. There are some very good juniors and novices coming up, along with exciting seniors, especially men and pairs. We have been spoiled with so many champions in the past, so we expect some of these younger skaters to become the best in the world. There's an awful lot of talent in Canada, but talent only goes so far. To become a champion takes much more.

Sandra, who has worked with more champions than just about anyone, has seen a common denominator among the champions and a common thread between those who haven't won. "Champions have that inner strength, that inner power, that mental staying power in the face of adversity. And every single one takes responsibility.

They never look for the excuse. They've never said, 'The ice was bad, I had a cold, my skates weren't tied up right, so and so said something horrible to me before I got on the ice, I looked up and saw whathisname and that threw me off, the choreography didn't feel right.' Every coach has heard all the excuses. Every single one of the people I have worked with, if they screwed up, will say, 'I screwed up. It was my fault.' That's why it's important that they also then reap the rewards. There is something else, and it's not a big secret. It's called training. All the champions trained. Really trained."

The perseverance, strength of character and plain guts skaters need to become champions gives them a certain bearing. Figure skating for almost fifty years has given heroes to a country where heroes are in short supply. From Barbara Ann to Elvis, none has ever let us down. Watching Elvis, Kurt, Josée, Herb and Isabelle and our other champions today, Barbara Ann says, "They're incredible and they're all nice young people. That's what I like. Look at Kurt at the Olympics. He just broke my heart, but he was magnificent, the way he handled it. He showed that even the best can have a bad day and rise above it. He made no excuses. He was a true gentleman, a true sportsman and made Canada and the world proud of him. We're very fortunate in Canada to have such wonderful young people representing us because, you know, when you go over to Europe, you're not just yourself, you are your country and you have an obligation to behave and compete the best you can."

In a sport like figure skating, the struggle to become the best isn't just played out on the ice. The unfairness of earlier days and the ever-present politics are enough to break the spirit of anyone who skates at the elite level. But our champions always survived with dignity and grace. Frannie tells parents who ask if she thinks their child has enough talent to go on, "You know, you can't guarantee success for them. But even if they don't make it to the top, it's a wonderful sport and it's the participation that develops the soul."

There is so much to be gained from skating. The sheer joy of doing it, of creating beautiful pictures and telling great stories through the medium of the ice is exhilarating. Over the long haul, how high you've jumped or how fast you've spun doesn't matter. There's something much more spiritual at work, something of such great worth that you can put up with the worst hardships of a cold and wearying life. As Toller says, "We all have frustrations, we all have disappointments, we all have unhappiness. But in the big picture, boy was it worth it."

Of all the gifts figure skating bestows, the greatest is the self-knowledge it brings even to people who seem far too young to have discovered so much. Elvis says, "The medal is amazing because that is what you're always striving for. It's always there. But I like the process of getting there because I know how much it made me a stronger person, how much I learned about myself, how much I can get through life and know that I can count on myself when I need to. When the chips are down I can count on myself and say, 'I can do this now.' And that's the whole reason why I'm here."

The dream of being a champion is entrancing. Becoming one is wondrously special, an achievement that can never be taken away. The word itself has carried me through many low points in my life. Like having a 'Lady' or 'Sir' in front of your name, the title stays around all your days, a delightful, shimmering source of strength tucked away in your soul. There is no shortcut to success and no flash of lightning coming down to bless the gifted, but there is a wonder to the strange, nebulous process that takes a host of human qualities and transforms them into something truly astounding. That's the enchantment of the sport and that's the secret of skating. It's magic.